"From atop Blair Mountain, Robert Shogan has conjured a vivid vision of modern America in the making in the bloody coal field struggles of 1920s West Virginia. Infused with the humane intelligence of one of our most distinguished political correspondents, this haunting tale restores a shocking chapter of American history to its rightful place in this nation's unfolding saga of democratic aspirations and shattered dreams. It is a rare gem of a book."

> —JOSEPH A. MCCARTIN, Georgetown University, author of
> *Labor's Great War*

"Robert Shogan sheds new light on this long-neglected episode of the labor movement's ongoing struggle for workers' rights. For too long, the significant Battle of Blair Mountain has been merely a footnote in American history books. Now, the real story of America's largest labor uprising—and the largest armed insurrection on U.S. soil since the Civil War—comes alive. As a native of Cabin Creek, W.Va.—and the great-nephew of the miners' commander, Bill Blizzard—I take personal interest in reading about my union's pivotal role in this historic rebellion for economic and social justice."

> —CECIL ROBERTS, president, United Mine Workers of America

"Bob Shogan has covered seven presidents and countless political campaigns. Now he tells the story of a forgotten chapter of American history—an armed uprising by 10,000 West Virginia coal miners against the coal companies that dominated their lives, exploited their labor, and controlled their state government. This book is a riveting refutation of the comforting conventional wisdom that there has never been class struggle in America."

> —DAVID KUSNET, chief speechwriter for former president
> Bill Clinton (1992–1994), and author of *Speaking American:*
> *How the Democrats Can Win in the Nineties*

"Here is a book about forgotten events that took place 80 years ago in a little understood corner of our nation. What a surprise that Bob Shogan has not only found ample documentary evidence to convince us of the historical significance of these battles between miners and mine owners in southern WV, but also spun a rip roaring tale full of shockingly vivid and down-to-earth portraits. When the tale is told, Shogan's conclusion seems irrefutable: our nation paid a heavy price in economic justice and social progress when state and federal authorities failed to ensure workers' basic freedom to form unions."

> —RICHARD L. TRUMKA, Secretary-Treasurer, AFL-CIO, and
> Past President, United Mine Workers of America

THE BATTLE OF
BLAIR MOUNTAIN

The Story of America's
Largest Labor Uprising

ROBERT SHOGAN

A Member of the Perseus Books Group

Copyright © 2004 by Robert Shogan.

Published in the United States of America by Westview Press, A Member of the Perseus Books Group, 5500 Central Avenue, Boulder, Colorado 80301–2877, and in the United Kingdom by Westview Press, 12 Hid's Copse Road, Cumnor Hill, Oxford OX2 9JJ.

Find us on the world wide web at www.westviewpress.com.

Westview Press books are available at special discounts for bulk purchases in the United States by corporations, institutions, and other organizations. For more information, please contact the Special Markets Department at the Perseus Books Group, 11 Cambridge Center, Cambridge, MA 02142, or call (617) 252-5298, (800) 255-1514 or email special.markets@perseusbooks.com.

Library of Congress Cataloging-in-Publication Data

Shogan, Robert.
  The battle of Blair Mountain : the story of America's largest labor uprising / by Robert Shogan.
      p.   cm.
  Includes bibliographical references and index.
  ISBN 0-8133-4096-9 (hardcover : alk. paper)
  1. Labor disputes—West Virginia—History—20th century.
2. Coal mines and mining—West Virginia—History—20th century.
3. Insurgency—West Virginia—History—20th century. I. Title.
HD5325.M615S49 2004
331.892'822334'0975448—dc22

                                                                    2004001648

Text design by Trish Wilkinson
Set in 11.5-point Janson by the Perseus Books Group

The paper used in this publication meets the requirements of the American National Standard for Permanence of Paper for Printed Library Materials Z39.48–1984.

10   9   8   7   6   5   4   3   2   1

For Ellen

Contents

Author's Note

"Labor, like Israel, has many sorrows," John L. Lewis observed during his reign as president of the United Mine Workers. "Its women weep for their fallen and they lament for the future of the race." Among labor's many costly defeats, the Battle of Blair Mountain arguably ranks as the most neglected.

When I first became interested in the Battle of Blair Mountain in the early 1960s, I thought it remarkable that so little had been written about this unprecedented episode in our development as a nation. The course of my professional life then took me in a different direction. When I returned to the subject, nearly four decades later, I found that more work had been done, all of it creditable. Yet the great uprising of the West Virginia miners remains only an afterthought in our historical consciousness, earning only a few sentences at most even in chronicles of the labor movement and no attention at all in more general accounts of the American heritage. This book is intended to help remedy this oversight. By looking into this dark corner of American history my hope is to cast light on the forces that shaped the American political and economic order in the 20th century and give the ordeal of the southern West Virginia miners its proper place in the story of our nation.

One reason for the continued obscurity of this episode up to now is our country's dominant middle-class ethos. This frame of reference discourages attention to struggles to achieve social and economic justice, if they threaten the sanctity of property values and the maintenance of law and order. As a result the significance of class conflict in the making of America is overlooked and misunderstood.

When the union coal miners confronted their adversaries, the 20th century had barely begun. The makings were already in place but had yet to assume the established pattern of the power structure we know today. Economic advantage and political control were up for grabs, in a no-holds-barred clash between business and labor. Both had emerged from the Great War bolder and brawnier than before, each eager for more, neither willing to give ground. Those were cruder times than now, with a good deal less artifice. With so much at stake the leaders on each side did not shrink from stating they intended to crush their enemies and from backing their rhetoric with action.

In West Virginia, where the level of hostility and violence between business and labor reached its zenith, the coal operators condemned the United Mine Workers union, the largest and most powerful in the country, as "revolutionary in character and a menace to the free institutions of the country." To meet this threat they deployed a private army of detectives and sheriff's deputies. And during one particularly bitter and bloody strike that set the stage for the Battle of Blair Mountain, the mine owners dispatched a special train, rigged with iron plate and bristling with machine guns to assault a tent colony that sheltered the strikers and their families.

For their part, the union leaders vilified not only the mine operators but the politicians who catered to their greed. "You can expect no help from such a goddam dirty coward," Mother Jones, one of the UMW's most ferocious organizers, told a crowd of union men who massed in the state's capital to seek the governor's support in their travail. "But I warn this little governor that unless he gets rid of these goddam Baldwin-Felts mine guard thugs there is going to be one hell of a lot of bloodletting in these hills." She was right about that. For years the union miners and the allies of the coal operators spilled each other's blood in the West Virginia hills until the miners were beaten into submission.

Though no such despotism as flourished in West Virginia in the 1920s survives today, the struggle between working people and their adversaries for political power and economic advantage rages on, and I believe the conflict in West Virginia provides lessons that illuminate the new battlegrounds of the 21st century.

Robert Shogan
CHEVY CHASE, MARYLAND
JANUARY 2004

Acknowledgments

I owe particular thanks to two native West Virginians who tilled the same fields before me, David Alan Corbin, now an aide to West Virginia Senator Robert C. Byrd, and Rebecca J. Bailey, now an assistant professor in history at the State University of West Georgia. The influence of their works on my own book is evident from the numerous citations in the reference notes. But in addition, along with encouragement and advice, Corbin supplied leads to a number of valuable sources. Bailey went to the great trouble of photocopying original material she had used for her dissertation for my use.

Joseph McCartin, Georgetown University labor historian, took time away from his own forthcoming book to read portions of this manuscript and make immensely helpful suggestions. The enthusiasm of Steve Catalano, my editor at Westview, and the steadfast counsel of my agent, Carl Barndt, made this book possible.

Similarly generous was Michael Workman of West Virginia University Institute for the History of Technology and Industrial Archeology who sent me a copy of the Institute's report on the Battle of Blair Mountain, which he had helped compile. My debt to the West Virginia University library goes back nearly four decades to 1964, when Charles Shetler, curator of the library's regional history collection, loaned to my local library, in Maplewood, N.J., the microfilm transcripts of the miners' treason trials so I could begin research on this work. Similar courtesies have been extended me by current members of the library staff, particularly Delilah Board, who made it possible to get the striking photos that illustrate the book.

Among others who went out of their way with various kinds of assistance were Gordon Simmons, cultural program officer for the West Virginia Arts Commission, Joe Geiger, assistant director of West Virginia history and archives, who sent me numerous back copies of that estimable publication *West Virginia History*, and Jim Zoia, aide to West Virginia Representative Nick Rahal, who managed to get me a copy of the 1921 Senate hearings on West Virginia's labor troubles. David Yepsen, of the Des Moines *Register* dug deep into his papers' morgue to find background on Iowa Senator William Kenyon.

The labors of Brandy Saverese, who researched the Jett Lauck papers at the Alderman Library of the University of Virginia, and Gena Wagaman, who collected relevant material from the treason trial transcripts at West Virginia University Library saved me precious time.

I benefited from the steady moral support of my daughters, Amelia Ford Shogan and Cynthia Diane Shogan. Cindy also put me in touch with Kevin Mack, who created the fine map to help guide the reader through the long struggle. My wife, Ellen Shrewsbury Shogan, read every page of this manuscript with a discerning eye and perhaps more important provided the encouragement and understanding that helped me complete ten previous books and have enriched my life for more than forty years.

THE BATTLE OF
BLAIR MOUNTAIN

THE FIELDS OF BATTLE

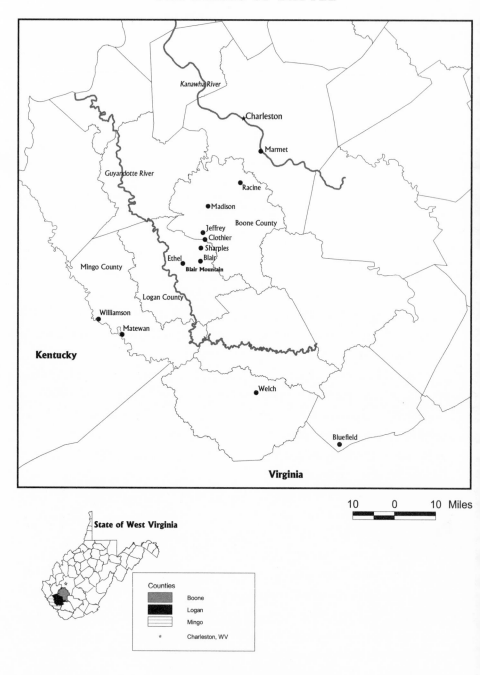

10   0   10 Miles

MAP CREATED BY KEVIN MACK

1

Matewan Station

ON A DREARY morning in May of 1920 seven men carrying Winchesters and pistols boarded the Norfolk and Western's No. 29 at Bluefield, West Virginia, bound for the little mining town of Matewan on the Kentucky border. All were hirelings of the Baldwin-Felts detective agency, personally selected by their boss, Tom Felts. Half a dozen or so others would follow by later trains. Nearly all "have been tried and can be relied on," Tom Felts had written to his brother, Albert, who was already posted in Matewan.

The railroad that transported the agents to Matewan was part of the reason for their mission. More than thirty years before, the well-tailored, smooth-talking agents of the Norfolk and Western had descended on southern West Virginia like locusts, their checking accounts fattened by funds from Philadelphia and across the sea in the City of London, and systematically bought up all the land they could lay their hands on. And not just the land. They were careful to secure the mineral rights, too. That was, after all, the point. On their heels came another invasion sponsored by the railroad. These men were a rougher sort, crude in dress and manner. They were construction workers, some 5,000 of them, and they set to work laying the Norfolk and Western trunk line, putting up more than sixty bridges and carving eight tunnels out of the Appalachian foothills, opening up the region and its fabulous deposits of coal. The 190 miles of tracks pushed through valleys of crooked streams penetrating a rugged wilderness that lacked even wagon roads. The hill country farmers turned away from their corn and beans, signed up for the mines and made their homes in cabins along the right of way. Their wives bought overalls and groceries in the company stores while their children played amidst the slag heaps that tarnished the once verdant land. Mules, horses and oxen hauled their work to the surface. Coal cars rumbled along the hillsides, dumping their loads at massive tipples, where it would be stored and then shipped out to markets around the country. Investors, well-fed men in rich tweeds and polished boots, came from all over to tour the valley, inspect the mines and lay out their money, certain of a bountiful return. The coal mines proliferated and thrived. No one could question the riches that lay beneath the earth. Some called the region the "El Dorado" of Appalachia.

Coal was big business, but now it was in big trouble. It was this crisis that called the Baldwin-Felts agents to Matewan. Baldwin-Felts prospered by doing the bidding of the coal companies of West Virginia, serving more or less as their private police force. Tom Felts was sending these men to Matewan, in Mingo County, because there, as in the rest of southern West Virginia, the coal companies, whose output fueled the national economy, and the United Mine Workers of America, the nation's most powerful labor union, were at each other's throats.

By this date, Wednesday, May 19, 1920, America had been at peace abroad for more than eighteen months. The last doughboys of the American Expeditionary Force had long since shipped out of Brest, bound for home, hoping to return to normalcy. The huzzahs from the victory parades on America's Main Streets had long since died out. But at home there was no peace between business and labor. The trade unions were up against it. During the war, with the help of Washington officialdom eager to keep production rolling, the unions had gained in prestige and numbers, gains that had translated into hard cash for the rank and file. But now labor was on the defensive. Struggling against rising prices, which shrunk their paychecks, and slumping demand, which threatened to take away their jobs altogether, many workers looked to their unions for salvation. But the nation's captains of industry would have none of that. Instead they were eager to reassert their prewar hegemony over the economy, rid the unions of their newfound illusions and power and boost their profits, already lifted by the war, to even greater heights. Looking at the world around them, the more prescient among the leaders of corporate America sensed that they were on the right side of history, at one of the great turning points in the nation's life story. The idealism that infused Woodrow Wilson's New Freedom and his crusade to make the world safe for democracy was in the process of being repudiated by a rigorous rightward shift, breathtaking in its scope. Its most conspicuous feature was the Red Scare launched by Wilson's own attorney general, A. Mitchell Palmer, which smothered dissent of all kinds. But the conservative trend was also marked by an enhanced reverence for free enterprise, its leaders and all their works, an attitude that served to reinforce the resistance of these worthies to the demands of labor.

The collision of labor's desperation with management's intransigence had triggered an unprecedented wave of strikes, more than 3,000 walkouts all told in 1919 involving more than four million workers. Steelworkers "hit the bricks," as did coal miners and printers. Even police walked off the job. "I really think we are facing a desperate situation," worried the normally sanguine junior senator from Ohio, Warren Harding. "It looks to me as if we are coming to crisis in the conflict between the radical labor leaders and the capitalistic system under which we have developed the Republic."

The following year, 1920, brought no letup in strife. Labor tensions mounted around the land, but nowhere were the stakes as high as in West Virginia on the day that Tom Felts dispatched his men to Matewan. Their journey was only fifty miles and took little more than an hour. But it would open a new and bloody chapter in the annals of American history. Their arrival would set off a chain reaction of violence that would rock the government of West Virginia to its foundations and at the same time challenge the Federal government in Washington, testing the will and nerve of the highest officials of the nation. It would take months to run its course and conclude only after 10,000 armed miners set out to defy the government of the state and the companies that controlled their lives in the largest armed uprising on American soil since the Civil War.

It was no accident that this upheaval would burst forth when and where it did, in Matewan in Mingo County. This county was the center of West Virginia's richest coalfield. Within twenty-five miles of the county seat, Williamson, about seventy-five mines produced twelve million tons of bituminous a year, a healthy share of total national production. Nearly all these mines were non-union, many opened during the past few years to meet the nation's growing demand for coal during the war.

When the war ended, the mines remained, productive and unorganized, to threaten the UMW's power elsewhere in the country by selling coal at a discount against the prices charged by unionized operators. Unless the UMW could organize all of West Virginia, the union's leaders realized, the nationwide strength it had spent nearly half a century building would dwindle and eventually disappear.

Sprawling beyond Mingo's borders, the Williamson Field reached across the Tug Fork of the Big Sandy River into Kentucky's Pike County to the west, and into the West Virginia counties of McDowell to the south and Logan to the east. Indeed, the coal seams in Logan were even richer than in Mingo and the mines employed more than twice as many men.

But Logan was the base of the mine operators' power. The operators subsidized Logan County Sheriff Don Chafin's department; in return Chafin's deputies did all they could to protect them against the union and its organizers. Outrage over the sheriff's strong-arm tactics had boiled over in the summer of 1919, about nine months before the Baldwin-Felts agents boarded the train for Matewan. Union headquarters in the state capital of Charleston, about fifty miles north of the Williamson field, seethed with stories that Chafin's deputies were beating and murdering the organizers the UMW had dispatched to Logan County, trying to cut out the boil that threatened its welfare and future. On Thursday September 4, angry miners began gathering in the town of Marmet, on the outskirts of Charleston, for a march on Logan County. By the next day, Friday, September 5, their numbers had grown to 5,000. Most were armed to the teeth.

This was enough to get West Virginia Governor John J. Cornwell to rush to the scene. Cornwell, a newspaper editor turned politician, had been elected on the Democratic ticket in 1916 with the help of miner support. He had won their votes by promising to give the UMW a fair hearing and curb the excesses of the guards hired by the coal operators. "Boys throw your support to me and I will do everything in my power to remove the gunmen from the state," Fred Mooney, secretary treasurer of District 17, which represented most of West Virginia's union miners, recalled the candidate saying. Cornwell had made token efforts to keep his promise, but in the judgment of the union men he had not done nearly enough. Actually Mooney, like other union leaders, believed that the mine guard system was so deeply entrenched that "only a superman, such as Oliver Cromwell or Napoleon Bonaparte would have been able to prevent its functioning."

Far from being a superman, Cornwell was only a hack officeholder and a journeyman orator, as he demonstrated when he arrived at Marmet on Friday in the dead of night and clambered on top of a soft drink truck to address the rebels. They crowded around the impromptu podium, and with the moonlight glistening on their gun barrels listened to Cornwell with fast-diminishing patience. Mindful that many in his audience had fought under their country's flag in France, Cornwell appealed to them as patriots and law-abiding citizens. "Boys do you not know that everyone of you is acting in violation of every law against bearing arms and that you are taking the law into your own hands?" he demanded.

That argument did not impress. "There is no law in West Virginia except the law of the coal operators," one miner shouted.

Ignoring him, Cornwell pressed on, vowing to crack down on the mine owners and their guards if only the rebels would take their rifles and go home. But those promises had an all too familiar ring to the miners. They heard Cornwell out, but when he finished and headed back to Charleston, they signaled their defiance by firing their weapons in the air, the din drowning out the protesting voices of Fred Mooney and the president of District 17, Frank Keeney.

Cornwell got the message. Back at the capital on Saturday, September 6, the governor put through a call to President Wilson's Secretary of War, Newton Baker, and asked for Federal troops to deal with the incipient rebellion. Since the birth of the Republic such requests had been considered a serious departure from constitutional norms and had required presidential approval. But when state national guards were called to the colors after the United States plunged into the Great War, worries mounted that governors would not be able to cope with domestic disturbances. To help them out in such emergencies, the intervention process had been simplified and expedited by eliminating the requirement for direct presidential involvement. Under the emergency policy known as "direct access," once Baker heard from Cornwell, he bypassed the Oval Office and instead sent word of the threatened uprising directly to General Leonard Wood. Wood, who had won his first star fighting Aguinaldo's guerrillas in the Philippines at the turn of the century, had been deemed too old for duty with the AEF in France. Instead he had been given command of the troops assigned to deal with labor disputes and other domestic disorders. Looking ahead to his prospects for gaining the 1920 Republican presidential nomination, Wood was eager for action and public attention. Within a few hours he reported to Baker that a force of 1,600 men had been assembled and was ready to march.

Informed of the deployment by Cornwell, Mooney and Keeney realized they faced the toughest challenge of their dual stewardship of District 17. Along with their Irish heritage they shared a common upbringing. Both had been raised in the mining camps of the state, worked in the mines since they were boys and joined the union early on. And both had been bloodied in the Paint Creek–Cabin Creek strike of 1912–1913. Back then thousands of miners in the Kanawha

Valley, just north of the Williamson Field, walked out demanding higher wages and recognition of their union, leading to what was, up to that time, the cruelest and most protracted dispute in West Virginia labor history. Keeney, sharp featured and square jawed, at thirty-five was the older by three years, the more articulate and the more aggressive. He was a quick thinker and also quick to anger. In 1912 he had fought against the local leadership's initial attempt to settle the Paint Creek–Cabin Creek strike as offering only meager gains to the union and for his pains was blacklisted.

But he returned in 1916 to take command of a full-scale revolt by members of the local who condemned District 17's leaders as "drunkards and crooks," then seceded, and formed their own local.

The burly, round-faced Mooney, though more deliberative and restrained than Keeney, was no shrinking violet himself. He too had attacked the original Paint Creek–Cabin Creek settlement proposal and after the strike finally concluded, had helped to foment the rebellion against the District 17 hierarchy. In the midst of his travails his wife died, leaving him to care for their three young children. Nevertheless Mooney along with Keeney pressed their insurgency. Ultimately an investigation by the national union confirmed their charges that the rulers of the local had sold out the rank and file during contract negotiations to line their own pockets. When District 17 elected new officers Keeney and Mooney agreed that Keeney, because he had led the secession movement, would seek the president's job, while Mooney would run for secretary-treasurer.

The two were strong willed but they were not pigheaded. Pondering the warning from Cornwell that the Army was on the way they realized they had no choice but to stop the march. They spent that day alternating between frantic phone conversations to Charleston, pleading with Cornwell for more time, and frantic speeches to their members, urging them to listen to reason. Finally, armed with a fresh promise from Cornwell to appoint a commission, headed by West Virginia's adjutant general, Thomas B. Davis, to investigate the allegations against the mine owners, the union men heeded the urgings of their leaders and agreed to disband.

Hopes for Cornwell's inquiry, never too bright to begin with, were further dimmed almost immediately. He seemed to give little weight to the miners' complaints. Instead, the governor told the *New York Times* that "some mysterious radical influence" was responsible for the march, sparking what he described as "false reports" of the rumors of atrocities against the union organizers. A fortnight after his interview with the *Times*, addressing a trade association convention in White Sulphur Springs, Cornwell underlined his suspicions of the labor movement, warning that radical labor leaders were at work on a deliberate plan to overthrow the government and install a communist system. "They do not intend to try to have their policies put into force through a popular vote," he said. "That would be too slow," and it would never happen. Laying the groundwork for the conspiracy, Cornwell said, was the union drive to shorten the work week, which he argued would inevitably reduce production and raise prices.

If Cornwell mistrusted the labor movement, his feelings were fervently returned by the leadership of the United Mine Workers. A few days after the miners' march had ended, John L. Lewis, then acting president of the union, publicly rebuked the governor. If Cornwell had properly upheld civil rights and civil liberties, Lewis wrote in a letter authorized by his union's national convention and released to the press, "it would not be necessary for free-born American citizens to arm themselves to protect their Constitutional rights." Meanwhile the convention's policy committee, in a militant mood, endorsed nationalization of the mines, and of the country's railroads, actions that only darkened the governor's already bleak view of the house of labor.

So it should have surprised no one when John L. Lewis called the mine workers out on a national strike set for November 1, 1919, that Cornwell could hardly wait to once again appeal for Federal troops; he acted two days before the strike was scheduled to start. The soldiers arrived in force, but life went on much as usual. Most union miners stayed out on strike; in Mingo County the non-union mines continued to produce coal. In the absence of serious disorder, the troops were withdrawn by mid-November. On December 10 the union sent its men back to work having gained a 14 percent wage increase and the promise that an arbitration commission would investigate their other demands, a pledge that turned out to have important consequences for the union's cause in southern West Virginia.

The fact that their own miners had stayed on the job fostered the belief among the non-union operators of Mingo County that they were invulnerable to the union movement, a state of affairs they credited to the high wages and favorable working conditions they claimed to provide. This view was given full-throated expression on the floor of the House of Representatives in Washington by Mingo County's own congressman, Republican Wells Goodykoontz. A freshman on the Hill, but a veteran servant of the mine operators, he spoke of the "genial surroundings" and high wages enjoyed by local miners. They had avoided the tentacles of the UMW, Goodykoontz informed his colleagues, because they were "the most happy, independent and contented of all our citizenry."

The real world was quite different from the picture Goodykoontz projected. In fact six mines had closed in Mingo County since the end of the war and miners still on the job were working fewer hours. Mingo County coal production in 1919 sank half a million tons below 1918. And though some miners were earning more—the average wage was almost 30 percent higher than before the war—this advantage was undercut by soaring inflation and shrunk dramatically in the eyes of miners when it was compared with the skyrocketing profits of their bosses, which neared 600 percent.

These circumstances encouraged John L. Lewis to lay plans for another organizing drive in southern West Virginia, though not in Logan County. Having assaulted that bastion in the summer of 1919 and been beaten back, the UMW's local strategists decided to infiltrate the mines in neighboring Mingo County instead.

Most of the Mingo County miners were descended from Scotch-Irish pioneers who had opened up this hill country a century before.

For most of that time the region was sparsely populated, inhabited mainly by subsistence farmers and hunters. Like mountaineers everywhere, they were proud, clannish and set in their ways. The harshness of their conditions tended to concentrate their minds on survival and little else. They were "a hard bitten lot," in the view of one of the early mine owners. "They drank and fought and gambled and whored." These West Virginia natives remained farmers at heart and they saw their work in the mines, irregular as it was, as merely a temporary expedient when crops were bad, a way to get through the hard times until they could return to tend their fields. Given this mind-set, the appeals of labor union organizers, with their talk of better wages and working conditions to be achieved in the long run, faced a hard sell.

The African-American miners who migrated to the southern West Virginia coalfields from the Deep South also posed a problem. They were relieved to have escaped the malignant racism of the Old Confederacy. A miner's pay was significantly better than a sharecropper's wages, and like their white co-workers, the black miners feared that heeding the siren call of the labor organizer would only cause trouble for them with their coal operator bosses.

Yet for all of these hindrances, the union leaders could not afford to ignore Mingo County. The Mingo County miners, white and black alike, were practical men and loyal to each other. If they could be convinced that the union would improve their lot they could be relied on to join, and to remain committed in the face of almost any adversity.

Not that UMW leaders anticipated theirs would be an easy road. Cornwell's paranoid view of organized labor was widely shared in Mingo County, particularly among the well-to-do, and by some war veterans, who having finished off the Kaiser were ready to crush the latest threat to American security posed by the Bolsheviki and their union allies. In October of 1919, as the mine owners were facing down the striking union, Mingo County veterans set up their own American Legion post, excluding ex-doughboys who sympathized with the union, and picked local businessmen and other UMW foes as their leaders. Most significant was their choice of a commander, Anthony "Bad Tony" Gaujot, who had won the Congressional Medal of Honor in the Meuse-Argonne offensive against the German legions. But he had earned his nickname as a leader of the mine guards in the Paint Creek–Cabin Creek strike, when his brutality made him notorious even among that ruthless bunch.

Nevertheless, the union pressed ahead, with Lewis himself traveling to Bluefield, to announce a campaign to organize miners throughout the southern Appalachians. "Now is the logical time for this work," Lewis said, "and the campaign will be pushed through to a finish." What made the timing particularly logical from Lewis's standpoint was his expectation, which turned out to be well founded, that the arbitration commission appointed as part of the coal strike settlement would agree to grant the union miners an additional wage increase. Given the economic hard times prevailing in Mingo County, it was reasonable to assume that the non-union miners would demand the same raise, thus adding to the momentum behind the union drive.

Another boost came from the mine owners themselves by the heavy-handedness of their dealings not only with their workers, but with their communities. Thus in January of 1920 an explosion in the headquarters of the Superior-Thacker coal company in Williamson rocked every building within a mile, smashing store fronts and living room windows. Remarkably, only one person died. The company denied any responsibility, though it did agree to pay 25 percent of the cost of property repairs. That same winter, the Hunt Forbes Coal Company refused to compensate the city for damage to the city streets from its lumbering coal-hauling trucks. About twenty miles to the north, in Kermit, the Gray Eagle Coal Company, weary of arguing with the town fathers about access to a public road, declared itself the winner in the dispute and posted armed guards to protect the property it claimed as its own on the contested land. Powerless to act, the citizens brooded and grumbled among themselves.

The notion that some of the inhabitants of Mingo County might take exception to such behavior apparently did not occur to either the coal companies or their supporters, among whom they could still count Governor Cornwell. A week after union leader Lewis had laid down the gauntlet to the coal companies in Bluefield, the governor hastened to that same city to reassure the business community. Praising the non-union mine owners for helping to break the 1919 strike, he warned a meeting of West Virginia builders that union success in organizing these fields would surely lead to nationalization of the industry. If he could not keep peace during the union organizing drive, Cornwell promised, he would quit his job, whereupon the assembled builders leaped to their feet to urge Cornwell to stay at the helm of West Virginia's ship of state.

In the minds of Mingo's miners, all such rhetoric was overshadowed when the arbitration commission recommended that union coal miners receive a 27 percent raise, an increase that would be denied non-union miners. Unrest swept the pits in Mingo, and non-union miners pressed their bosses for an increase. The response of the Howard Colliery at Chattaroy typified management's attitude. The Howard manager offered a modest increase but then boosted prices in the company store. When some miners complained, they were pistol-whipped by mine guards. At Burnwell Coal and Coke, one impatient miner posted a notice at the entrance. "To the miners of the Burnwell Coal Company: We shall have this 27 percent raise; we want this 27 percent raise which the government has granted us." The response from the president of Burnwell was not long in coming. He said, as one of his employees recalled, "he would let his mine go until moss grows over it, until it falls in the huckleberry ridge, before he would ever work a union man." Eighty of the ninety-two Burnwell miners walked off their jobs and sent two of their number to Charleston to ask District 17 for a charter; hundreds of other miners elsewhere in Mingo did much the same thing. In accordance with union policy, they were instructed by Tom Keeney to return home, reclaim their jobs and reopen the mines. Then, Keeney promised, they would be welcomed into the union. The discontents did as they were bidden. As the last week in April began, the organizing drive swept like wildfire through

Mingo County. The union counted 300 new members on one day, hundreds more the next. And its new members went into the mines proudly bearing their District 17 cards. But as fast as they joined, that was how fast the coal companies fired them, and rousted them from their company homes to boot.

Yet the organizing drive seemed to pick up energy from the outrage of the fired men. By early May union operatives in the field claimed to have formed fourteen locals and signed up nearly 3,000 of Mingo's 4,000 miners. It greatly helped that Mingo political leaders turned the county into sort of an organizing haven. They were a different cut from the coal company satraps who made up the regimes elsewhere in southern West Virginia. The highest ranking of this group was Mingo County Sheriff George T. Blankenship. Combining a reputation for honesty that appealed to the better citizens of town with a background in the Railroad Brotherhoods that won him the support of working people, Blankenship gained office in 1916 in an election that broke the back of the Republican machine that had long controlled the county.

Two years later the municipal elections in Williamson brought to power as mayor another union friend and Blankenship ally, Cabell Testerman. The mayor, who owned the town soda fountain and jewelry store, was a businessman, but he counted on the miners for his political base. Standing five foot five inches tall, weighing a portly 170 pounds, he did not cut a prepossessing figure. But he was not a man to be lightly dismissed, as he made plain after he won a court battle against political foes who brought charges of Prohibition violation against him shortly after his re-election in 1919. "I am the mayor of Matewan elected by the people for a second term which speaks for itself," he declared. "They can say what they please, fight when they please, but I am going to run the town according to the laws of this state."

Testerman had previously demonstrated his resolve to deal firmly with Matewan's rough-and-tumble environment by his choice as police chief of Sid Hatfield, a man regarded by the coal operators and many of the town's respectable citizens as little better than a thug, a man of "primitive scruples and dubious attainments." The miners, though, saw Sid, as they all called him, as their champion, a man who could be counted on to stand up for their side, even against the odds, in confronting the hired guns of the mine owners.

Having just entered his twenty-seventh year, Hatfield already was recognized as a dangerous gunman, an impression bolstered by his cold, close-set eyes and the menacing glare he cast upon his many adversaries. In part he owed his reputation as "The Terror of the Tug" to his family name, stamping him as a member of the clan that had waged the much celebrated feud with another mountaineer family, the McCoys. This bloody vendetta traced its roots back to Civil War border clashes. Back then William Anderson Hatfield, a crack shot better know as Devil Anse, led a band of Confederate marauders based in West Virginia while the McCoys fought on the Union side in Kentucky. The murders, kidnappings and arson perpetrated by both sides were much romanticized by the press. But many of these clashes were nothing more glorious than drunken brawls. After the turn of the century the feud guns fell silent and the clan rivalries and allegiances were blurred by time and intermarriage. As the Hatfields proliferated, so that many could no longer trace the bonds of kinship, some became quite respectable. One of their number, Henry, was even elected governor of West Virginia on the Republican ticket in 1912, and played a role, soon after taking office, in settling the Paint Creek–Cabin Creek strike.

Nevertheless the memories of Devil Anse's marksmanship lingered on and police chief Sid Hatfield of Matewan kept the legend alive, even though his relationship to the old Confederate was somewhat obscure. He was said to have been born out of wedlock to a drifter named Crabtree and the wife of a local resident named Jake Hatfield. But having been raised by Jake Hatfield as his own son, the police chief chose to call himself Hatfield and no one in Matewan was prepared to argue the point.

Whatever his lineage, Hatfield's loyalty to the miners had firm roots. He had grown up among them and worked alongside them, riding cars deep into the earth, then making his way through a maze of underground tunnels, with the only light coming from the safety lamp stuck in his cap. He had to be always on the watch for broken wires or stray timbers until he finally reached the chamber where he could actually mine the coal, swinging his pick, drilling and blasting, crawling through blackness, sweating on his knees as he shoveled coal into waiting carts. And always close at hand lurked the threat of a cave-in or blast of a violent death.

What set Hatfield apart from the other young men of the area was his skill at gunplay, exceptional even among the many hill-country men who took pride in their marksmanship. In the fashion of the legendary heroes of the Old West, Hatfield often carried two pistols, and it was said he could shoot with either hand with deadly accuracy. Sometimes, for the sake of speed, he would fire right through his pocket. To demonstrate his marksmanship he would throw a potato in the air, draw his pistol and split it open. About five years earlier Hatfield had engaged in what he liked to call "a little shooting match" with a mine foreman named Wilson. The unfortunate foreman did not survive the encounter. Questioned by authorities, Hatfield had claimed self-defense and was cleared of wrongdoing.

Hatfield's fists were also a formidable weapon. In his first year in office he had inflicted what the *Williamson Daily News* called "a good pummeling" on former Matewan Mayor "Squire" Andy Hatfield, whom Sid Hatfield had never forgiven for his testimony against him in a civil suit. Arrested for felonious assault, Sid Hatfield was released when no one pressed charges. Asked about the injury done to the "Squire," Hatfield demonstrated his scorn for the whole Matewan establishment. With a straight face, the police chief contended that the former mayor had been bending over to feed his swine, when "one of the pigs grabbed him by the nose and came very near biting it off," before Sid Hatfield could rescue him. "We hope our people can get along better in the future," commented the *Williamson News.*

Hatfield had been a heavy drinker until he realized that liquor got him into trouble and dulled his reflexes. When he was twenty-four he quit cold. Two years later Testerman made him chief of police. His new responsibility and his sobriety did not cause him to alter his other habits. Single and carefree Hatfield ran with the boys, excelled at pool and poker, chewed and smoked and had an eye for the ladies. One lady he was particularly interested in, according to local gossip, was Jessie Testerman, the twenty-six-year-old wife of Matewan's mayor. It was not hard to see why. The First Lady of Matewan was buxom and vivacious, with warm brown eyes and a coquette's smile. Once Hatfield became police chief he spent considerable time visiting with the mayor and his wife. Beyond that, some of Hatfield's detractors in town, of whom there were more than a few, claimed that he also managed to visit with Jessie Testerman when her husband was absent. And on occasion, it was said, Hatfield and the mayor's wife could be seen evenings, walking near the Tug, among the trees that lined the river bank. If the mayor himself had heard these stories, he gave no indication in his dealings with his police chief.

Working together, Mayor Testerman, Chief Hatfield and Sheriff Blankenship managed to serve as a buffer for the miners of Mingo against the power of the coal operators, whose rule elsewhere in southern West Virginia was unchallenged. Their role as protectors led to increased tension when the coal operators sought to counter the union's organizing drive by evicting union members from their company homes. The miners lived in these houses without leases and the company's legal argument for the evictions was that the tenancy of the miners was dependent on their employment. "It is like a servant who works in your house," S. B. Avis, a lawyer for the Williamson Coal Operators, explained. "If the servant leaves your employment, if you discharge him, you ask him to get out of the servants quarters. It is a question of master and servant."

But neither the miners nor Sheriff Blankenship accepted this master-servant theory. On April 27 Blankenship arrested Albert Felts, the detective agency's man in Matewan, charged him with illegally processing evictions and hauled Felts and twenty-seven of his men into magistrates court. Felts and his cohorts were released but only after agreeing to have Blankenship handle future evictions. Blankenship insisted that the companies give their tenants ample notice before acting, and with him at the controls, these ejections moved at a much slower pace.

Though frustrated by the sheriff's foot-dragging on evictions, the companies nevertheless pressed ahead on that front and deployed another weapon, so-called yellow-dog contracts, a tactic developed by the Hitchman Coal Co. in Wheeling, West Virginia, in 1907. Under these agreements, whose name signified the contempt in which they were held by union members, workers pledged not to join a union under penalty of forfeiting their jobs and, not incidentally, their right to live in company housing. If these contracts were violated, the coal companies not only fired the offending employee but went to court to get an injunction to stop the union from organizing. The yellow-dog contracts had been challenged in the courts by the UMW but after a prolonged legal battle had finally been upheld by the U.S. Supreme Court in 1917.

Hoping to boost the spirits of the embattled miners, the union's state headquarters sent two officials, Fred Mooney and William Blizzard, one of District 17's most determined organizers, to Matewan to conduct an outdoor rally. In a driving rain, some 3,000 showed up to listen to the prominent visitors who spoke while someone held an umbrella over each of their heads.

"Obey the law," Mooney admonished the good people of Matewan. But he also told them that the same law should bind the mine operators as well. The operators, he pointed out, had posted notices ordering miners to vacate their houses, and several of them had been ejected by Baldwin-Felts agents before the eviction proceedings had even reached the courts. These private detectives, Mooney told the crowd, had no right to assume the authority of duly appointed law enforcement agents.

The next day Mooney fired off a telegram of protest against the tactics of the mine operators to U.S. Attorney General Palmer. "Miners are being evicted without due process of law," Mooney wired. "One miner held up with Winchester while roof was torn from his home. . . . Cannot some action be taken by your department?" But Palmer, who many believed like General Wood had his eye on a run for the White House, was busy with his drive to defend the nation against the Bolshevik menace, and not incidentally promote his own future. He left the miners and operators to their own devices.

In Matewan, a few days after Mooney's futile telegram, a notice addressed to employees of the Stone Mountain Coal Company, signed by its superintendent, P. F. Smith, went up on the window of the company store. Smith reminded the miners that the houses in which their families lived were owned by the company and stated, in no uncertain terms, that miners who joined the union must leave these houses at once. It was to enforce this order that Tom Felts had ordered the dispatch of extra men from Bluefield into Matewan on May 19.

It was only natural that the mine operators should turn to the Baldwin-Felts agency when they had a tough and dirty job to be done. Founded in West Virginia thirty years before, the agency had gained a nationwide reputation for its dedication to union busting. In 1908 a West Virginia mine owner named Justus Collins, who pioneered the role of the detectives as strikebreakers, in a letter to an Alabama operator credited "these gentlemen" with having wiped out the union in the Williamson field. "Gentlemen" was not a term that everyone would apply to the Baldwin-Felts agents, certainly not the union miners. The detectives were a rough and harsh-tempered lot, many of them former policemen, others of a type often pursued by police. One union sympathizer labeled them as "nothing more than 'bums,' with psychopathic personalities." In 1913 when the UMW struck the southern Colorado coalfields, Baldwin-Felts agents riding in two armored cars strafed a tent colony of strikers with machine gun fire, killing one worker and wounding another. Later Tom Felts would claim that if there were machine guns used in the Colorado strike violence, they did not belong to the Baldwin-Felts agency and he knew nothing about who might have fired them. He had made the same denial about the machine guns used against union miners in the Paint Creek–Cabin Creek strike in West Virginia.

The Baldwin-Felts agents performed a variety of chores for the mine operators. Deputized by obliging sheriffs under West Virginia's permissive laws, they maintained order in the mining camps, collected rents, guarded the payroll and also kept out "undesirables," a broad category that included known criminals, professional gamblers, prostitutes, moonshiners and, certainly not of least importance, union organizers. Baldwin-Felts agents stirred particular hostility among the miners for their undercover work. Joining the workforce ostensibly as ordinary miners, they reported back to the company on the plans and remarks of their co-workers who appeared sympathetic to the union. These unfortunates were then fired and blacklisted so that other companies would not hire them.

West Virginia's law enforcement officials marveled at the zeal and ruthlessness of the Baldwin-Felts spies, likening the agency's network to the secret police of Czarist Russia. One of Tom Felts's most intrepid snoops, Charlie Lively, posing as a union sympathizer, went to great lengths to ingratiate himself among union members, even organizing several locals in Mingo County at the height of the union's campaign in the spring of 1920. A familiar figure at union meetings, Lively also found time to establish a restaurant in Matewan, which became a gathering place for union men. Even as he reported back to the coal companies, Lively "was loud in his denunciation of the gunman system and advised the miners to join the union and fight for their rights," Fred Mooney later recalled. Lively was much in evidence on the May evening that Mooney addressed the mass meeting of miners and afterward invited Mooney and Blizzard back to his restaurant. Lively and Mooney had been raised in the same Kanawha Valley town of Davis Creek, and had once belonged to the same UMW local. Lively could not have been more hospitable to his old friend on this rainy evening, urging Mooney to spend the night at his own home. But to Mooney, Lively's enthusiasm seemed a bit overdone, and he turned the invitation down, a decision that saved him from later regret.

Following the Paint Creek–Cabin Creek strike, the excesses of Baldwin-Felts agents as publicized by U.S. Senate hearings had shamed the West Virginia legislature into enacting legislation that supposedly curbed the detective agency. But the act failed to provide any penalty for its violation, thus leaving the mine owners and their detectives free to pursue business as usual.

Still and all, memories of the agency's role in the Paint Creek–Cabin Creek strike were fresh enough in May of 1920 that as the Felts brothers readied for trouble in Matewan, they thought it prudent to proceed with caution. Soon after he arrived in town, Albert Felts, the agency's field superintendent, approached Matewan's Mayor Cabell Testerman, to ask permission to mount machine guns on the roofs of some downtown buildings.

Despite the dim view some people took of his detectives, Albert Felts saw himself as a paragon of respectability. In Bluefield he lived in one of the town's "most picturesque homes," and he was a member in good standing of the Shriners and of the Elks. In trying to negotiate with Testerman, Felts was careful to couch his proposal in restrained and courteous terms. The chief concern of the Baldwin-Felts agency was helping preserve the peace in Matewan, Felts stressed.

The town seemed quite peaceful at the moment, Testerman pointed out.

But no one knew when there might be trouble, Felts argued. The machine guns would give his men command of the streets in case of a disturbance. And then the detective played his trump card. This was important for the job the agency needed to do in Matewan, he told the mayor, important enough that he would be willing to invest $1,000 in the mayor's goodwill. Would that help Testerman see things his way?

Testerman shrugged off the clumsy bribe and shook his head. The detectives were welcome to stay in town, provided they obeyed its laws, he told Felts. But no machine guns, not as long as Cabell Testerman was mayor.

Albert Felts took the mayor's refusal in stride. He remained in Matewan, keeping his eye on the union's activities and prepared for the confrontation he knew would be coming someday soon.

Once his brother told him that reinforcements were on the way, Albert realized that day had arrived. When the seven agents Tom Felts had dispatched to Matewan arrived, Albert Felts was on hand as train No. 29 pulled into the Norfolk and Western depot.

The station was just off Mate Street, the main thoroughfare of this town of only about 800 people, whose name its citizens pronounced as "Maitwahn." Lined by maple trees with whitewashed trunks, Mate Street had just a single block of businesses, dominated by the Old Matewan National Bank building on one corner. A few doors down, past Chambers Hardware, the Dew Drop Inn, and a couple of drug stores, a jewelry store and the pool hall was the Urias Hotel, which served as headquarters for the Baldwin-Felts men. Right across the street, in another office building, was the union's headquarters.

The hotel owner, Anse Hatfield, was such a good friend to the detectives that Tom Felts had written his brother Albert, just a few days before, suggesting that Albert "show Anse Hatfield a little attention and let him know that we appreciate the attitude which he has taken." The seven men who came in on No. 29 stopped off at the Urias and while they waited for the other agents due to arrive on the next train made quick work of the lunch Anse Hatfield served them.

Shortly after noon Albert Felts, who by then counted thirteen men in his party, including himself and another Felts brother, Lee, decided it was time to get to work. The detectives piled into three cars and drove to the Stone Mountain property on the outskirts of town, where they began clearing the miners' cabins, hauling the furniture out and piling it on the street, while the miners and their families stood by helplessly. The Baldwin-Felts men intended to finish in time to make the 5:15 train back to Bluefield.

But Felts and his crew were soon interrupted by Testerman and Sid Hatfield. Felts knew that both were friendly to the union, but of the two it was Sid Hatfield who most worried Albert Felts. Indeed the Baldwin-Felts agency viewed Hatfield as such a formidable adversary that Tom Felts had decided he would rather have the police chief with him than against him. In his pocket as he waited for Sid Hatfield to approach outside the homes of the evicted miners, Albert Felts carried a note from his brother, Tom, proposing that Hatfield be persuaded to change sides for a consideration, perhaps $200 to $300 a month. "Whatever arrangements you make," Tom Felts had cautioned, "must be understood and have this understood with Hatfield. If you make a deal with him I think you should suggest some means of bringing about a controversy or misunderstanding of some sort which will result in a split between him and the bunch which would look plausible and give him an opportunity of turning against them and telling them where to head in," Felts explained. "Because that is what we will expect if we make a deal."

Now, however, as Albert Felts and Sid Hatfield confronted each other in front of the evicted miners' cabins, was obviously not the time to reach any such agreement. Neither Hatfield nor Testerman was in any way conciliatory when they demanded to know what authority Felts had for the evictions.

The circuit judge in Williamson had given approval, Felts told them. But he had no written court order with him, and Hatfield and Testerman were not satisfied. Felts simply shrugged off their arguments and directed his men to go on with their work. Testerman, not one to swallow such affronts readily, was plainly indignant. "Well you don't pull anything like that and get away with it around here," the mayor snapped. Then he turned on his heel and together with Hatfield strode away.

Back in town about 1:30 P.M. Testerman and Hatfield immediately phoned Sheriff Blankenship's office in Williamson and asked the advice of Deputy Jesse "Toney" Webb, the sheriff's office manager. Webb put Testerman through to Wade Bronson, the county prosecutor, who told him the eviction orders were illegal and that warrants should be issued against the detectives. Testerman sent Charlie Kelly, one of the evicted miners, to Williamson to swear out the warrants.

Rapt listeners to these conversations were the Matewan phone operators, Elsie Chambers and Mae Chafin, the latter a cousin of the great enemy of the union miners, Logan County Sheriff Don Chafin, whose views of the mine workers union she shared. Mae lost no time in calling Anse Hatfield, the ally of the Baldwin-Felts men at the Urias Hotel to warn him. Anse, she knew, could be relied on to alert the Baldwin-Felts detectives.

By mid-afternoon the whole town knew that Charlie Kelly was due to arrive with the warrants Testerman sought on the 5:15 P.M. from Williamson, the same train the Baldwin-Felts men planned to take back to Bluefield. Fearing trouble, Testerman told Hugh Combs, a UMW loyalist, to select a dozen "sober-minded men" to back up Hatfield, as special officers. By about four P.M. Combs's deputies, duly sworn in by Testerman along with some other miners, began gathering at the railroad station. Nearly all were armed and while they waited cleaned their guns and checked their ammunition.

Meanwhile, Albert Felts and his men had returned to the Urias Hotel to pack. After they learned of Sid Hatfield's plans, they broke down their Winchesters and wrapped them up. Albert Felts and his two top deputies, C. B. Cunningham and Lee Felts, the only detectives who had licenses to carry small arms in Matewan, stashed their pistols on their belts as they walked to the station. They were almost there when Sid Hatfield once again appeared, accosted Albert Felts, and told him that he and his men were under arrest. The warrants, Hatfield said, were coming on the next train.

Felts laughed. "Sid," he said, "I've got a warrant for you too. I'm going to take you with me to Bluefield."

Hatfield laughed, too, and both men, smiling as if they were playing out a practical joke, walked down the street together, the other detectives trailing behind.

They all stopped when Testerman joined them in front of Chambers Hardware, across from the station, and asked to see Felts's warrant. Felts handed the mayor the warrant and Hatfield backed off into the hardware store. While Albert Felts still smiled Testerman studied the warrant, which in vague language charged Hatfield with taking a prisoner away from a local constable a few days before. Finally, the mayor declared: "It's bogus."

A bystander jeered: "It might as well be written on gingerbread."

Albert Felts still smiled and said nothing, but reached for his gun.

There would be nearly as many versions of what happened next as there were witnesses to the scene. By some accounts Albert Felts shot the mayor, then whirled and fired into the hardware store at Sid Hatfield. Others said that the first shots came from the store itself, and from Hatfield's gun, striking both Felts and Testerman. At any rate everyone agreed that the first men to fall were Cabell Testerman and Albert Felts.

Then all hell broke loose. Immediately Hugh Combs's deputies and some of the other miners who had been looking on raked the street with gunfire. Albert Felts, his brother Lee and Cunningham drew their pistols and returned fire, but they were badly outgunned. Most of their comrades, whose guns were packed away, scrambled for cover behind trees and fences. But Combs's men were relentless. One after another the Baldwin-Felts agents fell.

Detective Troy Higgins, a former Virginia police chief, ran for his life. But a miner named William Bowman, one of Hugh Combs's crew, took aim with his rifle and shot him dead.

Not everyone's marksmanship was that good. Art Williams, a miner and another special deputy, fired all the rounds in his .32 caliber revolver at Lee Felts but missed with every shot. Felts fired back with the same lack of success. Finally Reece Chambers, whose son Ed was a Hatfield crony and who had just seen Lee Felts shoot his brother, Hallie, opened fire with his rifle and Felts fell to the ground, mortally wounded.

Another detective and former Virginia police chief, A. J. Boohrer, managed to find his weapon and shot a miner, Bob Mullins, who had been fired that morning for joining the union. "Oh Lord, I'm shot," Mullins cried as he fell to the ground, mortally wounded. But then Art Williams picked up another gun he found on Lee Felts's body and shot and killed Boohrer, standing so close to him that Boohrer's blood covered his pistol.

So many miners fired at C. B. Cunningham that no one could claim clear credit for his death. His body was riddled with bullets, his head half blown off.

E. O. Powell, another of the unlucky seven who had arrived that morning on No. 29, also went down under a hail of bullets.

His comrade J. W. Ferguson staggered away from the station after taking a round from a miner's gun. A bystander helped the wounded man to a chair on the porch of a nearby home, but fled as a group of miners ran toward the house. When Ferguson's good samaritan returned a few minutes later he found the detective lying dead in an alley and a bullet hole in the back of the chair. The miners carried Ferguson's body to a burial ground on a litter fashioned out of Winchesters. As they passed through town one of the miners nodded at the rifles and said: "They brought them in here and they're going out on them."

Some of the detectives were more fortunate. One, John McDowell, running for his life, asked a woman bystander: "What's the best way out of town?" Pointing to the river, she said, "Split the creek." McDowell jumped into the Tug River and swam to safety in Kentucky. One of his colleagues, Bill Salter, took the same route, after first hiding for hours in a trash can until the violence had ended and the coast was clear. Another detective, Oscar Bennett, escaped because he had gone to buy cigarettes just before the battle started. When he heard the shots he sneaked on a waiting train and rode safely out of town.

By the time the 5:15 arrived from Williamson, bringing the warrants Hatfield wanted, it was all over. Nearly 100 rounds had been fired. Two miners and seven detectives including Albert and Lee Felts were already dead. The other six agents had escaped with their lives.

Mayor Testerman was mortally wounded. Put on a train for Welch, he died later that night, unable to comprehend what had happened. "Why did they shoot me?" were Cabell Testerman's last words. "I can't see why they shot me."

The bodies of the detectives lay on the street until Blankenship and W. O. Porter, the mayor of Williamson, arrived on the 7:15 P.M. train and saw to it that the corpses were put on a train back to Williamson.

Blankenship promptly deputized "every man in sight," and his posse patrolled the streets, keeping a close eye on each passing train. More Baldwin-Felts men might be on the way, the sheriff feared, and he wanted, as he said later "to protect the town."

The Baldwin-Felts men did not come, though one train that passed by did carry a contingent of state police who thought it wiser to delay their arrival in that bloody town until morning. But there was good reason for concern in Matewan and all of Mingo County. This place and its people were now fully caught up in a ruthless conflict between two old enemies. For the clash at Matewan Station that took ten lives and lasted twenty minutes was just the latest outburst in the struggle that had raged for half a century between the men who owned the mines and the men who worked beneath the earth.

2

"What Does Labor Want?"

"**I** HAVE ALWAYS found that if I could not make a living in one place, I could in another," John L. Lewis told a convention of Illinois miners when he was an up-and-coming UMW official. A plan to use union funds to provide for unemployment benefits was up for a vote and Lewis opposed it, using an argument about the work ethic that he might have borrowed from the local Chamber of Commerce. "Many men do not hunt work if they can make a living without it," he declared.

Lewis's views, expressed in 1909, a decade before he became UMW president, drew on his own experience in life and the labor movement. Born in 1880, he was the son of an Iowa miner who moved from one coal town to another to provide for his family. After a few youthful years as a miner and construction worker in the West, Lewis returned to Iowa, where he sought a place for himself among the middle-class gentry of the town of Lucas, marrying the schoolteacher daughter of a local doctor and trying his hand at business and then as a politician. After his grain-and-feed venture went sour and he lost a race for mayor, Lewis decided to go back to coal mining and to make a future for himself in the UMW. With the active support of his father and five brothers, Lewis quickly became president of one of the largest locals in the state.

When he made known his opposition to unemployment benefits, ten years before he became the UMW's president, Lewis was already embarked on a career path that relied less on comradely proletarian zeal than on his own energy, ambition and gifts for ingratiating himself with members of the union hierarchy. Friendly union leaders in Illinois helped him get a post as UMW lobbyist in Illinois, where he caught the eye of AFL President Samuel Gompers, who made him a national organizer for the labor federation. During the next few years Lewis rarely rested as he traveled around the land on political and organizing missions for the AFL and the UMW, assignments that gained him influential friends among labor leaders. In 1917 he was made acting vice president of the UMW. "Our ship made port today," Lewis wrote presciently in his journal. Without ever standing for election for office in the national union, he had positioned himself to be its leader.

This blend of pragmatism and individualism, which carried Lewis to the top of his union, reflected the forces that shaped the shaky status of American labor in a land imbued by the spirit of free enterprise. While business ruled the roost, the promise of abundant economic opportunity supposedly loomed for one and all. Optimism about their chances for economic and social mobility widely shared by American workers undercut the class consciousness and sense of solidarity that held sway among European laborers.

To be sure, workers had to deal with plenty of inequity. This was true for all workers, but particularly for immigrants, who learned that they often had to pay off the steel plant foreman to get hired, and even so generally got the job closest to the open hearth furnace. As for African-Americans, they learned early on that certain preferred positions, such as the better-paying craft jobs were out of bounds. In sum, injustice was a fact of working-class existence, almost every day and everywhere.

Even so, the knife edge of unfairness did not bite nearly as deep or as sharp in this country as it did in the lands where the immigrants came from, or in the case of black workers as it did deep in the heart of Dixie. And there was enough hope for economic advancement and improvement, buttressed by the pledge of political justice and equality embedded in the nation's fundamental charters, to curb resentment and restrain commitment to labor's challenge to the established power structure.

Given what they hoped were favorable prospects of ascending higher on the economic ladder, many workers had to ponder whether they were better off trying to exploit their own chances for advancement rather than committing themselves to improve conditions on the lower rungs. The labor movement of course had other huge barriers to overcome—the might of entrenched corporate interests, the widespread bias of the legislatures, the indifference if not outright opposition of the courts and a fractious and diverse workforce. But the internal ambivalence of workers toward trade unions contributed to the difficulties in overcoming these external obstacles and to American labor's slow and unsteady progress in redressing economic inequities.

Thus, frustration dominated the saga of the early trade unions as they hesitated and vacillated, shifting their energies from the economic arena to the political arena and back again, doing best in good times, and least, when they were most needed, in hard times. The labor movement did not gain a permanent foothold in the United States until late in the 19th century with the birth of the American Federation of Labor, a very businesslike labor organization. Established by a group of national unions in various trades in 1886, the AFL quickly staked out positions that symbolized labor's willingness to come to terms with the American way.

The new federation backed away from the broad and idealistic political reforms that had been dear to the hearts of the once potent Knights of Labor and other earlier national labor amalgams. Unions would continue to aim at political goals, the new federation decided, but only by working through the existing political parties rather than entering the political arena themselves. Under what was called the "new unionism," more mundane concerns close to home—wages, hours and the resolution of grievances—would now assume top priority.

This practical doctrine found its most articulate spokesman in Samuel Gompers, who emerged as the paradigm for the modern

American labor leader. Born in a London East End tenement at
the midpoint of the 19th century to the family of a Jewish cigar
maker, Gompers finished his formal schooling at the age of ten; he
began work, first as an apprentice to a shoemaker, then like his father, in a cigar factory. But his education continued long afterward.
In the United States, to which his family immigrated in the midst
of the Civil War, Gompers began to spend much of his spare time
at Cooper Union, the New York cultural and educational center,
absorbing knowledge at lectures and testing his wits in informal
debates.

Gompers also tried out his ideas on his fellow employees in the
cigar shop. Everyone contributed to the conversations, and also to
a fund for buying newspapers, magazines and books, which included the output of Marx, Engels and other socialist thinkers. But
when it came to socialism Gompers was fond of quoting the advice
of a fellow worker and ex-socialist. "Go to socialist meetings,"
Gompers remembered being instructed. "Learn all they have to
give. Read all they publish. Just don't join." He never did.

Also of great weight in shaping Gompers's outlook was the infamous riot in Tompkins Square in lower Manhattan where jobless
workers gathered to protest during the great depression of 1874.
Mounted police, drawn by reports that radical agitators had instigated the assembly, charged the crowd, swinging their clubs with
wild abandon, striking out at bystanders as well as protestors. Little public sympathy was forthcoming. Typical was the comment of
the *New York Times*, which found the flight of the protestors from
the charging police, "not unamusing" and portrayed the demonstration as the handiwork of alien troublemakers. Witnessing the
violence, Gompers, who also blamed the violence on outside agitators, took the lesson to heart. "I saw that leadership in the labor
movement could be safely entrusted only to those into whose
hearts and minds had been woven the experience of earning their
bread by daily labor," he later wrote.

Vowing to steer clear of radicalism, Gompers helped to rescue
his own Cigar Makers Union from near collapse by raising dues

and providing health and unemployment benefits. His success compelled other unions to adopt his businesslike tactics. It was only natural that Gompers should play a leading role in melding these national unions into a new organization, which by 1886 would become the American Federation of Labor, with Gompers himself as its first president. It was a post he would hold, with the exception of a single year, 1895, when sour economic times led to the election of a socialist dissident, until his death in 1924.

Throughout his rule Gompers continued to preach straight-ahead dollars-and-cents unionism. He spoke scornfully of "theorizers" and "intellectuals," whom he contended served only to sow confusion and dissension in the ranks of labor. Nevertheless, deep in his heart and in the back of his mind, he still cherished broader goals that reflected the idealism of his cigar shop seminars. "What does labor want?" he once asked rhetorically. "We want more school houses and less jails, more books and less arsenals; more learning and less vice; more leisure and less greed, more justice and less revenge, in fact more of the opportunities to cultivate our better natures to make manhood more noble, womanhood more beautiful and childhood more happy and bright."

But as time went on and the organization he headed became more entrenched as part of the economic system that ruled the nation, Gompers thought less about building a new Jerusalem and more about maintaining the power and influence of himself and his federation. It was Gompers's conviction that labor never could displace the capitalists on top of the economic heap that encouraged the barons of industry to negotiate with Gompers and his unions. And this was a reality he never forgot.

Many trade unions benefited from the order and cohesion that Gompers's approach brought to the labor movement, but none more so than the United Mine Workers. Early attempts at organizing coal miners had foundered on factionalism and internal rivalries, and were often disrupted by violence.

In 1874 the same economic conditions that led to the Tompkins Square riot that had so impressed Gompers triggered pitched

battles between police and Pennsylvania anthracite miners outraged by arbitrary wage cuts. Adding to the hostility on both sides
were dark stories about the role of the Molly Maguires, a secret society whose members allegedly sought to intimidate the coal operators as their forebears had once cowed landlords in Ireland with
threats of arson and murder. Ultimately it turned out that the coal
operators themselves had manufactured many of these threats as
an excuse to smash the unions trying to organize the mines. Meanwhile, though, mass trials in 1875 led to convictions of more than a
score of the Molly Maguires, no fewer than ten of whom were
hanged for murder.

The challenge of unionizing the coal mines was compounded
by the nature of the coal miner's job and of the industry. Digging
coal was like no other task in the new industrial economy. The
men toiled in subterranean chambers called rooms or places,
linked by tunnel corridors to the vertical shaft that served as entrance and exit for the mine. Each miner worked in his own room
under an earthen roof supported by layers of unmined coal and
wooden bulwarks, which the miner positioned. Because the tunnels were shallow, the miner usually had to lie on his side and
swing his pick against the lower part of the wall or "face" of his
room to get at the coal. After he had cut a three- or four-foot-deep
slit in the face, he placed a piece of wood under the cut to keep the
coal from falling prematurely.

Then, using an auger five or six feet long, he drilled holes
above the cut for an explosive charge. Once he had packed and
placed the charge, corked it with clay or dirt and attached the fuse,
the miner backed away to what he hoped was a safe distance and lit
the fuse. After the coal had been loosened by the blast, the miner
loaded it onto tram cars, being careful to remove the larger pieces
of slate and rock. The tram cars, mounted on tracks, were ultimately hoisted to the surface for shipment.

Not only was this work hard and tedious—it was laden with danger. Between 1890 and 1917 more than 26,000 miners were killed
on the job, many in explosions. About 12,000 miners were maimed

each year, some crippled for life. Sometimes hundreds died at a time; one blast in the little Illinois community of Cherry wiped out the town's entire population.

The miners could feel a distant kinship with their bosses, since in a sense they themselves were entrepreneurs. In most cases they were paid not by the day or the hour but by the ton, their earnings depending on how much coal they dug. The one compensation for the arduous and perilous ask was the freedom the miners enjoyed, unusual for workers in the industrial age. They set their own hours. If the operators established work schedules, the miners ignored them. Separated as they were into dozens of individual rooms the miners were hard to supervise.

The auxiliary workers, or "day men," who did not actually dig the coal but instead did the hauling and maintenance work, and made up about 30 percent of the workforce, were paid a daily wage. But they too were difficult to oversee since they often labored in remote sites, had little contact with foremen and relished their independence as much as the men who actually mined the coal.

At first glance the working conditions—isolation, danger and piece-rate compensation—would have seemed to make the chances of effective union organizing impossible. But other factors helped to draw the miners together, chiefly their resentment against the companies that controlled their lives, not only beneath the earth but above it. Miners worked in company mines with company tools and equipment, which they were required to lease, money that was promptly deducted from their pay.

The company stores that sold them food and other necessities charged exorbitant prices, which the miners had to pay, since there was no other available outlet. Just to guarantee the captivity of their consumers, coal companies paid the miners in scrip, which only the company store would accept. Even when wages rose, coal operators kept ahead of the game by boosting prices at the company store.

A couple of stanzas from Carl Sandburg's "Company Town" captured the essence of that life:

> *You live in a company house,*
> *You go to a company school,*
> *You work for this company,*
> *According to company rules.*
> *You all drink company water*
> *And all use company lights,*
> *The company preacher teaches us*
> *What the company thinks is right.*

In addition to imposing their will on the workers' lives, the mine owners often cheated on their own work rules, through a process called cribbing. A miner's pay was based on the tons of coal he mined. Each car that left the mines supposedly held a specific payload, such as 2,000 pounds. However, operators at times rigged the cars to hold more coal than the specified load, so miners would be paid for only 2,000 pounds when they actually had brought in as much as 2,500. In addition, some operators docked the miners for slate and rock mixed in with the coal. Since docking was imposed at the judgment of the checkweighman, hired and paid by the mine owner, miners were frequently cheated.

One reason for the appeal of a labor union was that it offered the miners a way to combat such chicanery. In bargaining with the mine operator the unions would generally insist that miners have the right to elect the pit committee and checkweighmen, who would represent the miners' interest in making sure they got an honest break from the company scales.

As one mine workers' ballad advised:

> *Union miners stand together,*
> *Heed no operator's tale.*
> *Keep your hand upon the dollar*
> *And your eye upon the scale.*

Still the autonomous nature of the job, and the idiosyncrasies of the industry, shaped the way unions were organized and did their business. "Coal mining is vastly different from any manufacturing or transportation activity," John L. Lewis pointed out. "It simply cannot be standardized because nature has refused to standardize rocks, slate, coal or men." Consequently miners from different regions tended to look after their own interests and found it difficult to make common cause with organized unions from other areas.

It was the mine operators who provided the impetus for the miners to band together. With the expansion of railroads, coal operators from various fields started to compete for each other's markets. Price changes now affected large producing areas and a great number of producers and the miners who worked for them. When Ohio miners joined in 1882 to form the Ohio Miners' Amalgamated Assn, their charter proclaimed: "It is evident that some step should be taken to check the evils that were fast accruing from insane competition, the heavy foot of which always rests upon the wage of the producer." But the problem extended beyond Ohio's borders and required efforts by management and labor that transcended state lines.

To cope with the crazy-quilt pattern of the industry, coal mine unionists in 1885 launched the National Federation of Miners; by 1890 the new organization had evolved into the United Mine Workers, which soon joined forces with Gompers and the AFL. Mirroring the expansion of the industry whose workers it represented, the UMW grew rapidly. But it faced a major problem in one state, West Virginia, where the union movement lagged far behind. This reality had been driven home to the union in 1897 when it staged a nationwide walkout in protest against wage cuts brought on by the depression that devastated the economy for most of the decade. Over 100,000 miners responded and the strike paralyzed the northern fields.

The non-union miners of West Virginia, though, held out. Gompers threw the prestige and power of the AFL into the fray, summoning labor leaders and supporters around the country to rally the West Virginia miners to the UMW banner. Among the labor luminaries who flocked to the Mountain State were Eugene

V. Debs, the founder of the American Railways Union, and the fiery "angel" of the miners union, Mary V. (Mother) Jones, then nearing sixty, who had already made a name for herself as an organizer in the mines of Pennsylvania.

The mine owners fought back. Company police jailed organizers and drove them from the state. Courts issued injunctions to stop the unions in their tracks. UMW President Michael Ratchford convened an emergency meeting of national labor leaders in Wheeling, who protested to the governor of the state against the violations of civil liberties and called upon labor organizations around the country to join the fight. Unions sent thousands of dollars to the state along with more organizers. Mass meetings around the country registered support for the miners' cause.

"The downtrodden miners of West Virginia will take heart," Ratchford wrote Gompers. "And as if by magic they will stand erect and assert their rights as free men."

But whatever magic Ratchford hoped to conjure up was no match for the economic and legal power of the mine owners. Trying to organize the miners over the opposition of sheriff's deputies and company police "was taking one's life in his hands," an organizer dispatched to proselytize the black miners of West Virginia's McDowell County later wrote. "While we never had any injunctions issued against us, we had men and Winchesters against us which were in most cases just as effective." John Mitchell, then vice president of the UMW, survived to become the union's president a few years later only by fleeing the gunshots of company guards, jumping in an icy mountain stream and swimming to safety.

Despite the resistance in West Virginia, the impact of the 1897 strike in the Midwest was powerful enough so that the union won a major victory there. The ensuing settlement had profound impact on the UMW mainly through one key element—the establishment of the Central Competitive Field Agreement between miners and mine operators in four states—Ohio, Illinois, Indiana and Pennsylvania. As a spokesman for the coal operators explained, the purpose of the agreement was to ease the pressures of competition between the mines in the four states: "The idea of this interstate movement was to establish as far as possible uniformity not only in the scale of wages, but in the conditions of mining, and as a result it was applied also to the selling price of coal."

The agreement did not fix the price of coal. But it leveled the playing field in the four states and made it possible for each operator to know what his competitors' costs were. The Central Field agreement won by the UMW opened the door for rapid growth of the union. By 1901 it would claim 250,000 members, making it the largest union in the country, a position that it would maintain for the better part of three decades.

Yet one cloud remained on the UMW's horizon—the coal mines of West Virginia. Said UMW President John Mitchell in 1900: "The principal disturbing feature of the coal industry which in any degree threatens the perpetuity of the peaceful relationship between operators and miners is the absence of organization or mutual understanding between the operators and miners of the State of West Virginia." Determined to expand the markets for their own coal, the West Virginia operators had refused to join in the Central Field Agreement and did all they could to oppose unionism. The United Mine Workers blamed this intransigence chiefly on U.S. Steel, which was one of the largest holders of West Virginia coal land, and notorious for its opposition to organized labor in its own industry. The union pointed out that through its subsidiaries and its corporate connections with the Pennsylvania Railroad, also a vigorous opponent of unionism, and the Norfolk and Western, U.S. Steel was a major force in the Mountain State's coal economy. But apart from Big Steel's anti-unionism, the coal producers of the state, including the independent operators who still produced most of the coal in southern West Virginia, had good reason to battle against the UMW, which could be traced to simple geography. While some West Virginia coal was said to be of higher quality than coal produced elsewhere, the truth was that it had to travel further to reach the industrial centers in the Northeast and Midwest than the product of competing states. Only by keeping the union out, allowing them to hold down wages, could the West Virginia producers make up for their increased transportation costs and gain a proportionate share of the market.

The stance of the West Virginia operators created a threat the union could not afford to tolerate. In 1902 the UMW launched a major effort to organize in the Kanawha–New River Coal field in central West Virginia and won a contract in that area. But unable to make gains elsewhere in the state, the UMW soon lost its foothold in the Kanawha area. The coal operators had formed the Kanawha County Coal Operators Association in 1903, the first such organization in the state, which relied on court orders and Baldwin-Felts detectives in Bluefield to block the union drive.

The UMW retreated, but meanwhile miner resentment against the low wages and heavy-handed treatment by the operators festered and mounted. In 1912, a decade after the UMW's retreat in the Kanawha Valley, thousands of West Virginia's miners, acting on their own, staged a walkout in the nearby Paint Creek–Cabin Creek area, demanding higher wages, the right to organize and an end to cribbing. Eager to exploit the opportunity, the national UMW pledged full support, imposed a special levy on its membership to help finance the strike and dispatched its vice president, Frank Hayes, to the state, along with the redoubtable Mother Jones, whom many miners remembered from her previous visit in 1897.

For a labor organizer, Jones's origins were improbable. A native of Ireland and a former schoolteacher, her life was changed in 1867 when a yellow fever epidemic wiped out her husband and four children. After that she drifted around the country, even working as a madam in a Colorado brothel in the 1880s. Then she began attending union meetings and discovered a talent for proselytizing. Her great strength was her showmanship; the skill and guile she displayed in her performances would have done credit to a Barrymore or a Bernhardt. Her white hair and rounded features gave her a grandmotherly appearance, an advantage she exploited as a license to infuse her diatribes against the mine operators with profanity that would have made a longshoreman blush.

Mother, as the miners called her, displayed her style during the 1900 strike against the anthracite operators when she organized miners' wives to march over the mountains late at night banging on tin pans with the goal of alerting the union picket lines to the strikebreakers trying to slip into work for the morning. Campaigning against child labor, in 1903 Jones organized a week-long march of child mill workers from Pennsylvania to the New York home of President Theodore Roosevelt, selecting the most physically stunted and scarred children she could find, as evidence of the abuses inflicted by their employment. Along with a theatrical flair, Mother Jones was endowed with enough courage to lead a march of strikers through the frozen and treacherous waters of mountain creeks and to stymie a belligerent guard by covering the muzzle of his loaded rifle with her hand.

For the Paint Creek–Cabin Creek strike, she drew on her full range of demagogic talents. In August of 1912, addressing hundreds of miners at a Sunday afternoon rally in front of the State Capitol, she demanded that the governor, Republican William Glasscock (whom she referred to for "modesty's sake" as "Crystal Peter"), drive the mine guards from the state. "You can expect no help from such a goddam dirty coward," she told the crowd, while a court reporter hired by the operators took down every word. "But I warn this little governor that unless he rids Paint Creek and Cabin Creek of these goddam Baldwin-Felts mine guard thugs there is going to be one hell of a lot of bloodletting in these hills."

The old scourge proved to be a sound prophet. Determined not only to crush the strike but also to rid themselves of the UMW once and for all, the operators imported strikebreakers from New York and the South and deployed some 300 Baldwin-Felts detectives to intimidate union organizers and leaders.

The Baldwin-Felts agents were everywhere. They threw up iron and concrete forts bristling with machine guns throughout the area, evicted the miners from their homes, destroying their furniture in the process, and then attacked the tent colonies in which the strikers took refuge. Their crowning gambit was the

"Bull Moose special," a train rigged with iron plate siding and machine guns, which they raced along the tracks one night spraying
bullets into the tents sheltering the miners and their families as
they drove along, a tactic they would, some months later, adapt for
use against striking Colorado miners and their families.

In the wake of the Bull Moose special's ride, the Cabin Creek–
Paint Creek miners retaliated in kind. Using weapons and ammunition provided by the national union, the strikers attacked a mine
guard encampment. The ensuing battle raged for hours and took
sixteen lives, mostly mine guards. In their fury the miners also
blew up the tipples of the mines being operated by strikebreakers
along with the trains carrying coal from the struck mines. They
met trains carrying new strikebreakers to the mines and sent them
packing.

In September 1912, a month after Mother Jones's fiery speech,
Glasscock did intervene, but not in the way she had hoped. Imposing martial law, the governor sent 1,200 state militia to disarm
both the miners and mine guards. The miners at first cheered the
arrival of the troops until they realized the guardsmen's real mission was not to restore peace but to break the strike. The soldiers
arrested more than 200 strikers without warrants and detained
them in makeshift jails. Still the strikers fought on. In February of
1913 Glasscock ordered the arrest of Mother Jones on a charge
of inciting to riot, and, despite the fact that she was stricken with
pneumonia refused to release her.

In March the newly elected Governor, Henry Hatfield, took
office, setting the stage for the end of the strike. Hatfield, too, was
a Republican like his predecessor and no great friend of labor. But
he was determined to get a settlement, even if it meant forcing the
operators to make concessions. He laid down terms including a
nine-hour workday, the right to shop in stores other than those
owned by the company, the right to elect union checkweighmen
and the elimination of discrimination against union miners.

The operators accepted, and so did the UMW officials. But
many rank-and-file miners were dissatisfied, because the settlement

ignored their two most important demands—recognition of the union and an end to the mine guard system. Despite the lack of support from the national UMW and many of their own local leaders and in the face of Hatfield's threat to deport men who refused to go back to work, the miners staged wildcat walkouts, blew up mines and tipples in protest and prepared to renew their strike.

The tide turned in their favor when a U.S. Senate committee that had been investigating the strike issued a report denouncing the arbitrariness of the governor, the intransigence of the operators and the abuses of martial law. Stunned by the public tongue lashing, and fearful of a new walkout by the defiant miners, Hatfield rushed to the scene and pressured the operators into granting the miners' original demands, including recognition of the UMW as their bargaining agent.

The end of the Paint Creek–Cabin Creek strike brought no genuine peace but rather an uneasy truce to the coalfields of West Virginia. The strike would have an enduring and polarizing impact on union and management for years to come. Though they had gained important ground, many miners still felt that they had been betrayed by their national union and their local officials, who they believed had been too willing to accept Hatfield's dictated compromise that ignored key union demands. Their resentment led to a search for new leadership among the more militant elements of the union and ultimately to the election of Tom Keeney and Fred Mooney as president and secretary treasurer, respectively, of District 17. "Keeney was all fire and dynamite," Mooney later recalled. "He asked for and showed no quarter."

It was an attitude widely shared among the miners in West Virginia, who were finding it hard to accept the moderate doctrine of new unionism preached by Gompers, with its emphasis on doing business with business, and also difficult for them to maintain their belief in the American promise of economic opportunity and equal treatment under the law. Following the Paint Creek–Cabin Creek strike, violence had come to be regarded as an almost routine and necessary tactic to deal with the brutal excesses of the mine guard system. After the end of the strike a miner wrote the *Mine Workers Journal* about the slaying of a mine superintendent who had "always kept the miners under an iron rule." Such slayings were justified, the miner wrote, because "as long as they believe in that infamous guard system, peace and harmony is in doubt."

For its part, management harbored at least as much hostility and mistrust. *Coal Age*, the journal of the coal operators, declared that the "so-called strike on Cabin and Paint Creeks was in reality an armed insurrection, formulated by agitators hired by the union and afterwards reinforced by socialists." The coal operators now saw the miners and their union not simply as economic adversaries but as a diabolical force seeking not merely unionization but domination of the West Virginia coal industry and of the United States. The Mingo County operators condemned the union as "unlawful per se, revolutionary in character and a menace to the free institutions of the country."

This perception was heightened when in 1912, the same year as the Paint Creek–Cabin Creek strike, the UMW adopted in its constitution a clause stating that miners were entitled to the "full social value of their product." This language redolent of the reform socialism that then intrigued some labor activists, beyond the reach of Samuel Gompers's influence, outraged the mine operators of southern West Virginia. They viewed the phrase not as harmless rhetoric but as a battle cry, confirming their suspicion that the mine workers union had in reality abandoned the labor movement and instead become a spearhead of revolution. "Their whole object is now and has been since 1912 to cripple all the protecting powers of government so that their armies can march unmolested into the territory of non-Union mines and shoot down the workman and destroy the mining plants at will," warned Harry Olmstead, chairman of the Williamson Coal Operators' Association.

So the battle lines were sharply drawn. Over the next decade the Great War would for a time transform the coal industry, and its fortunes would rise and fall. But one fundamental reality was unaltered. The miners of southern West Virginia and the operators of the mines remained on a course that left no doubt both would someday collide. The only questions were where and when. The answers turned out to be the main street of Matewan on May 19, 1920, where Sid Hatfield and the Baldwin-Felts agents shot it out, an explosion that would bring Harry Olmstead's nightmare of the marching armies of miners to the verge of reality.

3

Seeing Red

THE ECHOES OF the shots fired at the Matewan depot on
May 19, 1920, had hardly died down before the air was filled
with cries of outrage from the leaders of the United Mine Workers
and their allies. Their indignation was undiminished by the fact
that the miners had given better than they had gotten on the
streets of the town. Seven of the ten men who were slain had been
Baldwin-Felts agents. And when the smoke cleared, the detectives
had fled, leaving the field to Sid Hatfield and his union allies.

The union leaders, however, chose to focus not on the outcome
of the battle but on the circumstances leading up to it. The firing
of miners simply because they had joined the union. The ousting
of these men and their families from their homes. And generally,
the unfettered use of power by the Baldwin-Felts agents, the instrument of the mine operators.

All of these practices the union leaders had long condemned.
Now they saw in the violence at Matewan, which commanded front-
page headlines around the country, a chance to focus the attention
of the nation's leaders and of public opinion on the tactics that had
thwarted the union cause for a generation in West Virginia.

The first reports from bloody Matewan were fragmentary and
unclear. But in UMW headquarters in Indianapolis, John L. Lewis
did not wait for the details before he thundered his fury at both
West Virginia Governor John J. Cornwell and the operators of the

mines. "Press dispatches today tell of another shocking outrage in the long lists of such incidents that have been perpetrated in your state by private detectives in the employ of the coal corporations," Lewis wired Cornwell on the day after the shoot-out, making sure to send copies of his telegram to the nation's major papers. "Undoubtedly the American public must be astounded to know that such conditions can exist in any state in this union."

The recently formed American Civil Liberties Union joined in the assault. Established in 1917 as the National Civil Liberties Bureau, the organization's initial mission was the defense of conscientious objectors and critics of the war, whom the Wilson Administration prosecuted relentlessly. When peace returned, the group's lawyers were kept busy on behalf of the targets of various Red scares instigated by Federal and state governments, part of the pervasive paranoia over the Bolshevik regime that had just seized control of the Russian Czar's Empire. The ACLU's leaders saw the violence in West Virginia, not just as a labor dispute, but more fundamentally, as another challenge to the Bill of Rights. Condemning Cornwell's labor policies, the ACLU declared that the carnage in Matewan was an inevitable result of them. Cornwell's priority, now, the ACLU said, must be to reestablish free speech and free assembly in Mingo and Logan Counties.

The very next day no less a personage than the president of the American Federation of Labor, Samuel Gompers, added his voice to the chorus of protest. Gompers appealed to Republican Senator William Kenyon of Iowa, chairman of the Senate committee on education and labor, urging him to conduct an investigation of the violence in Matewan, as that same committee had probed into the Paint Creek–Cabin Creek violence in 1913. Denouncing "the invasion of West Virginia by an armed band of men in the pay of absentee owners of West Virginia mining property," Gompers charged that in West Virginia, "the blackjack and the pistol, the high powered rifle and the machine gun have been substituted for statute law, judges and juries." The bloodshed in Matewan, Gompers said, was simply a repetition of like outrages from West Virginia's past.

"The sense of justice of the American people must be outraged by such usurpations of power."

Reluctant to wait while Kenyon considered Gompers's plea, local union leaders turned elsewhere in Washington, and sought the help of the nation's chief executive, Woodrow Wilson. In a telegram to the White House Keeney and Mooney, the top officials of the UMW's District 17, protested the hiring of detectives by the mine operators, condemned Governor Cornwell and called upon Wilson "to take some immediate steps which will assure the miners of this state that the President is willing to investigate these terrible and disgraceful conditions."

It was not hard to understand why the union men would turn to the president for help in this critical hour. The man in the White House was the same leader whose New Freedom had once provided liberals with a battle cry and hope. "Here muster not the forces of party, but the forces of humanity," the schoolmaster president had declared as he began his first term in March of 1913. "Men's hearts wait upon us, men's lives hang in the balance, men's hopes call upon us to see what we will do."

But since that day much had happened to torment and transform this once inspirational figure. In May of 1920, when the UMW pleaded for his help in West Virginia, Thomas Woodrow Wilson was only sixty-four years old, even in those years an age not all that far removed from the prime of life. But for this sixty-four-year-old man, the energy and convictions that had driven his career were now lost in the past. His body was so eroded by the stroke he had suffered the previous fall while touring the country on behalf of the controversial Treaty of Versailles that he could barely grasp a sheet of paper in his right hand or utter more than a few sentences. And his spirit was so embittered by frustration and defeat that he could not muster the compassion to pardon the aging Socialist Eugene Debs, whom he had jailed for sedition during the war. Of Wilson, Norman Thomas, who inherited Debs's mantle as Socialist leader, said bitterly, that he "had proved recreant to every principle of liberalism which he once professed."

It was not just Wilson's personal condition that stood in the way of the mine workers receiving the help they sought.

A broad panoply of forces were at work, all of them it seemed undermining the prospects of not only the miners in West Virginia but all of those in the country who still shared a commitment to the principles to which Wilson had once seemed dedicated. The impact of this changed condition was underlined by the contrast with the political landscape less than a decade before, when Wilson became the first Democrat in nearly thirty years to gain the nation's highest office.

Woodrow Wilson had begun his climb in national politics at an important juncture in the history of American labor—just as the trade union movement was forging an alliance with the Democratic Party. In the late 19th century the Republicans, led by William McKinley, had been successful in winning the votes of workers by promising a full dinner pail and by delivering prosperity. And McKinley's successor, Theodore Roosevelt, helped to maintain labor's allegiance to the Republicans by championing legislative reforms that would protect unions and workers against the power of the corporate barons who had emerged in the industrial age. It soon became apparent, though, that the talk of reform was mostly just that. Roosevelt was unable to persuade his party leaders in Congress to give labor any meaningful relief. Labor grew even more estranged from the GOP when Roosevelt departed the White House to be replaced in the presidency and at the helm of his party by William Howard Taft, who did not even pay lip service to the idea of aiding labor. Taft's stance helped push labor and the Democrats into each other's arms. As the Democratic presidential nominee in 1912, Woodrow Wilson took his cue from his party's pro-labor platform, redolent with calls for curbs on the excesses of the giant corporations, and moved to bolster his ties with the trade unions. In response, AFL's leaders and operatives around the country bent every effort to turn out the workingman's vote for Wilson. John L. Lewis, for example, who had just been appointed an AFL organizer, campaigned for Wilson in New Mexico and Arizona.

With the help of labor, and the Bull Moose candidacy of Theodore Roosevelt, which divided Republican voters, Wilson captured the White House for the Democrats.

Mindful of labor's contribution to his victory, the new president selected as his secretary of labor, former Pennsylvania congressman and former UMW official William W. Wilson. The new secretary set a pattern for a number of his cabinet colleagues of consulting often with the AFL leadership, particularly on judicial appointees. As the 1916 election approached, President Wilson threw his weight behind measures to aid such varied victims of untrammeled economic power as merchant seamen, farmers, women and children. Most dramatically, the president averted a train strike by pushing through Congress legislation granting the rail unions their demand for an eight-hour day, which had the effect of raising wages by about 25 percent.

In the 1916 campaign Republicans accused Wilson of embracing Karl Marx. But their criticism was more than offset on the hustings by the energy and enthusiasm of the labor unions, who rallied behind Wilson everywhere, helping him squeak through to a narrow victory.

Labor's reward was a significant role in the massive task of organizing the economy for war. Even before the United States plunged into the conflict that had been raging in Europe since 1914, Wilson gave Gompers a seat alongside top corporate officials on the Council on National Defense, charged with responsibility for readying the nation's economy to meet wartime demands.

The war brought other benefits for unions. With munitions orders sparking the economy and labor in short supply, workers pushed back against their bosses. They changed jobs, joined unions and threatened to go out on strike. Unions also gained from the rulings of the National War Labor Board, created by President Wilson to implement labor policies for all war-connected industry. The new agency promoted the eight-hour day in some industries, raised wages, granted women equal pay for equal work and in other ways large and small fostered the spread of unionism. Between

1917 and 1920, union membership jumped by more than 70 percent from three million to more than five million, for the first time approaching 20 percent of the workforce.

For the coal miners and their union, the war took on special meaning because of the critical need for their output to feed the nation's war machine. "Scarcity of coal is the most serious danger which confronts us," Woodrow Wilson declared. Backing up his words, he ordered the draft boards of West Virginia to exempt all miners declaring that they were "the essential labor for the support of the government and the liberties of free men everywhere." The *United Mine Workers Journal* featured a statement from General Pershing asserting that the "work and support of the coal miners thrills us and helps to make our hearts more strong for the battle. I have always been certain that organized labor would stand steadfastly behind us until victory for democracy is achieved."

The government efforts to promote support for the war raised the political consciousness of the miners. The propaganda that called men to the colors and sold Liberty Bonds also spoke of overturning autocracy, demanded sacrifice and commitment and justified violence as a legitimate means to achieve righteous goals. Americanism became a surrogate for socialism, embodying the principles of equality and liberty that socialism itself championed.

For their part, the miners did not disappoint. Each week southern West Virginia set a new record for production. "Ours must be the superior will to conquer," inveighed the *Mine Workers Journal*. "Ours the grim courage to endure, to sacrifice and hold unfalteringly until the final victory sounds forever the doom of autocracy."

Over 50,000 miners ignored their draft exemptions and enlisted and 3,000 of these came home in coffins. But conditions were even more dangerous at home. Indeed District 17 President Frank Keeney wrote Wilson that the West Virginia miners had a higher death rate than the AEF. In 1918 mine explosions and accidents claimed the lives of 404 West Virginia miners. When thirteen coal diggers died in a mine explosion, the *Mine Workers Journal* declared that "these local boys died in the interests of democracy, they were exerting their manpower in the production of coal with which to help win the war."

With the mines now under the control of the Federal Fuel Administration, in return for a promise not to strike, the miners got a wage increase. It was a modest hike, particularly in comparison with the huge profits the operators were reaping. But more important was the dramatic growth of the union, whose organizing drives were fostered by the Fuel Administration's determination to regulate and stabilize the mines. By the end of the war the membership of District 17 had jumped from 7,000 in 1917 to more than 50,000, while nationwide the UMW's ranks expanded to take in nearly 500,000 of the country's 760,000 miners.

But if the labor movement in general did well during the war, other liberal causes suffered setbacks whose impact would carry over into the postwar era, leading to collateral damage to trade unions. In the early months of 1917 as he struggled with the decision of whether to lead his country into the conflict in Europe, Wilson worried that war would undo many of the reforms he had promoted in his first term. If the United States entered the war, Wilson told Josephus Daniels, his navy secretary, "you and I will live to see the day that the big interests are in the saddle." And he admitted to journalist Frank Cobb that he was reluctant to awaken "the spirit of ruthless brutality" that would infect "the very fiber of our national life."

Wilson himself did much to make his gloomy premonition come true. One of the early ominous signs was government's campaign against Big Bill Haywood's union, the Industrial Workers of the World, the radical fringe of the American labor movement. For conservatives and business leaders, reluctant to attack the more respectable Gompers and the AFL directly, the Industrial Workers of the World, or Wobblies as they were called, with their dedication to strikes and industrial sabotage, and their long-term goal of toppling capitalism made an ideal target.

Wilson ordered Federal troops who were already on duty in the West protecting industrial sites against German sabotage to ensure that union activism of the Wobblies did not disrupt the war effort. As things turned out the troops served as strikebreakers and provided a shield for local authorities and vigilantes to crack down on the Wobblies. Far from objecting the AFL encouraged this practice, in the belief that obstructing the "subversive" IWW would clear a path for patriotic AFL unions to move in. Instead, military rule drove out not only the Wobblies but also the AFL. Army officers in charge saw to it that in the interest of labor stability and continued production, the workers joined company unions. Meanwhile, in the fall of 1917 Federal agents raided IWW headquarters around the nation, and a Federal grand jury indicted nearly 200 IWW leaders on charges of sedition and espionage.

The success of the war on the Wobblies coincided with assaults on labor's allies all across the board, which gained legitimacy from a series of repressive laws Wilson prodded Congress into enacting. The most odious of these new statutes was the Espionage Act, prohibiting not only spying and sabotage but also public criticism that could be considered as harmful to the military. Its most celebrated victim was Eugene V. Debs, the perennial Socialist Party presidential candidate and longtime leader of the railroad workers. Debs was convicted after he ridiculed Wilson's claims that he was waging the war to "make the world safe for democracy." "This is too much even for a joke," Debs had remarked. That was enough for a Federal judge to sentence him to ten years in prison, an occasion that prompted Debs to deliver what would become his most memorable public utterance. "While there is a lower class I am in it," Debs told the court. "While there is a criminal element I am of it. And while there is a soul in prison I am not free." But Debs's idealistic rhetoric did not stop the wave of repression, which spread to state and local government.

In March of 1918 Russia's revolutionary rulers, who had overthrown the Czar, made a separate peace with Imperial Germany and deserted the Allied cause. The new Bolshevik rulers of the Kremlin called upon workers everywhere to rise up and put an end to the war of the capitalist oppressors. Nothing of the sort happened. But the threat, real or imagined, gave new impetus to the obsession with subversion, which persisted even after the slaughter in Europe ground to a halt on November 11, 1918. Even some supposed liberals, like Labor Secretary William Wilson, took the occasion of a Washington conference of governors and mayors on postwar planning in March 1919 to condemn the recent general strike in Seattle, and other walkouts in Butte, Montana, Lawrence, Massachusetts, and Paterson, New Jersey. These were not really "industrial economic disputes in their origin," Wilson claimed, but rather part of "a deliberate attempt to create a social and political revolution that would establish a Soviet form of government in the United States and put into effect the economic theories of the Bolsheviki of Russia."

The widespread belief in the connection between labor and violent revolution that Secretary Wilson's remarks mirrored had been fostered by the nation's wartime experience. Americans had emerged from the war militant in their patriotism and in their allegiance to what was often called "the American way." Though no one knew exactly what this credo meant, businessmen assumed that it stood for their right to bar union organizers from their premises. War stories of spies and international intrigue had fed the public's imagination and stretched its credulity. In their anxiety citizens did not it find hard to accept the notion that the struggle of American workers to improve their lot through collective bargaining was the leading edge of an armed revolution engineered by the rulers of Soviet Russia.

To be sure, in 1919, Russia's Bolshevik regime that Secretary Wilson spoke of fearfully was being racked by civil war. While in America's supposedly Red-ridden homeland, the *Atlantic Monthly* estimated the total members of the Socialist, Communist and Communist Labor parties at a not so grand total of 130,000. In other words the total membership of the parties of the Left amounted to barely more than two-tenths of one percent of the adult population. But such statistics were overshadowed in the spring and summer of 1919 by a series of genuinely alarming incidents of violence and near misses.

Alerted by the explosion of a bomb sent through the mail to the home of a U.S. senator, a conscientious postal clerk turned up more than thirty similar neatly wrapped infernal devices, which had been set aside because they lacked sufficient postage. Their addressees made up a pantheon of American business and government, including John D. Rockefeller, J. P. Morgan, Supreme Court Justice Oliver Wendell Holmes and Attorney General Palmer.

A few weeks after escaping that threat, whose progenitor was never discovered, Palmer was going to bed for the night when he heard a bang, as if something had hit his front door. Then came a blast. Rushing outside he found some human limbs, all that remained of his uninvited caller who had been blown to pieces by his own contraption. Nearby, investigators found a telltale clue, a copy of the radical publication *Plain Words*.

While the spate of bombings and attempted bombings lent credence to the specter of Red Revolution, it remained for the most part only a potential menace. A more immediate and tangible problem for the public, and particularly for the labor movement, was inflation, which had gained impetus from wartime shortages and continued to rage out of control following the Armistice. The notion that inflation might have at least as much to do with the soaring prices manufacturers were charging for their goods as with the wages they paid their hired help did not seem to occur to President Wilson. That summer he warned workers against going out on strikes, which he claimed "are certain to make matters worse, not better—worse for them and for everybody else." But discontented wage earners paid little heed to Wilson's warning, thus darkening Wilson's view of the labor movement even more. Indeed, as the strikes mounted, it was hard to distinguish the rhetoric and views of the Democratic President from those of his Republican opponents.

In September of 1919 most of Boston's policemen walked off their beats, demanding higher wages and affiliation of their union with the AFL. Vandals and looters went on the rampage and Boston papers called the striking men in blue "agents of Lenin" and described the city's plight as a "Bolshevist nightmare." Responding to a plea for help from the city's mayor, Massachusetts

Governor Calvin Coolidge dispatched the state militia to patrol Boston's streets. When asked about rehiring the strikers, who had been fired for leaving their jobs, Governor Coolidge delivered what would become a classic response: "There is no right to strike against the public safety by anybody, anywhere, anytime." That statement made Coolidge a national hero, gaining him the prominence that led to his selection as vice president and ultimately his ascension to the nation's highest office. But in substance and tone the words of the new champion of conservatism scarcely differed from those uttered by President Wilson, the erstwhile paladin of liberalism. A fortnight before his crippling stroke, Wilson branded the strike "a crime against civilization."

But there were higher stakes than the salaries of a few thousand policemen in the postwar industrial conflict that now challenged Wilson. Two of the country's most important industries—coal and steel—pitted powerful employers against their workers. These two businesses, together with the railroads, made up the backbone of the American economy. Coal and steel workers had watched with envy and admiration when only three years earlier Wilson had helped the rail workers win a historic victory, the eight-hour day. The steel workers too looked to Wilson for support as their nascent union sought to flex its muscles, convinced as their leader John Fitzpatrick put it "that the government would intervene and see to it that the steel barons be brought to time." But with the dismantling of the wartime labor agencies and his own increasing self-absorption and resentment, Wilson lacked the means or the inclination to play the role of friendly arbiter that labor sought. Instead, when more than half of the nation's steelworkers struck the steel mills in September of 1919, Wilson sent Federal troops and marshals to help break the strike.

The mine workers were in a better tactical position than the steel unions. First of all, labor relations in the industry were still governed by agreements reached during the war under the aegis of the Federal Fuel Administration. Then, too, the mine workers had an influential friend in Wilson's labor secretary, William Wilson, former official of their union. Finally, and not least, they had a formidable new leader in John L. Lewis, who in 1919 at age thirty-nine had become acting president. A hulking figure of a man, Lewis made an indelible impression because of his heavy jowls and bushy eyebrows, which would endear him to political cartoonists for decades. He employed his deep voice, to bully or charm with equal ease. He was a master both of caustic invective and soaring rhetoric, replete with biblical and Shakespearean references carefully calculated for their effect. He pleaded labor's cause, Lewis once said, "not in the quavering tones of a feeble mendicant asking alms, but in the thundering voice of the captain of a mighty host."

Indeed his mine workers, now more than 500,000 strong, filled that description. They were the nation's largest and strongest union, potent enough, many feared, to shut the coal industry down. And, like their new leader, they were in a militant mood.

When the union's delegates assembled in convention in Cleveland in September to lay out their demands on management, some of them chanted a ditty that reflected their bitterness at the turnabout in the government's attitude toward them since the Armistice.

> *We mined the coal to transport soldiers*
> *We kept the home fires all aglow*
> *We put old Kaiser out of business*
> *What's our reward? We want to know.*

But where the union saw ingratitude, their government saw only a menace to economic recovery. And this was a threat the Wilson Administration would not tolerate, as it had made clear even before the strike. Wilson had been felled by his stroke a month earlier, but a statement was issued in his name responding to the strike call issued by union president Lewis, condemning the union's action and warning that "the law will be enforced" and "the means will be found to protect the interests of the nation."

"There is no mistaking his meaning," the *New York Times* editorialized. "If words, that is to say reasoning and appeal do not avail, and local authorities confronted by disorder are unable to cope with it, the government will place Federal troops at the disposal of governors of States."

In the event, the Wilson Administration did not even wait for violence to break out to intervene. Playing a key role in the government's strategy, and destined to loom large in the history of that period was Attorney General Alexander Mitchell Palmer. Raised as a Quaker, Palmer was bright enough to have graduated from Swarthmore with highest honors at nineteen, and two years later to gain admission to the bar. Entering politics as a faithful servant of Pennsylvania's Democratic organization, he won election to Congress and in 1912 as the leader of the Pennsylvania delegation to the Democratic Convention, he helped to swing to candidate Wilson the delegates from the Keystone State he needed for the nomination.

That service was enough for Wilson to appoint him to the Federal bench and ultimately to make him attorney general. In the fall of 1919, with the president weakened by illness and distracted by events abroad, the nation shaken by domestic turmoil and no apparent heir to Wilson as 1920 Democratic standard bearer, Palmer saw an opportunity and seized it with both hands. Even before the coal miners walked out, the newly minted attorney general thrust himself to the center stage of the nation's affairs by persuading the stricken president to permit him to seek an injunction against the strike.

It is not clear that Wilson needed much persuasion. Josephus Daniels, Wilson's secretary of the navy, confidant and admirer, maintained later that had he been in good health, Wilson would have "nipped the injunction in the bud." It was true that the president was ailing. But the decision to enjoin the mine workers was of a piece with Wilson's rhetoric on the Boston police strike and his crackdown on the steel strike, both of which had preceded his breakdown.

At any rate Palmer got his way, getting a green light from the president and approval from the courts. Citing provisions of the Lever Act, which Congress had passed during the war to give government extra authority to deal with national emergencies, Palmer won an injunction against the strike on the eve of the scheduled walkout. Labor was furious. Its leaders had refrained from opposing the Lever Act only because they had been assured that it would not be used to prevent strikes. Gompers, who up until then had tried to talk Lewis out of the strike, declared the injunction a broken pledge and gave his full support to the strike.

For his part, Lewis charged that the president and his cabinet were the allies of "sinister financial interests." The injunction amounted to, the union chief added, "the most sweeping abrogation of the rights of citizens that has ever been issued by the Federal Court." Lewis's public outrage was echoed privately in the inner councils of the administration by Labor Secretary William Wilson, who threatened to quit, even going so far as to write out a letter of resignation to the president. The labor secretary's indignation was fueled not only by the violation of the promise to labor on the Lever Act but also by the fact that he himself was working furiously to reach an agreement at the bargaining table when Palmer acted, without any advance notice to his cabinet colleague. The old union man warned Palmer that apart from its unfairness, the injunction was impractical because it would not end the strike.

He was right about that. When the November 1 strike deadline came, even though the UMW leaders technically complied with the restraining order, the miners in the pits did not need the economic realities spelled out to them. Unbidden by their leaders, nearly 400,000 walked off the job, shutting down the industry. This defiance of the Federal courts served to confirm the public's fears that America the Beautiful was about to be engulfed by a Red tide. "Revolution Is Stake Radicals Play For in Strike of Miners," one newspaper proclaimed. "Red Bolshevism Directs This Blow Against the Nation," another headline blared. And the cartoonist for the *Post Intelligencer* in Seattle, one of the hotbeds of anxiety, depicted a monstrous foot labeled "Coal Strike" about to trample the Capitol dome in Washington.

With that sort of wind at his back, Attorney General Palmer was emboldened to push even harder against the coal strike. Back to court he went, gaining a new injunction, which went beyond barring the UMW high command from leading the strike by commanding them to take steps to cancel it. Under Gompers's leadership the AFL executive council decried the injunction, pledged its full support to the miners and urged the public to give its backing to the miners.

But John L. Lewis gauged his union's predicament differently. Reckoning that public sentiment was running against him, he canceled the strike, called upon the miners to return to work and declared: "We are Americans, we cannot fight our government." A generation later Lewis would bring outrage upon himself and make his union notorious by doing just that. But for the present, the public and the press hailed Lewis, only recently condemned as a tool of the Bolshevik conspiracy, as a labor statesman. Businessmen and politicians everywhere rejoiced in the end of the strike.

Except that the strike was not over. Tens of thousands of miners would not return to the pits. "This strike can't be stopped," declared Alexander Howatt, president of the Kansas miners, and a critic of Lewis's policies. "We'll call their bluff." The mutiny of the rank and file might have persuaded objective minds of the genuineness of the miners' grievances. But the majority of the press simply interpreted the continuation of the strike as further evidence of a Bolshevik plot. Lewis and other UMW officials were cited for violating the injunction and bound over to face Federal criminal investigation.

But none of this served to dig any coal. Winter was coming on, and as temperatures dropped so did the coal reserves. Schools and factories closed, electric signs dimmed and trains were cut back. Labor Secretary Wilson, talked out of resigning by his cabinet colleagues, argued that something needed to be done besides getting injunctions. It was his persuasion that led the administration to offer the unions a 14 percent increase with the promise that an arbitration commission would investigate their other demands.

Lewis knew that the miners wanted more. But he also knew the weaknesses of the union's position. Aside from the negative attitude of the public, the UMW had a more tangible problem—the non-union mines in southern West Virginia had continued to produce throughout the strike. Their output was steadily increasing as the West Virginia operators sought to take advantage of the opportunity their resistance to unionism had given them. Or as Harry Olmstead, chief labor negotiator for the Williamson field operators, later boasted: "The Williamson and neighboring non-union fields of West Virginia and Kentucky gave to the country practically all the supply of coal that was had and averted general disaster among the railroads and industries of the country."

Once again Lewis was ruled by pragmatism. He urged the miners to go back to work. Three months after they resumed digging coal, on December 10, the arbitration commission recommended the 27 percent wage increase that would cause such resentment among the non-union miners in West Virginia's Mingo County.

The end of the coal strike did little to allay public hostility toward liberals and radicals of all sorts, particularly those who were unfortunate enough not to claim U.S. citizenship. This was an environment perfectly suited to the inclinations and ambitions of Attorney General Palmer. In that turbulent summer of 1919, shortly after his own house was bombed, Palmer had gotten a special $500,000 appropriation from Congress to bolster efforts to ferret out subversives. For this purpose, Palmer used the funds to establish a new agency, the General Intelligence Division, and installed at its head an eager young agent named J. Edgar Hoover, who soon compiled a list of 60,000 purportedly dangerous radicals. The nation's new top Red hunter also sent to every newspaper and periodical of note in the country letters over Palmer's signature warning of "the real menace . . . of the Red Movement."

To root out this danger, in January of 1920 Palmer's agents swooped down on alleged nests of subversion around the country, arresting more than 4,000, and deporting hundreds. Often arrests were made without the formality of warrants. Prisoners were routinely held incommunicado and denied the right to legal counsel. But the few who questioned these procedures were drowned out by the patriotic majority. "There is no time to waste on hairsplitting over infringements of liberty," scolded the *Washington Post.* And the *Washington Star* chimed in by underlining the danger the country faced: "This is no mere scare, no phantom of heated imagination—it is cold hard plain fact."

If further validation of the raids were needed, Palmer himself supplied it. He claimed that the evidence from the raids served to prove that the domestic radical movement, presumably including labor unions, was dominated by radical aliens. Describing the prisoners caught in his net he declared: "Out of the sly and crafty eyes of many of them leap cupidity, cruelty, insanity and crime; from their lopsided faces, sloping brows and misshapen features may be recognized as the unmistakable criminal type."

Though Attorney General Palmer spearheaded the great Red Scare of 1919–1920, the person ultimately responsible was of course the president of the United States, Woodrow Wilson. Josephus Daniels and other admirers of the president later blamed the president's toleration of Palmer's excesses on Wilson's health. That argument had merit, up to a point. Since September of 1919 Woodrow Wilson had played only a limited role in the government he headed. The cabinet kept meeting, but without the president, at the call of its ranking member, Secretary of State Robert Lansing. But when Wilson learned of these informal sessions he viewed them as bordering on mutiny and summarily fired Lansing, replacing him with Bainbridge Colby, a New York lawyer bereft of foreign policy experience.

But just as important as his physical debilitation in shaping Wilson's attitude toward Palmer's excesses was the fact that what mental powers the president possessed were focused on his losing battle to save the League of Nations. When he did find time to consider the furor at home his reasoning seems to have been a mishmash. On one hand he still liked to think of himself as committed to the defense of free speech and other civil liberties. On the other hand, he grew to share in the fear of Bolshevism, which his attorney general sought to dramatize. Indeed in Wilson's case his antagonism toward Reds took on a personal aspect because he had come to regard the Bolsheviks as a prime force in opposing his own blueprint for international peace, including the League.

Yet Wilson, like many politicians before and after him, liked to have things both ways. In his own mind he wanted to see himself as a guardian of the nation's rights and liberties. In the same message to Capitol Hill in which he asked for a new sedition law, Wilson warned: "The seed of revolution is repression," and urged care and restraint in administering all restrictions on liberty, for whatever that was worth. Thus in April 1920, at the first cabinet meeting he had attended in more than six months, Wilson turned to his attorney general and said, "Palmer, do not let this country see red." "It was a needed admonition," observed Josephus Daniels, "for Palmer was seeing red behind every bush and every demand for an increase in wages." Needed it may have been, but Wilson's caveat certainly must have surprised Palmer, coming as it did from the same man who had given him every encouragement in his anti-Bolshevist binge.

This was the president to whom in the following month, after the slaughter in Matewan, the union miners of West Virginia appealed for help. Keeney and Mooney made their plea to Joseph Tumulty, Wilson's most trusted adviser on political matters, asking him to make an appointment with the president for John Spivak, a liberal journalist recruited by the ACLU to aid the union cause in West Virginia. Spivak, the District 17 leaders said, "represents all the organized miners of West Virginia."

Spivak had been dispatched to Washington once before to seek White House help in the fall of 1919 following the abortive union protest at Marmet and had met briefly with Tumulty. "From out of me poured details of the miners' difficulties, of organizers beaten and sometimes killed, of the Governor's refusal to enforce civil rights and of the miners' determination to exercise these rights, even if they had to use force," Spivak later recalled. In his zeal and naïveté Spivak hoped that Tumulty would promise immediate action. Instead all he got for his pains was a vague promise to look into the matter. "He seemed anxious to get rid of me," Spivak observed. Nothing came of that meeting.

Just as nothing came of the telegram that Keeney and Mooney sent in May of 1920, except for a letter from Attorney General Palmer. Claiming to be speaking for the president, Palmer wrote Mooney that Wilson lacked authority to intervene. Because Edith Bolling Wilson, the president's second wife, managed to shield her husband from most things in the world outside his sickroom, there is no evidence to suggest the president ever saw or even knew of the telegram from the embattled leaders of District 17. But given Wilson's postwar attitude toward the cause of organized labor, there is no reason to believe that he would have looked with favor on the miners' plea for help. At any rate, all that is known is that the president made no response and took no action.

The mine workers did get a response from another Washington politician, Iowa Senator Kenyon, to whom Gompers had appealed, contending that the national sense of justice had been outraged by the abuses of the West Virginia mine owners. There was a time in the not so distant past when Gompers's assessment might have been accurate, when political leaders and public opinion would have registered a protest and when Kenyon would have been moved to act. But that time was over and done with. A week after Gompers's appeal, he got Kenyon's response, but it was not the answer he was looking for. The violence in West Virginia was not an appropriate issue for Senate consideration, Kenyon wrote Gompers. Congress should first wait and see what action the state courts would take.

The message to the mine workers of West Virginia was clear. They were on their own.

4

"A Powder Keg Ready to Blow"

WHILE PUBLICLY decrying the conditions that brought on the May 19 shoot-out in Matewan, union leaders privately regarded the outcome of the violence as a precious opportunity. For years their organizing efforts in southern West Virginia had been stymied not just by the heavy-handed tactics of the Baldwin-Felts operatives but also by the intimidating specter cast by the detective agency. But now the bodies littering the street at Matewan Station served to undercut the aura of invincibility that had cloaked the detectives and repressed efforts at unionization.

It was no accident that in the immediate wake of what was becoming known as the Matewan Massacre, miners flocked to join the union fold. "Once these outlaws were out of the way there was a great rush for membership in the union," declared the *United Mine Workers Journal*. Mother Jones, who had been roving through southern West Virginia on behalf of the UMW, came to Williamson to add her personal brand of fuel to the fire. "I want to say to the robbers of Logan that Mother Jones is going in, we are going to clean up West Virginia," she declared. "I am not going to take any guns. I am going in there with the American flag, that is my banner and no rotten robber or gunman can meddle with me."

The national union threw its support behind the organizing drive with what counted even more than rhetorical inspiration— money. In response to a substantial grant from headquarters, Frank Keeney wrote to International Vice President William Green, who years later would head the AFL: "We have Mingo County nearly completed and are breaking into McDowell. I do not propose to be blocked, bluffed or brow beaten in this campaign until every miner is in the organization."

Late in June when the miners convened en masse in Williamson to rally behind the union, they instructed Keeney to make another effort to persuade the operators to bargain with the union. But lest anyone mistake their militance, they voted to call out their members on strike if coal operators continued to ignore the union's efforts to negotiate. Sure enough, starting July 1, 6,000 men struck twenty mines in Mingo and Pike counties with a daily output of 25,000 tons.

But as Keeney and his comrades would soon learn, whatever advantage they might have gained from the bloodshed in Matewan would prove to be temporary. While the union counted the battle of Matewan as a victory, Tom Felts had plenty of agents to take the place of the casualties of that encounter. And the coal companies would have no trouble finding other allies in their struggle against the union. Indeed by massive use of their economic power, the operators were able to enlist the resources of the state and Federal government against the union men, turning their contest with organized labor into a lopsided struggle.

Hoping to aid the UMW cause, the American Civil Liberties Union tried to drum up public support and provide legal assistance. But however well-intentioned, these genteel tactics proved ill-suited for the cut-throat nature of the struggle in West Virginia. The ACLU seemed "under the impression that there is some semblance of legal procedure here," Jonathan Spivak, the organization's man on the scene, groused in a letter to the ACLU president, Roger Baldwin. "There is not. You can't hold a meeting here, get pinched, and then fight it out in the courts. If you try to hold a meeting in the southern counties you'll never live to see the courts," Spivak said, and then added this warning: "This state is a powder keg ready to blow up any minute."

Like the miners, the operators saw this contest as a life-and-death struggle. And when the union made efforts to negotiate, the operators rejected them out of hand. Typical was the response of H. M. Ernst, assistant general manager of the Pond Creek Coal Co., to a telegram from Keeney, asking to bargain on behalf of the Pond Creek's miners, who had signed up for the union almost to a man. "We know of no organization among our men nor any differences regarding wages, working conditions and so forth," Ernst replied stiffly. "The feeling among our men and the company is unusually harmonious at the present time, but there is a very bitter feeling against your organization. In view of these facts we have nothing to discuss with you and must respectfully and emphatically decline your invitation."

Keeney, as he did right after the May 19 shootings, once again sought help from Washington, this time from the Department of Labor, asking the agency to mediate the dispute. In response, two agents from the department met with an official of the Coal Operators Association, whom they presented with a statement warning that "serious trouble," causing property damage and loss of life, threatened unless the coal dispute was settled. The best approach, the statement advised, was through collective bargaining, either with a union or some other method that assured the miners' representation.

The operators promptly rejected those terms and sent the Labor Department agents on their way. Instead of negotiating, the owners brought in strikebreakers by the trainload and began reopening the struck mines. "Are you in need of any miners?" one enterprising labor agency wrote the struck mines. "If so we can offer you for immediate shipment any number of experienced miners, with or without families of any nationality desired." Once they received an order, the labor agencies often did not bother to inform the workers they recruited that they would be going into the cauldron of a bitter struggle. Indeed, in some cases they told them they were be going to work for unionized mines.

The unions did not sit idly by and accept the newcomers. They put their own men on the trains entering Mingo County and saw to it that each train of scabs was greeted by a reception committee of strikers and organizers. "Upon alighting the men would be surrounded by dozens and perhaps hundreds of the strikers who would seek first to induce them to refuse to go further and accept transportation back," complained Harry Olmstead, chairman of the Williamson Coal Operators Association. "Should this matter of persuasion fail it was followed by a system of abuse, scathing denunciation, vilification."

Even worse, Olmstead contended that the strikers seemed to have the law on their side. Sheriff Blankenship, whose support for the union had already been demonstrated, sent his deputies to the train stations along with the striking miners to confront the strikebreakers imported by the mine owners and to underline the risks they ran. Stressing to the unhappy visitors the bitterness of the conflict they faced, the union representatives often offered to pay their carfare back to their homes. Indeed, during the first six months of the dispute, District 17 officials spent $14,000 buying return tickets for would-be strikebreakers. Some were in such a hurry to depart that they left their belongings behind them, and Keeney later collected twenty-two suitcases filled with the clothing of erstwhile scabs.

When, despite the efforts of the union, the operators managed to reopen nearly all the mines, under the protecting guns of the Baldwin-Felts guards, the union did not give up. Strikers continually harassed workers in the reopened mines, dynamited the tipples where the coal cars were unloaded and strafed the entrances with rifle fire from the hills. A favorite tactic of the union forces was to place tree trunks across the tracks used by the mine cars. When the drivers of the cars stopped and got out to clear the tracks, the miners fired at them from ambush.

The governor of Kentucky ordered units of the state's National Guard to Pike County, bordering Mingo, to patrol the mine fields on the west side of the Tug River. But West Virginia, unlike Kentucky, had never reestablished its national guard, which had been federalized during the war. Governor Cornwell was forced to rely on sheriff's deputies to keep order, with mixed results. In anti-union McDowell County, south and east of Mingo, the sheriff's office did what it could to aid the operators by protecting the trains bringing in strikebreakers, leading to repeated clashes with miners. On Independence Day of 1920, three McDowell County deputies were shot at by miners, firing on them from ambush with high-powered rifles, or so the sheriff's office claimed. But the miners said they only opened fire after they themselves were shot at while going to a union meeting. Two miners and two deputies were wounded in the skirmish. Two days later, in a firefight between a group of deputies and a half dozen miners with high-powered rifles, two men were shot and wounded on each side, with miners and the deputies each claiming they were ambushed by the other.

Antagonism intensified and led to more bloodshed. The home of McDowell deputy and mine guard Berman Hatfield, known for his brutal abuse of miners, was burned to the ground in early July. A few days later, Hatfield's bullet-ridden body was found near the railroad tracks in the town of Panther, near the Mingo County line, apparently shot from ambush. Soon after, miners erected a mock effigy of Hatfield's grave site on a sandbar in the Tug River near Matewan, a throwback to 17th-century English custom, signifying the depth of their hatred of the murdered deputy.

But in Mingo County itself the sheriff's office was a different story. The operators wanted Sheriff Blankenship's deputies to guide the strikebreakers through the threatening crowds of strikers and union supporters. But Blankenship, to the surprise of no one who knew him, refused. Since the sheriff had only had two deputies, the Red Jacket coal company sent him a list of its own mine guards, asking him to deputize them. Red Jacket, the largest coal operation in Mingo County, sprawling across 11,000 acres adjoining the Tug River and employing more than 1,000 men, and a leader in the use of yellow-dog contracts, clearly had much to gain from such an arrangement and had abundant resources to carry out its part of the bargain. But Blankenship refused to go along. He claimed the company's privatization plan would violate state law, a nicety sheriffs elsewhere in southern West Virginia ignored.

The sheriff's balkiness infuriated the mine owners. "They went after me," Blankenship later recalled. "They have always dictated to the fellows that have been in office, and when I got in there, I didn't take this dictation from anybody."

Unable to make headway with Blankenship, Red Jacket officials complained to Cornwell about the sheriff's behavior.

But it did them little good. Cornwell had no authority to issue orders to Blankenship or any other duly elected sheriff. The best he could do for the mine operators was to take a more subtle approach. In a letter to Blankenship, he asked the sheriff what steps could be taken to curb the disorders in Mingo County.

The answer from Blankenship was loud and clear: Everything was under control, "very quiet" in fact. "In view of the fact that practically all of the mines in this field are organized we can not conceive of any reason why there should be further disturbances," he told Cornwell. Yes, Blankenship had heard the same rumors that had evidently reached the governor's office—about mobs parading along the roads and such. But each and every time these reports had been investigated, it turned out to be a case of "so and so saw it and was telling me." Said Blankenship: "We have never been able to ascertain a single person who recognized any member of the supposed mob." Meanwhile the governor should rest assured that "every precaution" was being taken and anyone who actually violated the law would be dealt with severely. Just in case, Blankenship was securing extra deputies.

Given Blankenship's attitude, the only resort remaining to Cornwell and his coal company allies was West Virginia's new state police force. Warning that West Virginia was in danger of being overrun by Bolsheviks and anarchists, Cornwell had rammed through legislation creating the state police in 1919. Never one to underestimate a threat, Cornwell also pointed to the 8,000 inhabitants of the state who were citizens of nations with which, in the absence of a peace treaty, the United States was still technically at war. To blunt anticipated opposition from organized labor, the governor sent a letter to all the state's unions warning them that they could ill afford to be seen as offering "indiscriminate opposition" to a measure designed to protect the peace of the state and the safety of its citizens.

Besides, Cornwell claimed, creation of a state police force would encourage the legislature to act against two common practices abhorrent to organized labor—the private police forces created by the mine operators and the payment of deputy sheriff's salaries by the operators, notably in Don Chafin's Logan County.

Once Cornwell got his state police, he never returned to either of these two thorns in the union's side.

As it turned out, though, the 121-man force that came into existence in the fall of 1919 fell well short of meeting the high expectations of Cornwell and the coal companies, at least at first. This was in large part because of the independence of the first commandant, Jackson Arnold, a World War I combat veteran and a grandnephew of the Confederate idol General Thomas "Stonewall" Jackson. The limitations of the statute establishing the force prevented troopers from intruding on the authority of Sheriff Blankenship, or any other local sheriff, unless specifically ordered to do so by the governor. And given Arnold's insistence on running his own shop, Cornwell was reluctant to intrude on his authority.

As a result, mine operators complained bitterly to Cornwell that the harassment of their strikebreakers continued, while the state police stood by. "Is there no way by which the constabulary [state police] can stop this verbal vilification to which our men are subjected whenever their steps happen to cross the paths of the agitators?" an exasperated Red Jacket official wrote Cornwell in June of 1920.

No, nothing could be done, Cornwell responded, unless the law was changed in the future.

Meanwhile if the state police were turning out to be a disappointment to the mine operators, for the union they were proving to be a pleasant surprise. "Very fair," was the way Fred Mooney, District 17's secretary-treasurer, appraised the state police's initial responses to the strike. "They did not intimidate anybody." The only trouble came, Mooney reported, when some of the troopers "got hold of some of that mountain dew. Then one would get out of the way sometimes."

The union's positive view of the state police was reinforced when troopers arrested two mine guards who lived in Kentucky for possession of unlicensed revolvers and blackjacks. Their employer complained to Cornwell, claiming that his men had immunity from arrest in West Virginia. Cornwell took the issue to Jackson Arnold, who responded by pulling his men out of Mingo County. "So long as I happen to be Superintendent I propose to conduct it as I deem proper, regardless of attempts to dictate by letters of innuendo or otherwise," he wrote Cornwell late in June.

That of course did not suit the mine operators at all. They prevailed on Cornwell to get Superintendent Arnold to send about ten of his men back to Mingo and station them at one of the mines, "so that in case of any trouble they will be on the ground, and we will not have to wait three or four hours to get them from Williamson," one of the mine operators wrote the governor in mid-July.

Lest he seem insensitive to the niceties of the situation he added delicately: "Please do not infer that I am dictating to you." The truth was that Cornwell, like his predecessors in office, was so accustomed to taking orders from the mine owners that he may not have even noticed this latest example of high-handedness.

At any rate the mine operators at last found something positive in the role of the state police. But they were not satisfied: They wanted more. In a telegram to Cornwell praising the reassigned contingent of state police for achieving "peace and quiet," the relentless Harry Olmstead of the operators association added: "We anticipate this will be the result at most mines when sufficient protection is apparent. With enough men properly placed we believe this field would be at work on a normal basis in two weeks."

But Olmstead reckoned not with Jackson Arnold, who was as resolute as his celebrated ancestor. Whatever he might have thought about the coal operators before he took command of the state police, their habit of going over his head to the governor whenever it suited their purposes could scarcely have improved his opinion. Besides, this latest idea from Olmstead, which would have converted the state police force into a corps of mine guards, was simply bad police tactics. "I do not believe more men should be sent to the county," he told Cornwell when Olmstead's proposal was referred to him. He and his own ranking officers had concluded at a strategy conference that the best way to deal with Mingo's problems was to station twenty-five to thirty men at strategic locations so they could fan out and patrol the entire county. This strategy, he pointedly noted, has been "fully explained to those whose investments in the county seemed to entitle them to consideration." Instead of helping make his plan work, though, the mine operators had used the state police on hand as "stationary guards" and now wanted more men to use the same way. Implementing such a policy, Arnold told the governor late in August of 1920, would require 500 men, four times the existing strength of the department.

That settled matters for Cornwell. The day after getting Arnold's letter, he called for the Army.

Still taking advantage of the wartime short cuts for getting Federal intervention, which allowed him to avoid appealing to the president, Cornwell on August 28, 1920, sought help directly from Major General George A. Read, commander of the Army's V Corps area, or central department. "Disorders and threatened disorders are too numerous for the state police to deal with," the governor told Read. Based on more than a score of letters from local citizens claiming their lives had been threatened and "private information" about plans for the "commission of other outrages," he deemed "prompt action imperative" if lives and property were to be protected.

Read lost no time. He sent 500 men, elements of two infantry regiments stationed at Camp Sherman, Ohio. Within a few days they had moved out to the mines along a fifty-mile stretch of the Tug.

The call for Federal troops implied that conditions in West Virginia were out of control, which customarily in that state had led to a declaration of martial law. This was the precedent established by Governors Glasscock and Hatfield during the Cabin Creek–Paint Creek strike. Indeed the mine operators immediately demanded that the governor follow the example of his predecessors and make just such a declaration. But Cornwell, remembering that both those proclamations had been controversial, drawing a barrage of criticism both from within the state and also from the U.S. Senate investigating committee, held off.

Still no one could be sure what was in the governor's mind, and union leaders and their supporters were naturally concerned.

So also as it turned out was one of the leading jurists in the county, Mingo County Circuit Judge James Damron, who unexpectedly emerged as an influential and aggressive ally of the miners. As the circuit judge, Damron had early on involved himself in the storm set off by the Matewan shoot-out. Right after the battle he went to Matewan to personally assume command of the investigation. He sought first to prevent the flames of violence from spreading, ordering gun dealers to keep a record of their sales and cutting off new licenses to gun dealers. Most importantly he impaneled a special grand jury to investigate the violence and issued instructions that were in marked contrast with the outlook of the mine operators.

Infuriated, and shaken by the events of May 19, and egged on by Thomas Felts, who was grieving for his two brothers, the operators wanted nothing less than swift retribution against Sid Hatfield and his cohorts. Such an outcome would not only satisfy Tom Felts's urge for vengeance, it would drain the impetus from the mine union's organizing drive in Mingo. But as Damron spoke to the grand jurors, it became clear that he was taking a broader view of the May 19 shoot-out. The investigation should not confine itself to those few bloody minutes when ten men died, Damron concluded, but should also consider the full range of events leading up to the shooting—the union efforts to organize the miners and the eviction of the miners from their homes. There was reason to believe that these evictions were illegal on their face, Damron told the jurors, adding that there was evidence that bribes had been offered to officials of Mingo and Matewan if they would wink at the evictions.

Then the grand jury began hearing evidence. This was no easy task. While there was no lack of witnesses to the tragedy, the testimony most of them offered was obviously colored by whether they sympathized with the union and Hatfield or with the operators and the Baldwin-Felts detectives. Where did the truth lie? The grand jurors had such difficulty deciding that they chose to follow a highly unusual course. In July, when they had finished sifting through all the conflicting evidence, they handed down indictments against Sid Hatfield and twenty-two miners for conspiring to murder the detectives. At the same time they indicted four of the detectives who had survived the gun battle for the murder of Cabell Testerman and the two miners. County prosecutors decided to try Hatfield and the miners first, on the charge of murdering Albert Felts. The four detectives were ultimately tried in Greenbrier County, where coal mines and coal miners were few, and acquitted by a sympathetic jury.

It was the future of those proceedings that most concerned Judge Damron when he learned that Cornwell had called in Federal troops because he assumed that martial law would soon follow. If that should happen, Damron had to worry that the courts would be suspended and to wonder, in that event, what would be the status of the indictments the grand jury he appointed had labored to produce. Damron did not brood in silence about these issues; in a telegram to Governor Cornwell he expressed his "surprise at the thought of martial law in Mingo County," and passed on his concerns to Cornwell.

If such communication had come from any other jurist Cornwell might have been surprised, but given Judge Damron's background such behavior was only to be expected. Most of his
professional life, in law and politics, Damron had seemed to be
waging an unrelenting one-man guerrilla war against the political
hierarchy of the state, including the leaders of his own Republican
Party. In 1908 Damron had joined with a group calling themselves
the "old liners," who charged the "regulars" who controlled the
GOP with draining the public treasury with their expense vouch-
ers. Damron and his cohorts published their own newspaper, accusing the "regulars," led by Henry Hatfield, the Republican
governor elected in 1912, of ballot box stuffing and "hiring ruffi-
ans to bulldoze the decent" to gain political power.

Despite his apostasy Damron gained election to the circuit
court bench in Mingo and after the 1916 election returned to the
pursuit of the good government themes that had engaged him
early in his career. Over the protests of outgoing Governor Hatfield's allies, he gained a writ from the state supreme court allowing him to cleanse the voter registration lists of "illegal voters,
dead men, mules and tombstones."

Damron survived not only these political skirmishes but a murderous assault against his person. On February 1, 1917, a few
weeks before the United States entered the Great War, he was
shot and wounded, though not seriously, while walking home from
his office in Williamson. Suspicion fell against a local citizen who
supposedly bore a grudge against Damron because the judge had
imposed a three-year sentence on his girlfriend's uncle who had
been convicted in a shooting incident.

But Democratic Governor Cornwell thought that given Damron's checkered political background, there might be more to the
incident. He hired a team of private detectives whose only solid
conclusion after an eight-month investigation was that the initial
suspect was probably innocent. The Pinkerton agents identified so
many other local persons with a possible motive for trying to assas-
sinate Damron, from political feuding to personal revenge sought

by any one of a number of husbands whom Damron had cuck-
olded, that they gave up any hope of actually solving the case.

But all this was long forgotten by the late summer of 1920
when Damron, in the midst of campaigning for re-election to the
bench and with U.S. troops deployed in Mingo, wired Cornwell
about the possibility of martial law. That telegram brought a
prompt denial from Cornwell, who quoted from a telegram he had
sent to Wade Bronson, the country prosecutor, stating that there
would be no proclamation of martial law in Mingo County "if
public officials and private citizens cooperate in the enforcement
of the law, the protection of life and property and the punishment
of crimes that have been or may be committed."

Not content with Cornwell's response, Damron launched his
own personal inquiry into alleged incidents of violence, which he
suspected had been inflated or even invented by the mine operators to provide the governor with justification for martial law.
Looking into a report that "200 gunmen" had battled troops at
Chattaroy, Damron learned that the only shooting was done by
mine guards who had shot out the electric lights in front of the
company's store. Another reputed clash between miners and Federal troops boiled down to nothing more sinister than a soldier firing his weapon at what turned out to be a pig running around a
box car. Yet before the dust had settled, Colonel Samuel Burkhardt, the commander of the Army contingent, had rushed to the
scene in a special train. "In the meantime," Damron complained,
"news was being sent out from Williamson by some one to the effect that battles were being had between Federal troops and union
miners and that martial law was inevitable."

In their zeal to persuade the governor to proclaim martial law
the operators did not rest with publicizing incidents of violence,
real and imaginary. They also met with Colonel Burkhardt, who
was easier to impress than Damron. Beyond what the operators
told him, Burkhardt had alarming reports from his own intelligence officers, who had little sympathy for the union, particularly
when its tactics threatened property rights. One report noted that

the miners used "every character of intimidation with frequent instances of assault and destruction of property," to keep the mines closed. Taking a dark view of the organizing drive, the report claimed that the miners had "a well defined scheme for the employment of armed forces and the use of high explosives in the furtherance of their campaign of unionization."

With this information already in hand Burkhardt was quick to respond to the mine owners' complaints. "These gentlemen declare that conditions are, if anything worse now than ever before," Burkhardt obligingly wrote to Cornwell, echoing the operators' pleas for a declaration of martial law, pointing out that this would enable the mine owners to rely on the Army rather than the undependable sheriff's deputies or state police to crack down on strikers.

For his part, Damron was determined to resist this cavalier approach to the Constitution. Mindful of the coal operators' campaign to pressure Cornwell, Damron fought back in remarks to the grand jury he had convened to investigate the Matewan shoot-out. Rebutting Cornwell's assertion that the alleged failure of county officials to cooperate with state police justified calling in the Army, Damron argued that if a county officer failed to discharge his duty, he should be removed from office, rather than "resorting to the extreme measures that have been resorted to in this county." To demonstrate his own impartiality, Damron ordered Sheriff Blankenship to dismiss deputies who were suspected of union sympathies and replace them with neutral officers. He canceled every pistol license in the county and vowed to keep the peace by calling out a posse of deputy sheriffs to deal with any violence.

Partly because of Damron's statements, Army Secretary Newton Baker asked Cornwell to agree to the withdrawal of Federal troops. But Cornwell was reluctant to comply without the endorsement of the operators, and they were steadfastly opposed to any such thing. Calling Damron's proposal to substitute deputies for soldiers "utterly impractical," Red Jacket coal's William N. Cummins wrote to Cornwell on October 6 that any deputy given that duty would have to live with the consequences afterward. "It must be remembered that with the lawless, radical union agitators which the condition here has landed upon us, there is no such animal as a neutral," Cummins added. "There are but two attitudes, for and against."

It was easy to see why the operators wanted the Army to stay. Under the "direct access" policy, the Army had been dispatched to deal with twenty-nine so-called domestic disorders, nearly all stemming from labor disputes. Though the Army as a matter of form directed its troops to be impartial between management and labor, as the official Army history of the Federal role in domestic disorders concluded, "the presence of troops in areas of labor unrest usually served to intimidate workers and break strikes." This was certainly the case in Mingo County. As Red Jacket's Cummins acknowledged, even with the governor refusing to declare martial law, the presence of Federal troops had "vastly accelerated" the mine owners' efforts to get their struck properties back into production.

For supporters of the mine workers, and the labor movement in general, this was nothing to cheer about. "The saddest day I had was speaking at a number of points from Bluefield to Huntington, West Virginia," Navy Secretary and Wilson confidant Josephus Daniels confided to his diary after a campaign trip on behalf of fellow Democrats late in the fall of 1920. With snow on the ground, Daniels wrote, the miners and their wives and children had been evicted from company houses and were suffering. "Worst of all, men in the Army uniform were being used by the mine-owners under the pretense of 'preserving order.' When I saw shivering children living in shabby tents it aroused my indignation to the boiling point." When he returned to Washington Daniels recounted his experience to his colleague Newton Baker, who according to Daniels, "was as indignant as I." At any rate, on November 4, the soldiers began returning to their Ohio barracks and by November 20, their departure was complete. But they did not stay away long. Violence flared again in their absence. In the week following the withdrawal of the troops, miners and strikebreakers clashed at least four times in Mingo County, at Borderland, Kermit and twice at Chatttaroy, all small mining towns.

Cornwell once again appealed to General Read for troops. "The state government is totally unable to cope with the situation," he claimed. Read made plain his weariness with dispatching troops to put out fires in West Virginia that only blazed again once the soldiers left. But with Secretary Baker's approval he ultimately gave Cornwell what he wanted. On November 28 Read deployed a battalion of the 19th infantry regiment commanded by Colonel Herman Hall to West Virginia, whereupon Cornwell, to appease the operators, proclaimed a limited state of martial law. This decree placed the sheriff's department and the state police under military command but kept the civil courts open to try all offenders, thus avoiding the use of a military tribunal, which had provoked such indignation during the Paint Creek–Cabin Creek strike. It was a finely drawn distinction, which the *New York Times* described as "military control," rather than martial law.

Whatever the legal state of affairs was called, it clearly worked against the interests of the strikers. The soldiers set up headquarters in the county courthouse in Williamson and their mules and trucks filled the streets of the town. Their commander, Colonel Hall, banned all public meetings and demonstrations, and also banned the carrying of firearms. Within a week some 500 rifles and pistols had been collected.

Meanwhile the union received another blow—this time from courts. Responding to a petition from Red Jacket coal company, a Federal judge issued an injunction against the union, banning it "from in any way or manner interfering with the said contracts of employment" between Red Jacket and its workers, referring to the yellow-dog contracts pledging not to join the union that miners had to sign when they were hired. Red Jacket superintendent Cummins lost no time in exploiting the injunction. He mailed a copy to Matewan's new mayor, E. K. Beckner, along with a note referring to "the activity of certain vicious and disorderly characters," which he claimed had made it unsafe for Red Jacket workers to pass through the town. Any interference with these men, Cummins wrote, would amount to a violation of the injunction. Sure enough when three union members were charged with assaulting two Red Jacket workers, instead of facing a trial by jurors who might have been sympathetic to their cause, they were called before a Federal Court judge and given sixty days in jail for violating the injunction.

By early December, five months after the start of the strike, the operators claimed they had raised production to about 80 percent of normal. They boasted that they were helped not only by labor they had imported but also by some ex-strikers who had returned to their jobs after signing yellow-dog contracts. Hundreds of other union men had given up on the struggle and moved away. But about 2,500 of the original 6,000 strikers stayed on in Mingo County, most of them living in tent cities the union had helped put up.

To pay for groceries the union gave each striker $5 a week for himself, $2 more for his wife and $1 for each child. The union also tried to arrange for free medical care and for credit at clothing stores. It was little enough to get by on. A *New York Times* correspondent who visited the largest of the tent colonies, at Lick Creek, near Matewan, found many of the children who were playing in the debris-strewn streets seemed anemic and underfed. Their meals were cooked on open fireplaces, thrown together from boulders and mortar.

Nevertheless some of their parents still talked bravely and confidently. "We are all Americans and good enough to hold out for our rights, even though it's tough to live this way," Martin Justice, one of the leaders of the Lick Creek colony, declared.

With few other weapons at its command, the union was counting on the plight of the hundreds of tent colony families to win public sympathy, through coverage in a number of the nation's important newspapers and magazines. Neil Burkinshaw, of *The Nation*, in an article titled "Labor's Valley Forge," described the "appalling" conditions in the tent colonies. "Huddled under canvas that flapped and strained at the guy ropes, in the high winds I found hundreds of families gathered about pitifully small fires. In most cases the tent dwellers were living on the bare frozen earth, the most fortunate having simply a strip of oil cloth or carpet as floor. Several children have died of pneumonia and it was pitiful to see any number of new-born babies there—and worst, many women pregnant."

In his peroration, Burkinshaw struck just the right note from the union's point of view. "The miners of Mingo County are fighting one of the gamest fights in the history of industrial war, fighting for a principle—the emancipation of themselves and their children from the worst economic serfdom in America."

This sort of journalistic rhetoric naturally infuriated the mine owners, so much so that the Williamson Coal Operators Assn. issued a statement charging the union with compelling its members and their families to endure the hardships of the tents in order to "excite the sympathy of the public." "The UMW agitators furnish transportation for men who come into the fields for employment back to other fields and obtain work for them," the operators charged, "while requiring their members' wives and children to shiver and suffer in the tents."

Actually of course no one was "required" to stay in the tent colonies. The miners who lived there after being evicted from their company homes had little other choice, unless they were willing to go back to work on the mine owners' terms. It was true that UMW leaders hoped to use the hardships endured by the tent city dwellers to dramatize the union's struggles in southern West Virginia. They had little else to give them hope.

In their desperation, the union leaders had tried to persuade Cornwell to bring about a conference with the operators, which might produce a face-saving way to end the strike.

But the governor was in no mood to help the UMW find a way out of its difficulties. He was still smarting from the public criticism heaped upon him by the union and its supporters. "The governor of West Virginia has failed miserably to give all citizens equal protection of the law," charged William Green, international secretary treasurer of the UMW. "Property rights have been made superior not human rights." The *New York World* was even more condemnatory in an editorial right after Cornwell had made his second request for troops in three months. "Under our system political bankruptcy cannot reach more degrading levels," the paper asserted. "With its whole body of officials incapable, with the mass of inhabitants destitute of resource, and with no military or constabulary force strong enough to meet rival mobs and subdue them," the *World* demanded: "What claim has West Virginia to consideration as a self-governing state?"

To answer such criticism, Cornwell took advantage of an invitation to address the Southern Society, a group of Dixie civic leaders and businessmen at New York's Waldorf-Astoria on December 8, 1920. Introduced as the "law and order governor," Cornwell quickly conceded that the Mingo County strike had brought serious violence to his state. As the *New York Times* noted in its account of the talk, labor violence had taken forty or fifty lives in the county since spring. But Cornwell pointed out that there had been violence elsewhere in the country, right there in New York City, for example, and cited the 1919 bomb blast on Wall Street the previous September that had killed twenty-nine persons and injured more than 200 others. It would be unfair to judge New York by that tragic event, Cornwell said. And just as unfair to judge his own state by the violence in Mingo Country.

Venturing into foreign policy, Cornwell pointed to what he regarded as the much greater horror taking place in the Bolshevik state that had replaced the old Russian Empire, a country with which some Americans now wanted to establish diplomatic relations. "I believe the hand as stained with blood as if it were the hand of savages should never be grasped in friendship," Cornwell said. Diplomatic recognition by the United States of the Kremlin regime "would accelerate immeasurably an undesirable campaign here against our institutions."

Then the governor launched an attack on what he considered the root of West Virginia's troubles—the United Mine Workers.

"If John L. Lewis wants the respect of the people for his union he has got to cut out the rough stuff," Cornwell declared. "I say the labor unions must respect the law and must put out the radicals from their midst."

That was music to the ears of his affluent audience. They clapped and cheered as Cornwell continued to pound away at the radicals. "Radical organizations," he warned, "are growing all the time and it is our duty to combat them everywhere—in business organizations, in civic organizations, in the churches and schools." The governor noted with approval Samuel Gompers's efforts to rid the AFL of radicals but stressed this was not enough. "The job of Americanizing America shouldn't be left to Gompers," Cornwell cried. "It's everybody's job."

The truth was that even if Cornwell had been willing to try to pull the UMW's chestnuts out of the fire by seeking a compromise with the mine owners, the latter were in no mood to parley. "We are opposed to the UMW," a spokesman for the operators explained, "because it has proved an entirely irresponsible organization which does not abide by its contract obligations and is directed by men who seem bent on making trouble and never hesitate at violence and disorder as a means to the attainment of their ends."

The mine owners could easily afford to castigate the union. Things were going their way. They were winning the strike, and the governor of the state was on their side. But the mine owners were not the sort of men inclined to leave anything to chance. Judge Damron had been a thorn in their side all through the turbulent weeks following the shoot-out. If he continued to play that role, he could cause them serious trouble, both as a spokesman for critics of their tactics and as a jurist.

But for this problem as with many others they had a solution on hand—money. On October 31, 1920, in the midst of his struggle with Cornwell over martial law, and as trial neared on the case against Hatfield and his co-defendants, Damron announced that he had quit the bench. He offered no explanation at first, but one was not long in coming when the operators announced that the legal team they intended to deploy to aid the prosecution in the Hatfield murder trial had gained a distinguished recruit, someone who would not suffer for lack of familiarity with the case. He was none other than former County Judge James Damron. As the main battlefield in the struggle between the union and the operators shifted to the courtroom where Sid Hatfield would be tried, Judge Damron would now help prosecute the defendants whose indictments he had overseen.

5

"It's Good to Have Friends"

A CCORDING TO THE official record, the murder trial to
punish the wrongdoers in the gun battle at Matewan Station
pitted the Mingo County prosecutor against Sid Hatfield and the
twenty-two miners charged with the killing of Albert Felts. That
was the heading on the trial papers when the legal proceedings began, January 26, 1921. But in truth that particular confrontation
was overshadowed by the long and bitter conflict between the
mine owners and the mine workers' union.

At the heart of the courtroom battle was not the guilt or inno-
cence of the defendants. The mine owners knew from the start
that the odds were heavily against any Mingo County jury convict-
ing their friends and neighbors of a murder charge when the victims were Baldwin-Felts detectives. For the coal operators, the real
objective of the trial was not legal but political—not to gain a verdict from the twelve good men and true in the jury box but rather
to build support among the public for their campaign to destroy
the union. This reality was well understood by the leaders of the
union, who were just as determined to convert the trial into a rallying point for their drive to organize.

Neither side was shy in stating its stake in the proceedings.
"This trial is a direct result of the barbarous warfare waged on
members of the United Mine Workers by the coal operators of
Mingo County," William Green, the UMW's national secretary,

declared. The UMW, Green pledged, would give the defendants "full moral and material support." Indeed in January 1921 the UMW levied a $1-a-month assessment on its 500,000 members to support the strike in Mingo County, and a similar battle for union recognition in Alabama, adding to the $1.3 million already spent on behalf of the southern West Virginia miners.

As for the mine owners, the Williamson operators association issued a statement branding the UMW as "the most tyrannical of all labor unions." The union sought not only to enlist new members, the operators charged, but more ominously "to so organize the coal mines that they will control the production of coal and make it impossible to operate a mine without their sanction."

Bearing out the rhetoric was the dominant role each side played in the courtroom contest. The union assumed the responsibility for the defense of Hatfield and the miners, hiring John J. Conniff, one of West Virginia's canniest criminal lawyers to serve as chief counsel for the defense and assigning Harold W. Houston, the general counsel of the UMW's District 17, to back him up. For their part the mine owners, carrying the load for the prosecution, recruited a pair of former judges, not only the recently resigned Judge James Damron but also former state supreme court Justice Joseph M. Sanders, and supported them with S. B. Avis, a long-time counselor to the Williamson Coal Operators Association, and John Marcum, a veteran criminal lawyer. If the mine owners needed any help in making ends meet, Tom Felts, seeking revenge for his brothers, had offered to pay a share of the costs.

Within the borders of this broad struggle for economic power, the trial touched off another and more personal conflict, something close to a civil war within the town of Matewan, which pitted miner against shopkeeper, neighbor against neighbor, and in some cases children against their parents. At the center of this storm was Matewan's police chief, Sid Hatfield, whose dramatic personality dominated the public perception of the trial. His principal role in the Matewan Massacre had by itself made him a national figure, a hero to the miners, a villain to union foes and many other Americans who considered themselves law abiding. But other events that followed in the wake of the May 19 shoot-out added to the police chief's notoriety, hardening and intensifying the feelings about him on both sides.

On June 1, 1920, only twelve days after the Matewan battle, Hatfield and Jessie Testerman, widow of the late mayor of Matewan, quietly slipped into Huntington, more than 120 miles north of Matewan, and got a marriage license. Their plan, as they explained later, was to wed that evening, but no minister was available. So they took a room in Huntington's Florentine Hotel, figuring they would be protected from discovery by Huntington's distance from Mingo County and its considerable size; its population of 75,000 made it the largest city in the state.

They failed to reckon with the relentless Tom Felts. Determined to avenge the death of his two brothers and the other agents who made up the cream of his detective corps, Felts kept Hatfield and Jessie Testerman under constant surveillance. No sooner had the couple checked into their hotel than Felts was on the phone to his friends on the Huntington police force. Within less than an hour two Huntington officers were knocking on the door of the Hatfields' hotel room. Both Hatfield and his bride-to-be were unceremoniously taken off to city jail, where they were booked on a charge of "improper relations" and locked in separate cells.

Determined to assure that the hapless couple got the attention he felt they deserved, Tom Felts called a press conference in another part of the town to reveal what he claimed was the real truth behind the Matewan shootings. "Hatfield and the late mayor's wife had been having an affair," Felts asserted. "Hatfield shot Testerman to get him out of the way. The charge that Albert Felts killed Testerman is a dirty vicious lie."

If the reporters who then rushed to the Huntington jail expected to find a penitent Hatfield they were mistaken. Eager as ever to improve upon the truth, Hatfield at first claimed that he and Jessie were already wed. At any rate, he contended, they had known each other for a long time and had done nothing improper. As the reporters must have realized, even if the star-crossed pair wanted to indulge their passion in their hotel room, Tom Felts's alacrity had probably deprived them of the chance. As for Felts's accusation that it was Hatfield who had shot the mayor, the police chief trampled that notion into the dust. Albert Felts was the one who had done that deed. "Felts shot from the hip," Hatfield said. "He carried two guns. Any other statement is foolish."

His inamorata was more forthcoming. No, they were not married, the widow Testerman acknowledged, but soon would be. That was their reason for coming to Huntington. After all, the musty old Florentine Hotel was not the sort of place for a romantic fling. The truth was, she said, her husband, the late mayor, had always considered Sid Hatfield a good friend to them both and had even advised his wife that if anything happened to him, she should feel free to marry Hatfield.

When Hatfield and his fiancée appeared before the local magistrate, he imposed a $10 fine, which would be remitted if the couple married that day. Hatfield submitted his marriage license, dated the day before and His Honor did the honors. Sid and Jessie left town as husband and wife.

Another contretemps that entangled Hatfield was more difficult to shrug off. This was directly linked to the forthcoming trial and involved Anse Hatfield, the keeper of the Urias Hotel. Anse had always been a good friend to the Baldwin-Felts detective agency, so it was no great surprise that he testified before the grand jury investigating the May 19 shooting, offering evidence, it was widely said, that was particularly damaging to Sid Hatfield and his cohorts. The prosecutors made no secret of their dependence on Anse's account of events that day to help make their case.

But this was never to happen. One hot August night, about three months after the Matewan shooting, while the innkeeper was on the porch of his hotel, a bullet ripped through his chest, came out his back and lodged in the jaw of Dr. Edward Simpkins, a local dentist with whom he was chatting. Hatfield claimed to be sitting outside the late Mayor Testerman's store, a hundred feet away, when he heard the shot. He ran to the hotel, Hatfield claimed, to search for the assailant.

Meanwhile a state trooper found Fred Burgraff, one of the miners accused in the May 19 shooting, near the railroad depot, holding a rifle. The trooper ordered Hatfield to arrest Burgraff.

A few days later Anse Hatfield's family claimed they had received a note threatening his life because of his grand jury testimony.

Sid Hatfield denied any knowledge of this note, or other threats sent to other witnesses. But he soon found himself charged along with Burgraff with Hatfield's murder.

Anse Hatfield's slaying heightened tension in the county as the trial approached. Concerned about the possibility of other attacks on prosecution witnesses, the V Corps commander, General Read, asked War Secretary Baker to persuade the White House to proclaim martial law, strengthening the legal hand of the Federal troops in Mingo. But by now Baker was under continuing pressure from organized labor and its supporters, who objected to the presence of the Army. Running out of patience with West Virginia's governor and with its local officials for their failure to keep order, Baker turned Read down.

In explaining that decision, Baker cited the constitutional basis of the legal framework that had governed Federal intervention in state affairs until he, Baker, disrupted that process. "The rule to be followed," he reminded Read, "is that the public military power of the United States should in no case be permitted to be substituted for the ordinary powers of the states, and should be called into service only when the state, having summoned its entire police power, is still unable to deal with the disorder." To be sure, "the rule to be followed" cited by Baker was exactly the proposition that he had undermined at the start of the war with his direct access policy. Read was scarcely in a position to point this out to the Secretary of War, and Baker himself chose to ignore the contradiction. Instead he took this opportunity, two years after the end of the war to rescind his own policy of direct access occasioned by the wartime emergency and reaffirmed the prewar strictures governing requests for Federal troops. These required that appeals for military intervention should be made through the War Department to the president himself. And while he was at it, Baker ordered Read to pull the Army out of West Virginia.

For Governor Cornwell this was shattering news. He knew the withdrawal of the troops would mean he would have to face the outrage of the mine owners. In some desperation, he pleaded with Baker to change his mind, or at least delay his decision. With the Matewan shooting trial coming up, Cornwell warned Baker, the danger of violence was greater than ever. He pointed out that at the start of January, Federal troops had been fired upon from the Kentucky Mountains, apparently a protest against the reopening of two nearby mines. If the soldiers would stay through the trial, the governor pledged he would get the legislature to reestablish West Virginia's National Guard so that the state could keep order in its own house.

Baker relented, but only to a degree. He ordered the withdrawal of three companies of the troops by mid-January 1921. Another company would stay until mid-February.

So the Army was much in evidence when heavyset, florid-faced Judge R. D. Bailey, who was Damron's successor, gaveled the crowd that filled the rustic wooden courtroom overlooking the Tug to order. Colonel Hall was seated behind the judge while in an adjoining chamber a sergeant of Company G, 19th Infantry was on alert. All it would take would be a signal from him to bring a squad of armed regulars into that hall of justice. Outside, troops kept a path clear through a throng of curiosity seekers for those who had official business before Judge Bailey.

But even the U.S. Army could not steal the spotlight from Sid Hatfield, who remained the cynosure of all eyes. With a new mayor running Matewan in place of Cabell Testerman, Hatfield lost his job as police chief but had been promptly elected as constable of Magnolia District, the largest of Mingo County's six districts. With his new badge, Hatfield continued to provide good copy for the journalists from papers all over the nation who crowded the courtroom. On the first day the normally rumpled constable looked almost dapper in a new brown suit. His new wife was by his side, wearing a jaunty air and a rope of pearls around her neck. But Hatfield spoiled the overall effect by carrying a gun in each pocket, something that might have gone unnoticed except for the presence in the courtroom of the man who had become Hatfield's most dedicated enemy on earth, Tom Felts. Spotting the telltale bulge in Hatfield's pocket, Felts informed Judge Bailey, who issued a stern warning that firearms were strictly prohibited. From then on deputies searched everyone who entered. Hatfield continued to bring his weapons, but obediently checked them at the door.

The constable scored well with the press by making himself readily accessible and answering questions freely. "I reckon you thought I had horns," he told one reporter with a grin. "It's the limit what I read about myself." To satisfy the media, "Two Gun Sid," as he had been dubbed after the May 19 shoot-out, patiently posed for pictures brandishing his two pistols, but always smiling. Indeed the papers began to call him "Smiling Sid." As for the bloodshed in Matewan that was the reason for the trial, Matewan's police chief dismissed that "as just a little free-for-all."

Judge Bailey took away some of the merriment when on the first day of trial he abruptly suspended the bonds of the defendants. At the end of each session, instead of going to their homes, they were confined to the small jail behind the courthouse. But this turned out to be less than an ordeal.

The wife of the jailer took Jessie Hatfield into her home, so the bride could be close to her new husband. The jailer brought in new mattresses and allowed the defendants to go back and forth between each other's cells, while they played dominoes and visited with their families. "This ain't a jail," Hatfield told the reporters. "This is the Matewan Hotel."

The next day, the prosecution won the first skirmish. A defense motion to dismiss the indictments was rejected, whereupon Judge Bailey called upon the defendants to plead to the charge. "Not guilty," they shouted in unison.

The trial had been in session only three days when violence threatened to interfere as a result of local resentment against the Baldwin-Felts detectives who were much in evidence in the town. A report reached the judge that 1,000 armed union men were planning to march on Williamson to protect the prisoners from the Baldwin-Felts "thugs," as many of the miners called the detectives. After a conference with attorneys for both sides and representatives of the union and the companies, Bailey arranged for the detective agency to withdraw its men and relative calm returned to Williamson.

Still a more fundamental problem remained—getting a jury. The interlocking family relationships made it difficult to find veniremen who were not related to any of the defendants. When the name "Anse Hatfield" was called from the list of veniremen, a lawyer declared, "He's dead, your honor." But two men in the courtroom, each bearing the name of the slain hotel keeper, stepped forward.

Ties to the union and resentment of the Baldwin-Felts agents also complicated matters. The prosecution had underlined this difficulty at the start by getting Judge Bailey to strike all union men from the jury panel. One earnest citizen, striving to show his lack of bias, announced: "I am not a union man nor a Baldwin-Felts thug." To his apparent surprise he was excused. By February 5, ten days after the start of the trial more than one thousand men had been called, one hundred questioned, and not a single juror had been selected.

This impasse stirred talk of allowing women to serve on the jury. After all, the 18th amendment had just given female citizens the right to vote. "The only hope I can see is in the enactment of a law by the legislature next month that will permit women to serve as jurors," one jury commissioner told the *New York Times*. But no one really wanted to wait a month, and there was little enthusiasm among legislators for such a break with custom.

Yet another possibility was allowing Negroes to serve on the jury. After all, this was not Virginia, the capital of the Confederacy, but West Virginia, which had broken away from the Old Dominion at the start of the Civil War. But when it came to race, the mores of the Deep South still prevailed. Judge Bailey himself put an end to the idea of an interracial jury.

The defense spread the word that prosecution was deliberately stalling on jury selection in the hope that the legislature would act on proposed legislation to permit juries in murder trials to be selected from other counties. A jury chosen anywhere but in Mingo County would certainly improve the prosecution's chances of getting a conviction.

Ultimately, persistence paid off. On February 10, after two frustrating weeks, a twelve-man jury of teachers, farmers and laborers was selected. Two days later, prosecution launched its case.

The foremost casualty of the ensuing courtroom conflict was the truth. Witnesses for each side swore to versions of events that flatly contradicted each other. In most cases it was difficult to tell who was lying. But it was clear that for as long as the trial lasted, mendacity ruled the day.

That soon became apparent when the prosecution called as witnesses the Matewan phone operators, Elsie Chambers, the daughter of defendant Reece Chambers, and Mae Chafin, Logan Sheriff Don Chafin's seventeen-year-old niece, who had overheard the phone call from Hatfield and Mayor Testerman to deputy sheriff "Toney" Webb, seeking warrants for the arrest of the detectives.

For the defense the most troubling part of their testimony, sworn to by both women, was that in talking to Webb, Hatfield was supposed to have vowed: "We'll kill those sons of bitches before they get out of Matewan." On cross-examination defense counsel Conniff sought to undermine Elsie Chambers's credibility by getting her to concede she had fallen out with her father, Reece, one of the defendants, and that she had not lived at home for the past four years. And he tried to suggest that Mae Chafin was confused about what she had heard. But a measure of damage had been done.

The prosecution then moved its case right to the spot of the initial shots with the testimony of Joe C. Jack, a coal company guard. Jack claimed to have arrived in Matewan shortly after four P.M., just before the shooting started. He headed for Chambers Hardware store, where he encountered Reece Chambers and Sid Hatfield and sheriff's deputy Hugh Combs, among several hangers-on. Hatfield was talking about the evictions of the Stone Mountain miners and mentioned that he expected warrants for the arrest of the detectives on the next train from Williams.

Both Combs and Hatfield spoke ominously about their expected encounter with the detectives. Combs said if he could not get the detectives "lined up" for arrest, he would "get a gun and kill half dozen of them" himself. Reece Chambers, slapping the rifle he was holding, said: "This here will get them." But it was Sid Hatfield who was the most ferocious, Jack testified. Even if the warrants "Toney" Webb sought were not issued, the police chief supposedly vowed, "we will go out and kill the last damned one of them."

Jack left town on No. 16, the same train the detectives had hoped to take to Bluefield, and returned on Friday, May 21, two days after the shooting. One of the first people he encountered was Chief Hatfield, who asked Jack if he knew anything about the shooting. No, Jack told him, he knew nothing about it.

Hatfield looked Jack straight in the eye. "Are you sure you don't know anything about it?" he asked.

Yes, Jack said, he was sure.

Hatfield stared at him. "That is what I call a man," he said, with evident satisfaction.

In his cross-examination, defense attorney Conniff did everything but call Jack an outright liar. First he got the witness to acknowledge that he had not testified before the grand jury or told anyone about what he had now claimed to have seen on May 19 until he met with the prosecutors shortly before the trial. "I was telling them tales all along," Jack said of his conversations with Hatfield and the miners. He kept his knowledge to himself, he claimed because, if he spoke out, "I was told I would be did the way Anse Hatfield went."

Who told him that? Conniff wanted to know.

"Mr. Hatfield sent me that word." Bearing the message, he said, was a Matewan housewife, Mrs. Stella Scales.

"How did Sid come to send you that word when you told him you didn't know anything about the shooting?"

"I don't know nothing about that."

Not till the trial was already underway—Jack did not remember exactly when—did he finally tell the story of what he had supposedly seen to S. B. Avis, the coal company lawyer working with the prosecution.

Until then, Conniff asked, "there wasn't anybody on earth knew what you told here today, was there?"

"Not the straight of it, no."

"Not the straight of it?"

"No sir."

"Well," Conniff asked archly, "did they know anything about the crooked of it?"

The spectators rewarded Conniff with the laughter he sought and Avis indignantly objected for the prosecution.

Soon after, Conniff completed the rout of Jack by calling to the stand Stella Scales, the woman Jack had claimed had passed on the threatening message from Hatfield. Not only did Scales deny passing on any such message, she claimed she did not even know Hatfield. She finished off her few minutes in the limelight, with a flourish, asking to be introduced to Hatfield. She then marched into the ranks of the defendants and made a display of shaking hands with the police chief, who introduced her to his wife, sitting nearby.

By now anxiety among the lawyers at the prosecution table was increasing. Over more than a week of testimony they had called more than a dozen witnesses. But their case was wobbly.

The atmosphere of fear and intimidation in Matewan in the wake of Anse Hatfield's murder had kept some people from coming forward. Most of the key witnesses seemed flawed in one way or another. Elsie Chambers had turned against her father; Mae Chafin was suspect because she was kin to Sheriff Chafin; Joe Jack had come across as little better than a buffoon.

But the prosecution and the mine owners were not without resources, notably money and power, and both were brought to bear on the trial. To strengthen its case against Hatfield and his cohorts, the coal operators' lawyers fell back on one of the favored strategies for prosecuting a conspiracy case—getting one of the alleged conspirators to switch sides. In this instance they offered a twofold incentive—not only would the charges be dropped against any of the defendants willing to transfer his loyalties, but he would also get a reward of $1,000. After taking informal soundings among the defendants, the prosecutors found a logical target in Isaac Brewer, who conveniently was related to two of their number, James Damron and James Marcum. The deal was closed during a weekend recess, and immediately after Brewer stunned his erstwhile comrades by taking the stand against them.

For the prosecution the importance of Brewer's testimony was the double burden of guilt it imposed on Sid Hatfield. Not only did Brewer claim that he had seen Hatfield shoot Albert Felts, but he also contended that the police chief had voiced threats directed against Mayor Testerman. According to Brewer, Hatfield was angry because the mayor had been unwilling himself to issue a warrant against the detectives, forcing Hatfield to get the warrants from the sheriff's office in Williamson. Indeed the chief was so furious that he told Brewer he "would cut the mayor in two with a bullet" if Testerman "messed around" in Hatfield's dealings with the detectives. Claiming to be in Chambers Hardware store on the afternoon of the battle, Brewer swore that Hatfield whispered to him, just before the first shots were fired, "Let's kill every damn one of them."

Hatfield shot Albert Felts, as Brewer told the story. Then Brewer himself was shot in the hand and chest by detective Cunningham. As the wounded Brewer lay on the ground he saw another defendant, William C. Bowman, stand over the fallen Felts, aim his pistol and fire. "Now I guess you'll die," Brewer remembered Bowman snarling at the mortally wounded Albert Felts.

One question Brewer did not answer: Who shot Testerman? He conceded he did not see that happen. But the prosecution found another way to deal with that issue when it played its trump card, by calling C. E. Lively, who had wined and dined the union faithful at his Matewan eatery, all the while earning his pay as a Baldwin-Felts informer.

Calling Lively represented something of a gamble; like their other star witnesses he was tarnished. If Joe Jacks was an oaf and Isaac Brewer a turncoat, Lively was a professional charlatan and his testimony about the confidences he had heard from the defendants while posing as a union sympathizer was derived from treachery and deceit.

In addition, Lively was the eyewitness to nothing that mattered in the trial. He had been in Charleston on the day of the shooting, trying to further ingratiate himself with the UMW leaders.

All he could impart in the courtroom was hearsay, the stories that the defendants had told him, well after the smoke had cleared. Was the value of this tainted secondhand testimony worth the damage Lively's underhanded tactics might do to the prosecution's case?

The fact that the prosecution decided that the gain outweighed the cost underlined the struggle for public opinion, which was the mine owners' true concern in the trial. Whatever the jurors believed about Lively, his version of events would be transmitted by the press and would gain the attention of newspaper readers in the state and around the country.

In the next few hours Lively would share with the jurors the admissions of no fewer than five of the defendants about their actions on May 19—Art Williams, Fred Burgraff, Bill Bowman, Reece Chambers and Hatfield.

Williams supposedly told Lively how he had emptied a .32 caliber Smith and Wesson at Lee Felts, missing with every shot, then shouted at Reece Chambers, who was armed with a rifle: "There, shoot that God-damned son of a bitch, I want one of his guns." Chambers did as he was told and having better aim than Williams hit Lee Felts, who fell to the ground. Williams raced over to where Felts lay and picked up a gun lying nearby. But it was empty of shells. He then tried to pull another gun out of Felts's hand, finally kicking it free. With that Williams ran down the street, saw one of the detectives leaving a house, pressed his gun against the man's head and shot him dead. Blood spurted on the gun, Williams recalled for Lively's benefit, and he had to clean off the weapon when he went home.

Fred Burgraff told Lively of slaying another detective in an alley. "Did he die game?" Lively wanted to know. No, Burgraff, told him, the detective begged for his life. But Burgraff concluded that the victim was too far gone. "The god damned son of a bitch, he had to die."

Bill Bowman had been at work on the day of the shooting but arrived back in town just as the trouble started, Lively testified Bowman told him. He ran to the corner of the post office and saw a detective running down the street and fired at him. He aimed to hit him on the side and the man seemed to jump two or three feet up in the air, then fell to the ground. Then the detective jumped up and Bowman fired again. "And it was his last jump."

Reece Chambers "never said very much," as Lively recalled. But Lively did hear him say that he had shot Lee Felts, "and that he had a right to do it," since Felts had just shot Reece's brother, Hallie Chambers, another of the defendants. "Lee put up a game fight and was about the only one who stood toe to toe and fought," Chambers supposedly told Lively. "The others tried to run."

Lively's most important testimony from the prosecution's point of view had to do with Sid Hatfield. Lively said that before the shoot-out during a conversation about the possibility that the detectives might come to Matewan to evict miners, Hatfield had said: "They better not come down here and try anything like that, they would all get killed."

After the shooting Hatfield told Lively that he himself had shot Testerman, right after shooting Albert Felts, giving the reason that the mayor was "getting too well lined up with those Baldwin men." But the prosecution was not satisfied with that answer. They knew that Lively had a more intriguing explanation for Hatfield's shooting the mayor.

"Had he ever said anything about anything that Testerman had that he wanted?" Avis asked the witness.

"Not outright, he never did," Lively testified. "But he did say something that had led me to believe in my own mind that he did have something he wanted."

Furious, Conniff leaped to his feet. "Objection," he cried.

"Sustained," said Bailey.

Avis tried a different tack. "Don't tell us what your conclusions were, just what the words were."

Remarkably, the defense failed to object at this outpouring of surmise piled upon hearsay. So Lively plowed ahead. "Well at one time before this Sid and I were talking. I asked him if he was married and he said, 'No,' and a poor chance to get married. Another man had the woman that he wanted."

"I took it more of a joke than anything else," Lively said.

"You must be crazy about that little blonde," Lively supposed told Hatfield, apparently not having any idea who was the object of the police chief's affection.

"She is not a blonde, she is a brunette," Hatfield replied. "I will have her if I have to wade through hell to get her."

So there was the gravamen of the prosecution case. The real reason for the bloody battle at Matewan Station was not the eviction of the miners but Sid Hatfield's murderous lust.

In his cross-examination Conniff did all he could to emphasize the Judas-like aspects of Lively's role. Questioning Lively's attitude toward the United Mine Workers, which he had joined in 1902, about ten years before going to work for the Baldwin-Felts agency, Conniff asked: "You took the obligation of a union man, didn't you? You took an obligation you never intended to keep?"

"I didn't give the keeping of it any consideration at that time," Lively responded.

"Do you mean by that you paid no attention to the obligation?"

"Very little."

Time and again Conniff used the words "deceit" and "falsehood" as he hammered away at the witness. "With a union card in your pocket you were working against the union, weren't you?" he challenged Lively, who was shielded by the prosecutor's objection from having to answer.

Conniff pressed him about the union meetings he had attended. "What was your purpose?" he demanded.

"More to hear the speakers than anything else," said Lively. "Yes I like to hear an orator whether he suits me or not."

His response drew hisses in the courtroom and a skeptical rejoinder from Conniff. "Give us the real reason."

Lively hemmed and hawed until finally the judge directed him to answer. "In order to be more able to associate with and have the confidence of the people, of the defendants, that had been in the Matewan murder, massacres or whatever you might term to call it," he said. "I realized that no man can make an investigation of a case as serious as that unless they have the absolute confidence of those concerned."

Exactly what had Lively told the defendants to gain their confidence? Conniff wanted to know.

"I told them it was a good thing they were killed," Lively said. "That they ought to have done it—that they done a good deed—talking along that line."

The restaurant he had opened in Matewan in July of 1920 paid its own way, without any help from Baldwin-Felts, Lively claimed. But he acknowledged that all that time he was on salary from the agency—$225 a month, plus expenses. "Your purpose was to give Baldwin-Felts value received for what they were paying?" Conniff remarked, in what was more of a statement than a question.

"My purpose was to get the real true evidence, without regards to who it hurt or who it favored, to have justice brought in," Lively claimed.

Next Conniff targeted Lively's recounting of his conversations with Sid Hatfield about the shootings, pressing Lively to repeat the reason Hatfield had given for supposedly shooting Testerman, that the mayor was "too well lined up" with Baldwin-Felts and the mine owners. "What did he say that Testerman had done that indicated that?"

"He never said what he had done."

Conniff asked Lively whether Hatfield had ever mentioned that the Baldwin-Felts agents had offered the mayor $1,000 to allow them to put a machine gun in town. No, Lively said, that had never been mentioned to him directly, though he had heard Hatfield talk about it to others.

Then Conniff painstakingly took Lively through the joint involvement of Testerman and Hatfield in the events of May 19.

He reminded him that Testerman and Hatfield had both confronted Albert Felts at the evictions and warned him he was breaking the law, that Testerman had later called the county prosecutor to alert him to the evictions, that Testerman had recommended to Hatfield that he get the prosecutor to draw up the warrants for the arrest of the detectives. And as the day neared its bloody crisis, Testerman had come to the Matewan Depot, late that afternoon, to inspect the warrant Albert Felts had for Hatfield's arrest, he had asked Felts to accept a bond in lieu of the arrest, and that after looking over the warrant, he pronounced it "bogus," almost his last words before he was shot to death.

"Now you tell the jury what if anything Sid said to you that gave him the impression that Testerman was 'lining up with the other side'," Conniff said.

"Well he never said anything to me; never gave me any reason why that Testerman was lining up with the other side," Lively admitted.

"That statement that he shot Testerman because he was lining up with the other side, that is an absolute falsehood, isn't it?" Conniff fairly shouted at the witness.

The prosecution objected but this time Judge Bailey ruled in favor of the defense.

Now Conniff's manner was calm and deliberate. "Answer my question?" he demanded.

"Put that question again, please."

"I will make it plain for you. Your statement that Sid Hatfield said he shot Testerman because he was lining up too much with the other side, is an absolute falsehood, isn't it?"

"No."

"You said that because you were getting $225 a month and expenses, didn't you?"

"No, I said that because Sid Hatfield said so."

Avis objected as expected and Bailey sustained him. But Conniff was satisfied. He had poked enough holes in the prosecution's arguments to clear the way for his own case for the defense.

The story of the Matewan shoot-out that Conniff's witnesses presented was so much at variance with the version presented by the prosecution that it seemed at times as if their testimony was describing an entirely different episode.

In the defense's version, it was not Sid Hatfield who fired the first shot but rather Albert Felts. And it was not Felts who was the first victim but rather Mayor Testerman. This was the story told by Dan Chambers, three of whose blood relatives were on trial. Reece Chambers, one of the principal villains according to the prosecution's script, was Dan Chambers's great uncle, and Hallie and Ed Chambers were his second cousins. Still another defendant, Clare Overstreet, was his brother-in-law.

Dan Chambers had a good vantage point on the afternoon of the shooting. He was in Chambers Hardware store, standing "a couple of feet" from Sid Hatfield, when Albert Felts attempted to arrest the constable with the warrant that Testerman had pronounced "bogus." No sooner had that word been spoken, Chambers remembered, than Albert Felts "jerked a gun from his right hip and fired," mortally wounding the mayor. "He grabbed himself and staggered back."

More shots were fired, "a roar of shots," Chambers remembered, and he prudently ducked out of the way, obscuring his view.

But he did see Sid Hatfield pull his own gun from under his belt. Under fierce cross-examination from the prosecution, including an elaborate attempt to reconstruct the shooting by using attorneys from both sides to impersonate the principals, Dan Chambers stuck to his story. Ultimately attorney Avis in his exasperation resorted to the same tactic used by his counterpart on the defense, simply calling the obdurate witness a liar in everything but name only.

"Isn't it a fact, Mr. Chambers, that you were not inside the store at all?" Avis challenged.

But Chambers was unmoved. "If I had not been in there, I wouldn't have been telling you so."

Along with contradicting the prosecution's version of the shooting, Conniff's witnesses also challenged the claim that Hatfield and his cohorts had been planning to massacre the detectives. Sheriff's deputy "Toney" Webb testified about his conversation with Hatfield on the afternoon of May 19, during which two prosecution witnesses, Elsie Chambers and Mae Chafin, had testified that the police chief had vowed: "We'll kill those sons of bitches before they get out of Matewan."

Were those Hatfield's words? Conniff asked his witness.

"No sir," Webb replied. "I never heard Sid Hatfield make such a statement in my life, whether over the telephone or otherwise."

Instead of Hatfield, Webb testified, it was Albert Felts who had exhibited murderous intent. Three weeks before the Matewan shoot-out, Webb was dispatched to the Burnwell Coal company's housing, where Felts and his men were evicting miners from their homes. "What the hell are you doing here?" Felts demanded.

"I am an officer and go where I damned please," Webb replied. Webb then called the county prosecutor, Wade Bronson, who told him the evictions were illegal. When Webb informed Felts, the detective asked him to come into the office of the coal company. A desk inside was covered with guns, one of which Albert Felts patted.

"How do you like the looks of these?" he asked Webb.

"It looks more like home than any place I have seen since I left Letcher County, Kentucky," Webb replied good-naturedly.

Felts then suggested to Webb that he was making a mistake by not coming to the agency's headquarters in Bluefield to discuss Webb's future. "He said that he wanted to talk to me for sometime; that I was a young man, and was pursuing the wrong course, and I was a damned fool to take the course I was taking."

Webb was unmoved by this blandishment. "It's not the first time, Albert, that I have been called a damned fool," the deputy remembered saying. "But my instructions are, if you evict any more people here, I am going to arrest you."

"Don't you think it is a big job to arrest 243 men?" Felts shot back, referring to the size of the coal company's full staff.

"That may be," Webb conceded. But if he had to, he would try it, because that is what the prosecuting attorney had told him to do.

Webb turned to go, but Felts pounded the table with his fist. "Webb, I want to give you to understand that I am going to break this goddamned union on Tug river if it sends 100 men to hell and costs $1 million."

Webb stood firm. "If you evict these miners by due process of law I will help you," the deputy told Felts. "Otherwise if you evict these people without due process of law I will have to arrest you." Whereupon Webb left.

The defense rested.

Summing up, Conniff made a point of confronting the controversy over Sid Hatfield's marriage to Cabell Testerman's widow, condemning "the dragging of Mrs. Sid Hatfield's name in to this case." The lawyer scoffed at Lively's accusation. "It is ridiculous to believe that Sid Hatfield killed Testerman because he married the mayor's widow two weeks after his death," he said. "Would Sid have gone out alone and precipitated a fight with 13 men armed to the teeth, merely to gain his prize?"

Testerman himself deserved better treatment, Conniff told the jury. "A monument should be erected to this man who died a martyr to his duty." Conniff recalled testimony that, before he went to the depot that fateful afternoon, Felts told Testerman, "Mayor, I hope there is no hard feelings between us." Speaking directly to his opponent, Joseph Sanders, who would make the final argument for the prosecution, Conniff said: "Judge Sanders, when you close this case, let me remind you that just before Judas Iscariot betrayed his savior for 30 pieces of silver he affectionately kissed him. So did Felts affectionately shake hands with Testerman."

"Amen," some one in the courtroom cried out.

In his closing Sanders spoke for four hours, reminding the jurors of the damning testimony presented against the defendants, making particular point of Lively's testimony about Hatfield's yen for the former Jessie Testerman. But the former supreme court justice must have known he was waging a losing battle.

It was dinnertime Saturday, March 19, ten months to the day from the Matewan shoot-out, when Sanders finished and Judge Bailey gave his instructions to members of the jury. They deliberated for a few hours that night, got the day off Sunday and resumed their discussions on Monday. In *Thunder in the Mountains*, Lon Savage recounts the story that as the talks reached a decisive point, one of the jurors, a farmer from the remote little town of Gilbert, pointed out the window at the mountains, where the foliage was just beginning to green. When the trial began in January, the farmer recalled, the mountains had been sere and brown. He was prepared to sit there, he said, until the mountains turned brown again, and then green once more, before he would vote to convict any Matewan boy. While that much-repeated tale may be apocryphal, the reality it reflected was soon made evident. After forty-six dreary days in court, no one on that panel was ready to stay longer in the interest of gaining a conviction. Before lunch on March 21, 1921, the jurors delivered their verdict, acquitting all the defendants.

Each of the defendants had to put up a $10,000 bond for appearance in the next term of court on the charges of killing the six other Baldwin-Felts agents. But this did not mar their jubilation.

A special train took Hatfield and the others back to Matewan, where they were greeted, reported the *New York Times*, "like heroes."

It took Hatfield an hour to make his way through the admiring throng the 100 yards from the Matewan depot to his home and when he got there his hand was swollen from being shaken. "This is the happiest day Matewan ever knew," someone in the crowd cried out.

"At least for me it is," said Hatfield. "It is good to know you have so many friends."

The sense of relaxation would not last for very long, however. For while the union and its supporters had triumphed in the courtroom, they had, only a few months earlier, suffered a major blow on another battlefield, the political arena, and now they braced for the grievous consequences of that defeat.

6

"War, Insurrection and Riot"

WHILE SID HATFIELD and the miners had reason to be grateful for their friends in Mingo County, the situation was very different in Charleston, West Virginia's capital. Indeed, when the new governor, Republican Ephraim Morgan, and the new legislature arrived there to take over the state government in March of 1921, just as the jury in Hatfield's trial was reaching its verdict, anyone friendly to Hatfield or to the UMW cause in general would have been very hard to find.

Not that the miners wasted any tears on the departure of John Cornwell from the governor's office. But their bitter experience with Cornwell's reign had led the union and its supporters down a risky political course, the costs of which they were only beginning to bear.

In the spring of 1920, even as they were mounting their drive to organize the mines of southern West Virginia, the mine workers union and its allies had plunged into a separate but related contest in the political arena. It might seem surprising that in the midst of their critical campaign to win new members, the forces of labor would divert attention and resources to some other objective. But if the union and its backers had learned any lesson in the past few years, it was how important political power was to their chances of success.

They all remembered that they had helped to make Cornwell the first Democrat to hold the governorship of their state in the

20th century. Now they saw in Cornwell a man who too often used his power to curb their potential in the state. His view of the UMW seemed darkened by his increasing fixation with the threat of left-wing radicalism, an obsession reflected in his speech in 1919 warning that organized labor was conspiring to impose communism upon the United States.

Looking back on the struggle over unionization in West Virginia near the end of his term Cornwell would say: "I had no part and parcel of it so far as lending aid or sympathy to either side went. It seemed to me to be my sole duty to preserve order, in so far as I was able to do so."

To West Virginia's disappointed union leaders, who had helped to put Cornwell in office, that chilly neutrality represented a betrayal, and they were not shy in making their feelings known during his tenure. John L. Lewis had called for his resignation. Fred Mooney had berated Cornwell as a narrow partisan and said his administration had been thoroughly discredited. Frank Keeney had written to Secretary of War Newton Baker to complain of Cornwell's bias.

Some rank-and-file members were more compassionate. "While no money could hire me to vote for you again," one UMW member wrote, "still I respect you and your laws as a true American should." But Cornwell was too seasoned a politician not to realize that such mild admiration did not promise much for his political future. Stripped of the labor support that had helped win his narrow victory, plagued by glaucoma, which badly impaired his vision, and worried about the need to provide for his family's future, he announced that he would take his leave from politics as his term ended.

With Cornwell departing the scene, the Democrats faced a year in which the tides nationally were running against them, and settled on a little-known political timeserver, Arthur B. Koontz, whom union men viewed as Cornwell's stooge, as their choice for governor. On the Republican side, the party's favorable prospects for victory set off a bitter three-way contest for the nomination.

Most of the GOP establishment backed Ephraim Morgan, a conservative state judge from Marion County in the northern part of the state. But the previous Republican governor, Henry Hatfield, threw his support to Paul Grosscup, an oil and gas executive from Charleston, who also had the backing of the mine owners of southern West Virginia.

To the left of both of these contenders was a respected veteran of the law and of government, Samuel B. Montgomery, who had bona fide liberal credentials. He was a former leader of the state federation of labor, counsel for the United Mine Workers, and commissioner of labor in the Hatfield Administration. Given these choices, it was not hard for UMW leaders to conclude that Montgomery represented their sole hope. So they turned their backs on their former allies in the Democratic Party and mounted a major effort to help Montgomery win the Republican nomination.

On primary day, May 25, the week following the Matewan massacre, the early returns showed Montgomery running strong among GOP voters, and many in District 17 headquarters were jubilant. But later results showed he had finished third, behind Morgan, the winner of the nomination, and Grosscup. Montgomery lost even in Mingo County. On the following day, when the union field workers returned to headquarters, Keeney chided them. "You guys didn't make much of a showing," he remarked.

"You should get a look at the river and you'll see what sort of a showing we made," was the reply from one disillusioned field man. "The ballots are still floating. They didn't even bother to turn them in." Union men claimed that in the open-shop counties the ballot counting was monitored by company guards, who were also deputy sheriffs, and who made it their business to invalidate as many Montgomery ballots as possible.

In the general election, the union forces, seeing little to choose between the two major party candidates, again backed Montgomery, who ran as an independent. A banner hung across Matewan's main street reflected labor's sentiments. It urged support for James M. Cox, the Democratic presidential candidate and his young running mate, Franklin D. Roosevelt of New York, the Democratic candidates for county and district office and Independent Samuel B. Montgomery for governor. Montgomery campaigned in Matewan, making a particular point to visit with the local hero, Sid Hatfield. In the statewide balloting he got 81,000 votes, 15 percent of the total. It was a respectable showing in itself. But its main significance was that it denied victory to the Democrats, whose candidate, Koontz, got 185,000 votes, compared with 242,000 for the victorious Morgan. Most politicians concluded that Montgomery's vote, nearly all of which presumably would have gone Democrat, had enabled Morgan to regain the governorship for the GOP.

When the last ballot had been counted, the union forces realized that the state house in Charleston had become enemy territory. Whatever Cornwell's faults, at least they could remind him about the promises he had made to gain their support; the 52-year-old Morgan, whose service on the state's public service commission had stamped him as a faithful servant of West Virginia's business interests, and his fellow Republicans had not even pretended to any sympathy with the union cause. And in the wake of labor's support for Montgomery, the Democrats who remained in the legislature had no reason to do trade unions any favors.

Cut off from the levers of power in Charleston, the UMW turned to Washington for help, making another bid for a Senate investigation. Senator Kenyon had turned down just such an appeal right after the Matewan shoot-out the year before. Nevertheless in February of 1921, with the union men still walking picket lines amidst intermittent violence, Frank Keeney came to Washington to personally lobby the senators and the press. "The Constitution has been kicked into the discard in West Virginia," Keeney told reporters, insisting that the blame "can be laid at the door of the operators' gunmen." Keeney scoffed at charges that the miners had been shooting at state troopers and soldiers. "Let me tell you these miners are crack shots, and if they ever shot at a trooper more than twice he wouldn't be alive." What the union wanted, Keeney said, was "for a committee of senators to decide who is doing the shooting."

The Senate did not respond. Instead, in the weeks before the legislature convened, new violence hardened public attitudes against the UMW. On February 19 a sustained gun battle between union miners and company guards at the Willis Branch coal company in Fayette County, about fifty miles east of Mingo, had brought an appeal for more state protection from the company. A few days later, Cornwell visited the nearby community of Willis Branch along with governor-elect Morgan and declared that the town had been "shot off the face of the map." Homes that had not been burned or blasted with dynamite were riddled with bullets. The townspeople had fled and only stray dogs roamed the streets. Faced with what he would soon have to deal with, Morgan seemed shocked. "It is inconceivable that such conditions could exist in this day and age," he said.

The not-guilty verdict that freed Hatfield and his co-defendants late in March generated a burst of euphoria on the union side. Hailing the verdict, the *UMW Journal* predicted that "it will really result in the complete elimination of the brutal gang of gunmen" who had ruled labor relations in West Virginia. To exploit the verdict and the celebrity of Sid Hatfield, the union produced a silent movie called *Smilin' Sid* after the sobriquet he had acquired during the trial, which showed Constable Hatfield, his two guns on his belt, swaggering through the tent colonies and mining camps at the head of a squad of fearless union men.

But the rosy mood in union ranks was soon darkened when the newly elected legislature convened in 1921. One of the first items of business was passage of a bill, sponsored by State Senator Joseph Sanders, one of Sid Hatfield's prosecutors, which made it possible to draw a county court criminal jury from the citizens of another county, thus nullifying the advantage union leaders and sympathizers, such as Hatfield, enjoyed in pro-union counties. A similar proposal had been defeated the previous session when labor still had some friends in the capital. The bill was too late to help the prosecution of Hatfield for the Albert and Lee Felts murders, but neither the union nor the operators doubted there would be more such trials. Among other blows dealt the union cause were measures doubling the size of the state police force, thus strengthening the governor's hand in cracking down on strike-related violence, and setting the stage for reactivation of the national guard, in belated keeping of the pledge Cornwell had made to then War Secretary Baker earlier in the year.

With the cards stacked even more in their favor now than before the elections, the coal companies stepped up their importations of strikebreakers. For their part, the union miners, more desperate than ever, struck back with increasing fury.

All through the early days of that spring, union snipers, many hidden in the hills on the Kentucky side of the Tug, kept a steady rain of fire on the mining camps manned by strikebreakers. The White Star mining company at the town of Merrimack near Matewan was a particular flash point. Despite continuous sniping intended to shut down the mine, the company brought in fresh strikebreakers and maintained production. The strikers blew up the mine's power plant, but White Star made repairs and resumed operations. Finally on Thursday May 12, 1921, one week short of the first anniversary of the Matewan shoot-out, the violence escalated and the union launched a full-scale attack, laying siege to the town. Scores of miners in the hills above the town cut down telegraph and phone lines and trained their guns on the buildings, the mines and the strikebreakers. The union attackers used a cow horn to control the assault; one blast signaled the start of shooting, with three blasts firing ceased.

Strikebreakers returned the fire, and the shooting soon spread. By one reckoning, some 10,000 shots were fired during the long day and night. Bullets ripped into the walls of nearby homes in Matewan, and in state police headquarters shells tore through a wall and smashed a mirror. Women and children hid in closets and fled their homes, for leaving the shelter of a house was dangerous. In Matewan, Harry C. Staton, a former justice of the peace and local prohibition officer, who had testified against Sid Hatfield in the Matewan shoot-out trial a few weeks before, was shot dead as he walked along the railway tracks near his home, and police arrested Calvin McCoy, a miner who had been one of Hatfield's co-defendants.

Under orders from Governor Morgan, units of the recently expanded state police hurried to the scene in newly acquired automobiles. Although Colonel Arnold was still nominally in command of the state force, his background as a holdover Cornwell appointee and his reputation for independence did not stand him in good stead in the new administration. To handle this critical assignment in the labor hotbed of Mingo County, Morgan picked his own man, Captain J. R. Brockus.

Then forty-five years old, Brockus had enlisted in the U.S. Army as a private in 1890, served seven years in the Philippines, taken part in the China relief expedition in 1900, commanded an infantry battalion in France in the Great War and left service wearing a major's gold oak leaves. An old AEF comrade had recruited him for the state police, which he joined with the rank of lieutenant. He won rapid promotion to captain thanks in part to his natural aggressiveness, a trait that, when displayed a few months later that year, would leave its mark on history.

But on this May Thursday in 1921, Brockus would encounter mostly frustration. The cars carrying him and his troopers to the battlefront in Merrimack bogged down in the spring mud. They put chains on the tires but finally abandoned them and set off on foot. Some of his men then came under sniper fire from both sides of the river and found themselves trapped, about one half mile west of the mining camp village of Sprigg, unable to move in either direction. It took five hours before they could escape, thanks to a long freight train that shielded them as they scurried into the woods, and then retreated back to Sprigg.

Another state police detachment headed for Sprigg on a passenger train, which also came under sniper attack. Terrified passengers huddled on the floor. The conductor refused to make the scheduled stop at Sprigg, and carried the troopers half a mile east of the town to the protection of a tunnel. But no sooner did the troopers leave the train than the heavy fire forced them also to flee into the woods.

At the close of the day, Brockus's report to headquarters was grim: "The situation is serious, and unless steps are taken to disarm all persons on both sides of the river officers will be ambushed, houses shot up and murder committed by the wholesale."

Brockus complained that he lacked the legal authority to restore order. "Arms and ammunition are being purchased daily from the local merchants and shipped in by express," he told his superiors. "Under the present conditions we have no authority to take a rifle from a man whom we might meet on the public road with a load of ammunition going directly to the firing."

The gunfire continued throughout the day and into the night. In Matewan the streetlights went out, and fearful families around the county slept on floors or in cellars. The next day, Friday, May 14, fighting spread to other towns along the Tug River and across the Tug into Kentucky, pitting union miners against strikebreakers and state police along a ten-mile front. One strikebreaker, Ambrose Gooslin, was wounded and another, Dan Whitt, was killed as they crossed railroad bridges over the Tug River. Both were shot at daybreak. But the gunfire was so intense that Gooslin lay on the bridge for hours until nightfall when friends finally dragged him to safety. He died two days later.

Normal life came to a halt in Matewan and the surrounding area. Stores and schools closed their doors and strikebreakers fled for their lives. At the height of the battle, Sid Hatfield patrolled the town with his friends, all heavily armed. Confronting the superintendent of the Stone Mountain Coal Co., who was overseeing the unloading of a rail car, Constable Hatfield ordered him to stop to avoid an attack by snipers. When he refused, they argued and Hatfield knocked the superintendent down. Some said he hit him with a rifle while Hatfield claimed he used only his bare hands and had "just slapped him down." At any rate another criminal charge was filed against the constable.

Late on Friday, May 13, the second day of fighting, a deputy sheriff under flag of truce made his way to the outposts of the union miners in the mountains behind Matewan and won from them a promise to stop shooting if their foes would also lay down their guns. With that to go on, Brockus dispatched a well-known local physician, across the Tug to Kentucky to negotiate with the strikebreakers. After crawling a half mile under fire the doctor parleyed with the non-union miners, who agreed to call a truce. He returned to Matewan Saturday night May 14, where a relieved Brockus spread the word that the bloodshed was over.

The sustained outbreak of violence came to be known as the "Three Days' Battle." Frank Keeney later described the episode as "a shooting bee." No one had an exact casualty count, but estimates ran as high as twenty deaths on both sides and Keeney was told on good authority that for eight days in the wake of the battle "they were bringing dead men out of the woods."

Less than three months after the last elements of the 19th Infantry had been withdrawn, following the murder trial in Williamson, Federal troops once again were needed in West Virginia, or so Governor Morgan believed. Early in the Three Days' Battle, Morgan had appealed for troops to General Read, commander of V Corps, a request that was backed up by Governor Edward Morrow of Kentucky. Since the direct-access policy had been revoked earlier that year, Read had no choice except to pass the request along to the White House. Meanwhile Republican Senator Howard Sutherland of West Virginia hurried to see the new president, Warren Harding, to support Morgan's appeal. When Harding failed to respond immediately, Morgan pleaded for help again, this time directly to Harding himself. He made no attempt to disguise his impatience: "Are we compelled to witness further slaughter of innocent law abiding citizens with no signs of relief from the Federal government?"

Morgan may well have assumed that Harding, a solid Republican supporter of business interests, would leap at the opportunity to use the power of Federal government to crack down on the excesses of organized labor. But if Morgan did believe that, it was because he lacked an adequate understanding of who the nation's 29th chief executive was and what he intended to do with his presidency. Harding, who had been in office barely two months when Morgan sought to burden him with West Virginia's problems, was the quintessential middle-class man of postwar America.

Warren Gamaliel Harding believed in getting along by going along, without making a fuss or muss. A small-town newspaper publisher, he was a trustee of the Trinity Baptist Church, a member of the board of directors of almost every enterprise of consequence in his hometown of Marion, Ohio, a leader of fraternal organizations and charitable causes. His life exuded an aura of respectability that offered no hint of the future scandals that would besmirch his presidency. Harding harbored no ill feeling toward anyone and instead sought to make friends on all sides. Despite his many and diverse activities, he found time to organize the Citizen Cornet Band, available for both Democratic and Republican rallies and took an active part. "I played every instrument but the slide trombone and the E-flat cornet," he once claimed.

He had an easy manner. People liked him and he did nothing to antagonize them. If the Republican bosses who helped him get elected wanted to make decisions about policy and appointments, he saw no reason to object. His matinee idol features, genial manner and particularly his sonorous voice and grandiloquent style helped him climb the political ladder. After one Harding speech on the floor of the Ohio Senate, the *Ohio State Journal* observed: "The speaker's address was rich in grace of diction and his manner, earnest and forceful throughout, rose to the dignity of true oratory."

But these gifts carried him only so far. Though he moved from the state senate to the lieutenant governorship, when he ran for governor he failed. Then in 1912 when many Republicans bolted their party and backed TR on the Bull Moose ticket, Harding stuck with the regulars and delivered the speech that nominated his fellow Ohioan, William Howard Taft.

Taft was doomed. But Harding's loyalty to his party made up for whatever else he lacked in leadership gifts. Grateful Republicans rewarded him with their nomination to the U.S. Senate in 1914, the first year that senators were publicly elected, and Harding won easily over the Democratic candidate, State Attorney General Timothy S. Hogan, who fell victim to a wave of anti-Catholic feeling. "This is the zenith of my political ambition," Harding declared on election night. The U.S. Senate he found to be a "very pleasant place." But Harry Daugherty, his longtime friend and political manager, had higher ambitions for Harding than the senator had for himself. That Harding continually denied ambitions for the presidency did not disturb Daugherty.

"He will of course not say that he is a candidate," Daugherty wrote a friend. "He don't have now to do much talking or know much. Presidents don't run in this country like assessors, you know." Others looking at the man's inner self might not necessarily see in Harding the qualities that would suit him for the office designed for Washington and graced by Jefferson and Lincoln. Daugherty, though, relied on the externals, which made Harding seem attractive and appealing. "He looked like a president," Daugherty pointed out. And in the mediocre Republican field of 1920 and in the postwar mood that gripped America, that was just about enough.

Gaining nomination from a previously deadlocked Republican convention as a compromise choice, through backroom conniving that Daugherty had foreseen, Harding laid out his vision of the nation's future. "America's present need is not heroics, but healing," he declared, "not nostrums, but normalcy, not revolution, but restoration, not agitation, but adjustment, not surgery, but serenity . . ." And so on and so forth. It would take only a quick glance at Harding's s alliterative list of dos and don'ts to realize that intruding the majesty and power of the Federal government into what was essentially a local dispute was not likely to comport with his view of appropriate presidential actions.

Refusing to be stampeded by Morgan's entreaties, Harding conferred with his secretary of war, John Weeks, then signed two separate proclamations of martial law, one for Kentucky and one for West Virginia, but did not issue either, pending further word from General Read. Read alerted the 19th infantry and Colonel Hall to the possibility of a return to Mingo County. Meanwhile, he sent his own intelligence chief, Major Charles Thompson, to Charleston to gauge the extent of the emergency.

Thompson met with Governor Morgan, with Mingo County officials and with the coal operators. It was indicative of the prevailing attitude among Army officers toward labor unions that Thompson made no attempt to consult with union officials. It did not take him long to conclude that the miners had caused a serious disorder. The question was whether the Federal government needed to intervene in either state. The answer for Kentucky, as Thompson soon realized, was obviously no. The governor of that state, as Thompson learned, had at his disposal a fully organized National Guard, including five companies of infantry and three troops of cavalry along with 300 deputy sheriffs. That certainly seemed sufficient.

West Virginia was a more complex matter. Its forces were puny by comparison with its neighbor, since despite the preliminary action by the legislature earlier in the year, the state had not yet gotten around to reestablishing its National Guard. But Thompson concluded that West Virginia's failure to act was no excuse for it to seek Federal aid. "Authorities have not taken sufficiently active measures," the major reported to General Read "and for purposes of both politics and economy, they have decided to rely on Federal protection."

Thompson had another reason to advise against giving Morgan the troops he wanted. Twice before the Army had been sent to West Virginia to restore order, only to see violence erupt after the soldiers were withdrawn. Thompson believed that it would take a full declaration of martial law—putting the Army in full charge of law enforcement—for the arrival of the soldiers to achieve long-term results.

Harding was not prepared to take any such drastic action.

After meeting with his cabinet, he had a telegram sent to Governor Morgan explaining his decision. "The Federal government is ever ready to perform its full duty in the maintenance of the constituted authority," the wire said. But it added that the president felt he would not be justified in sending troops "until he is well assured that the State has exhausted all its resources in the performance of its functions." And of this, the White House made clear, Harding was far from convinced.

In the wake of Harding's rebuff, Morgan finally did what he should have done all along, make use of West Virginia's emergency public safety law, enacted in 1919. This allowed him to transfer authority for law enforcement in Mingo County from the sheriff's department, whose deputies even under Blankenship's replacement, A. C. Pinson, were suspected of siding with the strikers, to the decidedly less sympathetic state police, under Captain Brockus. On May 18, Pinson, in an official warrant submitted to Brockus, asserted that the labor disputes in the county had led to numerous breaches of the peace. "Murder by laying in wait and shooting from ambush has become common." And since "there is now imminent danger of riots and resistance of the law," which could not be suppressed by his own forces, the sheriff added, the resources of the department of public safety, which managed the state police, were required to restore order.

That same night, Mingo County authorities called a mass meeting in the county courthouse at Williamson to solicit volunteers for a "vigilance committee," also dubbed a "law and order committee," to reinforce the existing state police. The cream of Mingo's middle class, some 250 businessmen, doctors, lawyers and every clergyman in town, answered the summons. They were the "better citizens" of Mingo County, "the men in business there and who have property there and were clamoring for protection," as Brockus would later describe them.

The meeting opened with a chorus of "America." "My country 'tis of thee, sweet land of liberty," sang the assembled "better citizens." Dr. J. W. Carpenter, minister of Williamson's First Presbyterian Church and leader of this law and order rally was well suited to the task, having often denounced the union leaders and their sympathizers as no better than murderers from his pulpit. President Harding had admonished Mingo County to use its own resources to clean its own house, Carpenter reminded the attentive burghers in his audience. Now each upstanding citizen must do his duty, just as many did during the Great War. "It is just as much a patriotic duty to clean up Mingo County as it was France," the Reverend Carpenter declared. As for himself, let no one think that because of his status as a man of God he was not ready for this secular challenge. "I don't know a thing about a rifle, but I am sure I can wield one, or a baseball bat if necessary."

Lant Slaven, a partner in the law firm of Goodykoontz, Scherr and Slaven, whose client list was laden with coal operators, sounded the same note of civic responsibility. "Who knows how soon they will be firing on Williamson?" he asked. "There may be some losses among us, but who here would not be willing to sacrifice for the sake of law and order in Mingo County?"

Major Ike Wilder, commanding Kentucky guardsmen on duty along the Tug, showed up in full regalia, including spurs, to pledge his state's full cooperation. Sheriff Pinson, who had just gotten off the phone with Morgan, passed on the governor's enthusiastic endorsement and read a telegram: "No time should be lost in placing under arrest every person in the county who has engaged, aided or abetted in the recent murders, attempted murders and destruction of property."

Just before the meeting closed, Captain Brockus arrived from a quick trip to Matewan, and strode to the podium like Caesar mustering the Roman legions. "Unless you have a rifle on your shoulder and are ready to do your duty, then we will have no order in Mingo County," the captain declared. "Unless you show up to take your place, then there is no hope, but I know you will." Brockus called for those men willing to serve the cause of law and order to stand. The response was overwhelming. "It seems to be unanimous," Brockus declared triumphantly.

The next day, May 19, 1921, Morgan proclaimed martial law. It was the first anniversary of the battle of Matewan, and the terms of Morgan's proclamation underlined how much ground the union and its members had lost since then. The governor declared West Virginia to be in a "state of war, insurrection and riot" and cited the inability of local law enforcement to maintain order. In one note of caution, intended to avoid judicial reversal of his decree, Morgan allowed the civil courts to function. But his edict banned the carrying of guns, ruled out public assemblies, meetings or processions and prohibited the publication of a newspaper or pamphlet "reflecting in any way upon the United States or the State of West Virginia or their officers or tending to influence the public mind against the United States or the State of West Virginia." Appointed as the governor's chief agent in charge of administering the martial law was Major Thomas. B. Davis, adjutant general of the state of West Virginia, who as a result of his new responsibilities would soon become known as the "Emperor of the Tug River."

A man with the build of a stevedore and the face of a bulldog, Davis by the time of his appointment already had a long and stormy personal history in West Virginia law enforcement. Though the news would have shocked the union workers he fought against throughout his public career, Davis had once been a union man himself. Raised in Huntington, West Virginia, his first job out of high school was as an apprentice machinist at the Chesapeake and Ohio railroad yards, and he rose to become president of Huntington's machinists union.

But in 1898, when the United States waged its "splendid little war" against Spain, Davis signed up with the 1st West Virginia Voluntary Infantry. He never heard a shot fired in anger, instead spending the war being shunted from one training camp to another. But Davis had developed a taste for military life. When his regiment was disbanded in 1899, he joined West Virginia's national guard, or state militia as it was called, and by 1910 had been elevated to the rank of major and given command of the 1st Battalion, 2nd Infantry.

It was the 1912 Paint Creek–Cabin Creek strike that first thrust Davis into the center of West Virginia's labor strife, revealing his nonchalance toward civil liberties. The military commission that had held sway over defendants charged with violating Governor Glasscock's martial law decrees selected him as its provost marshall. Despite the fact that the civil courts in the martial law district were open, the military commission, sitting in the town of Pratt, in Kanawha County, ruled on offenses ranging from larceny, adultery and disorderly conduct to disobeying sentries and perjury. A nearby freight terminal served as a bullpen to hold prisoners, among whom was Mother Jones. On occasion the commission tried as many as thirty prisoners at a time, dispensing with such formalities as indictments or juries. Davis saw to it that those convicted were hustled off not to the county jail but to the Moundsville State Prison.

With Davis's active assistance, the commission rode roughshod over the civil courts. When the county circuit court issued an order forbidding enforcement of the commission's sentences, Major Davis, acting on orders from Governor Hatfield, who had by now succeeded Glasscock, blocked the county sheriff from serving the writ on the national guard officer who headed the commission.

In May of 1913 after a pro-labor newspaper, the *Socialist and Labor Star*, editorially denounced the "coal barons" and attacked Governor Hatfield for arresting a union lawyer and suppressing the *Labor Argus*, sister paper to the *Star*, Davis led a raid on the *Star's* offices. Bearing warrants from Hatfield himself, Davis and his posse of Guardsmen and sheriff's deputies forced their way into the paper's offices in Huntington, overpowered a guard and wreaked havoc, destroying type and printing equipment. From there Davis and his commandos invaded the editor's home, seizing correspondence and books and rummaging through his files in a search for the paper's subscription list. The editor and assistant editor were imprisoned for two weeks, when they were finally released with no charges filed against them. The *Star* brought suit against Governor Hatfield, Davis and the officers on the raid, charging trespass, unlawful suppression of the paper and conspiracy. The state supreme court, laden with Glasscock appointees, rejected the suit, holding that the governor's actions could only be reviewed via impeachment proceedings.

Davis resigned from the militia in 1915. But when the United States plunged into the Great War, Davis once again donned a uniform, this time as West Virginia's adjutant general, with the rank of major and the responsibility of providing security for the state's factories and transportation lines. Since the national guard had been federalized and shipped out of the state, Davis had only the special deputy police force created to meet the wartime emergency to command. When that force was abolished at war's end, Davis retained his post as adjutant general. And in September 1919, after the miners' march on Marmet, it was Davis whom Cornwell appointed to head the investigation into their grievances. He also gave Davis an additional assignment, one that Cornwell had not discussed with the union leaders—to decide who was to blame for the march.

Davis seemed to take the second part of his assignment more seriously than the first. After weeks of hearings producing over 600 pages of testimony, and months of other inquiries, Davis delivered his conclusions, which by this time the union must have expected. As to the union's "wholesale indictment of conditions in Logan County," Davis found no foundation for that at all. But he had no difficulty assigning responsibility for the armed march: It was the fault of the UMW for issuing a letter based on unfounded information that inflamed the miners.

A few months later in the summer of 1920, when Federal troops were dispatched to Mingo County, Davis returned to action. This time he served as Cornwell's liaison with Colonel Burkhardt, the commander of the troops from Camp Sherman, with whom he traveled through the county, laying out a plan for assignments of the soldiers.

The new declaration of martial law following the Three Days' Battle returned Davis to prominence, and he did not delay in making his presence felt. On May 20, the day after martial law was declared, Davis arrived in Williamson, met with Brockus and Pinson and ordered distribution of the proclamation. The next order of business was to vet the list of volunteers for the vigilance committee. Davis and Brockus selected a committee of seven longtime Williamson residents and instructed them "to cross off those they were not absolutely sure of; that is that they could be relied upon to be issued a rifle and ammunition and go out in the interest of law and order." Each vigilante was given a Regular Army rifle, shipped down from Charleston, eighty rounds of ammunition, a badge and a striped armed band. All told some 780 men gained appointment as volunteers, more than 200 from Williamson.

Serving without pay, they needed to be ready at a moment's notice, Brockus warned; four quick blasts of the Williamson fire siren, repeated three times, would call them to action.

Conspicuous by their absence from the ranks of the vigilantes were union members, farmers or blacks. In explanation Brockus claimed that he recruited only men who lived close by so they would be ready to respond to any outbreak of violence in the city. "Now it is out of reason to expect to go out there in the country and get a farmer to repel an attack at Red Jacket, for instance," he said.

In implementing the martial law regulations, it was Davis who decided what was a crime and how it would be punished, without the nuisance of warrants or hearings. In his approach to law enforcement, the Emperor of the Tug appeared to pick up where he had left off during the Paint Creek–Cabin Creek strike. While the rules laid down by Morgan sounded strict on their face, their severity seemed to depend on whether or not a union man was the perpetrator. For example, all union meetings were banned; in fact if as many as three strikers gathered in one place, they were told to move along. Meanwhile the Salvation Army and the American Legion and similar organizations conducted their assemblages and ceremonies as usual.

On the second day of martial law, May 20, Davis banned distribution of the *West Virginia Federationist*, the state AFL's newspaper, for an article blaming Morgan, county officials and coal operators for the Three Days' Battle, and several strikers were arrested for reading the *United Mine Workers Journal*. The next night Davis and Brockus led a raid at UMW headquarters in Williamson's River View Hotel and arrested a dozen men, who were in the process of doing nothing more menacing than arranging relief payments to strikers, and carted them off to jail, in some cases for six days.

The broad sweep of the martial law rules, as interpreted by Davis and his minions, inevitably led to a legal challenge. On the afternoon of May 23 Brockus led a detail to an ice cream parlor near union headquarters in the River View Hotel, where they arrested A. D. Lavinder, a UMW organizer, on the charge of carrying a pistol. Lavinder claimed he had a permit for the gun, but the police insisted that under the martial law edict, all such permits were null and void. They told Lavinder he needed to go with them to Davis's headquarters.

Lavinder, a feisty sort, was not impressed. "If the adjutant general wants to see me, he can come to union headquarters," he said. Whereupon the troopers hustled him off to jail, and his appearance when he arrived there made it clear that on his way over his captors had found physical expression for their displeasure with his behavior. Furious at this abuse, UMW lawyers filed a petition for habeas corpus on Lavinder's behalf against the sheriff of McDowell County, in whose jail Lavinder was held because of overcrowding of the Mingo County jail.

While that legal controversy simmered, tension mounted in Mingo. On May 24 Sid Hatfield arrived in the county seat of Williamson to answer charges growing out of his fracas with the mine superintendent in Matewan in the midst of the Three Days' Battle. On hand to meet him were Brockus, Davis and a contingent of armed vigilantes. But Hatfield got off the train on the wrong side, eluded his hostile reception committee and received a hero's welcome from a multitude of admirers as he marched down the street to the courthouse.

Meanwhile, with much less fanfare, a shipment of Thompson submachine guns arrived in Mingo County and were distributed to state police. Nearly every day now, union miners were being arrested for carrying union literature, for speaking against martial law and for carrying arms. Held without bail or hearing, they overflowed the Mingo jail. Brockus had to send them, like Lavinder, to prisons in adjoining counties.

These conditions in West Virginia were drawing increasing attention outside the state, creating an opportunity for labor leaders and their liberal allies to renew their demands for a Senate inquiry. This time they chose to target a figure well known for his willingness to defy the Republican establishment that ruled the world's most exclusive club, Senator Hiram Johnson of California. Hard-driving, humorless and often ham-fisted in his approach to issues, Johnson's fealty to conscience and principle was unquestioned even by his foes. He had established that reputation early in his career as an assistant district attorney in San Francisco. When a colleague prosecuting corruption charges against a leading political grafter was shot down in open court, without blinking Johnson took over the case and gained a conviction.

In 1912 he risked his political future by breaking with the GOP regulars to run as Theodore Roosevelt's vice presidential candidate on the Bull Moose ticket. After six reform-filled years as governor of California, he had come to the Senate in 1916, where his integrity remained remarkably intact. In him the labor leaders found what they needed, sympathy for their cause, a willingness to act and a powerful voice. On May 24, as the West Virginia state police were taking inventory of their newly arrived submachine guns, Johnson introduced a resolution calling for an investigation of violence in the coalfields of southern West Virginia.

The next day, in West Virginia, disorder claimed more lives. Snipers from one of the strikers' tent colonies lodged themselves in the Kentucky hills and fired into the Big Splint colliery, between

Borderland and Nolan. A state police detachment arrived on the scene, together with Kentucky guardsmen, and came under fire. One trooper and one guardsman were killed, and one of the snipers was mortally wounded. Two men were arrested and another escaped into the hills. Brockus sent a posse after the escapee, who was brought back to West Virginia without benefit of extradition. "We do not know the state lines down there and we don't care," one trooper told the *New York Times*. "The prisoner was lucky to get into the lockup alive."

The outbreak at Big Splint drew increasing attention to the tent colonies of strikers, particularly the settlement at Lick Creek, which was by far the largest. A *New York Times* story out of Williamson datelined May 26, the day after the Big Splint violence, reflected the attitude of Davis and his cohorts toward the strikers and their families. The story pointed out that the violence at Big Splint occurred only a short distance from Lick Creek. "The question of what to do with these colonies, now regarded as perhaps the chief obstacles in the maintenance of peace in the Mingo coal fields is one of the most difficult confronting the authorities," the story added. "The colonies are presently free from close surveillance that many persons think they should be subjected to. The Lick Creek and Nolan colonies are on the shore of the Tug, making escape into Kentucky for tent dwellers a comparatively easy step." Though the story was sparing in quoting officials by name, given the views expressed, it was not hard to identify the "authorities" and "many persons" expressing concern about the tent colonies as Major Davis and his aides.

Meanwhile, Davis left his command post at Williamson to go to the state capital to meet with Morgan and other state officials about the problem of the tent colonies and about handling the dozen or so cases stemming from martial law arrests. Not surprisingly, Harry Olmstead, spokesman for Williamson Operators, accompanied Davis and participated in all the meetings. Actually with Davis on hand, Olmstead's side was already well represented. The adjutant general let it be known to reporters that the measures put into effect so far were "too gentle," and that he planned to get the governor to approve "a tightening of the reins by military authorities."

What Davis had in mind was to create a sort of predecessor of the Gulag. He contemplated expelling the union families from the tent colonies, commandeering their tents and resettling the erstwhile occupants in new camps under military control, at what he considered a safe distance from the strike zone and the refuge of the Kentucky border. Judging from what happened later, it seems probable that a raid on the Lick Creek colony was also on the agenda.

But for the moment, Davis held off any new aggressive move. With the Senate resolution hanging fire on Capitol Hill, he did not want to give forces lobbying for the investigation additional ammunition. Instead he was content to put on a show of strength in the Williamson Memorial Day parade, when state troopers, led by Brockus, marched to the colors. They were joined by a substantial contingent of the American Legion and the newly formed vigilante corps, or Law and Order Committee as its creators preferred to call it.

A few days later, on June 4, Major Wilder, concluding that his 300 Kentucky National Guardsmen were no longer needed, withdrew his force back to Pike County. But that still left Davis in charge of a formidable force—some 800 state troopers, vigilantes and coal company guards, all equipped with weapons, not to mention a fair number of strikebreakers who were carrying weapons for their own defense, a violation of the martial law decrees, which Davis chose not to notice.

In this environment an explosion of new violence seemed only a question of time. The clock began ticking on the morning of June 5, when nervous Lick Creek colonists fired at an auto carrying five passengers whom they took to be hostile vigilantes. Immediately, Brockus and Sheriff Pinson swept down on the colony and arrested about forty miners. There was no resistance, though eight men fled into the woods. Arriving on the scene, Major Davis issued a stern warning: "If there is any more shooting up there you can just line up on the road because we are going out and bring everybody in. You are not going to stay in jail two days either. You will stay longer."

Given the bellicosity of that visit, when Davis and Brockus returned to Lick Creek nine days later, supposedly to arrest a miner charged in a shooting incident, they could hardly have been surprised at their reception. The suspect they were hunting, standing on the porch of his home, opened fire on their car with a pistol. Then snipers began blasting away from behind rocks and crags on the hills.

Davis was ready for that. He ordered a trooper to rake the hillside with one of his newly issued tommy guns. The trooper was reluctant so Davis repeated the order, with emphasis. This time the trooper obeyed, firing half of the two rounds in his clip. The snipers responded. The trooper emptied the clip at the hills, and the sniping stopped. Then Davis returned to Williamson and sounded the call to battle—four blasts repeated three times on the fire house siren. Within ten minutes about seventy members of the Law and Order Committee responded. Davis loaded them into twenty cars and drove up Sycamore Creek, which parallels Lick Creek. Brockus meanwhile alerted the state police to seal off the only exit roads from the colony. His plan was to herd all the snipers in the hill back into the tent colony and its environs and trap them there.

Starting at the top of the mountain, Brockus and his men formed a skirmish line about a mile long, and proceeded downhill, searching for snipers. As they approached the fence bordering the colony they came under fire. "It was rather hot for a time," Brockus recalled later. After about fifty to seventy-five shots were fired, Brockus suddenly heard a cry for help. It was one of his troopers, James A. Bowles, who had been dispatched with a party of fifteen vigilantes to sweep the other side of the hill, which Brockus believed to be lightly defended. But Bowles spotted a group of armed miners in a wooded valley to the rear of the tents, just as they noticed him.

Both sides began firing. Bowles shot and killed a miner, Alex Breedlove, in cold blood, according to the miners, and was himself shot through the shoulder, again according to the miners, by one of his own men. A wild scene ensued. An enraged Brockus ordered his men to drive the miners and their families out of the tents, while the Law and Order vigilantes ransacked the tents, slashing the canvas, smashing the furniture and driving the miners and the families to the road. The women and children were released but forty-seven of the men were lined up on the railroad track and marched down the road to Williamson. There they were herded into a single jail cell and held for four days, when eight of them were charged with violating the martial law edict and the rest released.

The uproar caused by the death of Breedlove and the assault on the tents led to a visit to the colony on June 15 by Judge Bailey, who two months before had presided over the Matewan shoot-out trial, an assistant county prosecutor and an attorney for the miners. As they were inspecting the area, a vigilante in a passing car, who mistook the officials for miners, paused to shout: "If you damn red necks haven't got enough, we will give you more of it."

Even as Major Davis's tactics heightened antagonisms on both sides, the state's efforts to crack down on the miners suffered a legal setback. On June 14, the same day as Brockus's raid on Lick Creek, the state supreme court, ruling on appeals by A. D. Lavinder, arrested in the ice cream parlor case, held that the martial law proclamation was invalid. Imposition of martial law required the existence of an official military force, such as the National Guard, for its enforcement, the court held. "There was no actual militia organization or force representing the state government in Mingo County," the court pointed out. Though Major Davis, who held a military commission, was directing the civil authorities, "they were not enrolled, enlisted or organized as a military force." While the ruling was based on technical grounds, the opinion stated the court's disapproval in broad terms. The governor could not "by a mere order convert civil officers into an army and clothe them with military powers . . . set aside the civil laws and rules by his practically unrestrained will," the court said. Using reasoning that must have stunned Davis because of its contrast with the *Labor Star* decision by the same court a decade earlier, the justices declared: "Power in a chief magistrate to effect such result would be suggestive of the despotism of unrestricted monarchial government . . . preclusion of which is one of the chief aims . . . of constitutional popular government."

That left Morgan in a lurch, and in dire need of a military force the court would recognize as legitimate. West Virginia's legislature had finally gotten around to reestablishing the National Guard, but those units would not take the field until late July. In the meantime the governor made use of an all-but-forgotten statute to set up a temporary militia that would meet the requirements of the state court's ruling.

On June 27, two weeks after the court handed down its ruling in the Lavinder case, Morgan issued an order supplementing his martial law proclamation, directing the sheriff of Mingo County to create an "enrolled militia" of 130 men, drawn from all county residents. Until the National Guard was activated these units would enforce the martial law edict. Meanwhile the vigilante force would be disbanded, though many of its members would serve in the temporary militia, which also would be commanded by Major Davis. Given the make-shift nature of this enrolled militia, the court's ruling weakened Morgan's hand at least temporarily. More significantly, it also raised further questions outside the state, particularly in Washington, about the credibility of his governance.

Ever since Hiram Johnson had introduced his resolution calling for a Senate probe of West Virginia's labor unrest, he and the UMW's friends in the nation's capital had been monitoring the state looking for fresh ammunition. Brockus's ill-fated raid on Lick Creek combined with the supreme court's overturning of martial law and its rebuke of Morgan gave them what they wanted. On June 21, a week after the Lick Creek raid and the supreme court decision, Johnson rose on the floor of the Senate to demand his colleagues respond to "the existence of a state of civil war" in West Virginia. The day after his resolution had been introduced, he pointed out, there had been more killings in West Virginia. "This never would have occurred," Johnson contended, if the Senate had acted and appointed an investigating panel earlier. "Do Senators wish to see some of the scenes of the place where this civil war exists?" Johnson asked and referred his colleagues to news photos of the tent colony "showing men and women living simply under God's canopy in tents and in many cases guards have slashed so as to destroy the only abode that these poor people have."

Just the previous day, Johnson reminded the Senate, Nebraska Senator George Norris had denounced the tactics of British troops waging guerrilla warfare against Irish Republican militants. Johnson also recalled the stories of alleged atrocities by the Kaiser's troops against women and children during World War I. Such episodes were more than matched by the accounts of violence against innocent women and children in West Virginia, Johnson claimed. "There never has been in our history, if these stories be accurate, anything like the conditions that obtain today in this territory at our very doors."

This time the Senate did not delay. Johnson's resolution was readily adopted and the Senate instructed the chairman of its labor committee, Iowa's William Kenyon, to do what he had resisted doing a year earlier, "make a thorough and complete investigation of the conditions existing in the coal fields of West Virginia in the territory adjacent to the border of West Virginia and Kentucky . . . and report its findings and conclusions thereon to the Senate." One year after the shoot-out in Matewan, the struggle between the mine workers and the coal companies was to shift to yet another domain, the time-honored halls of the United States Senate.

7

Mr. Hatfield
Goes to Washington

IT WAS A TYPICALLY torrid midsummer day in Washington, the kind of weather that made foreign offices around
the world classify the city a hardship post for their diplomats. The
capital suffered along with the rest of the East. In New York a
bricklayer working on a Broadway office building keeled over and
died and the director of a motion picture being shot in the Hotel
Ambassador in midtown Manhattan collapsed and fell down a
flight of stairs. Washingtonians, including the members of the
U.S. Senate, being more accustomed to the heat, went about their
lives as usual, though at a sluggish pace.

So it was on Capitol Hill. At first glance the Capitol building
itself, with its darkened hallways underneath its cast-iron dome,
appeared cool, at least by contrast with the sweltering streets outside. But this proved to be a temporary illusion, as the members
and staff of the Senate Labor Committee realized as soon as they
entered the committee's high-ceilinged hearing room. Despite the
slatted blinds shielding the windows against the blazing sun, and
the electric fans that stirred the turgid air, the heat and humidity
had transformed the chamber into a soggy oven. Yet, for the leaders of the United Mine Workers of West Virginia, there was no
place else they would rather be on July 14, 1921, as the hearings

ordered by the Senate into the labor struggle in the West Virginia coalfields commenced.

From the start of their organizing drive in southern West Virginia, the union men knew the odds were stacked against them because of the economic and political power of the operators. But they were impelled forward by the hope that if their struggle could generate enough national attention, public opinion and the influence of the Federal government would turn the tide in their direction. Certainly in midsummer of 1921 the union needed whatever help it could get. For the operators seemed on the verge of breaking the strike, if they had not already done so. As the hearing commenced, the operators boasted that the output of the Williamson field mines had all but returned to normal, and were operating at 96 percent of their regular capacity of five million tons a year.

Though the UMW leaders stoutly denied such claims, their actions tended to belie their words. In a letter to Governor Morgan only a few days before the start of the Senate hearing, union leaders had made a compromise offer of sorts. The proposal, as the union described it, amounted to scrapping its demand for a union shop, under which the operators could only employ union members, and agreeing to accept an open shop, an arrangement in which union and non-union men would work side by side. But the operators felt themselves to be in such a strong position that they did not even consider the union tender or dignify it with a direct response. Instead Harry Olmstead, the representative of the Williamson operators, had responded only with a press release in which he declared that the operators would not deal with the union in any "shape, manner or form."

If the union had any basis for its hopes of countering this conservative tide in the forthcoming proceedings, it was in the presence, as chairman of the committee, of the junior Senator from Iowa, William Squire Kenyon. Though less flamboyant and strident than California's Hiram Johnson, whose resolution had set the hearings in motion, Kenyon was himself a respected member of the small but influential band of Senate Republican progressives. The son of a Princeton-trained Congregational minister, Kenyon was born in Ohio but raised in Iowa, the home state of John L. Lewis, and an early stronghold of the UMW. Though the Reverend Kenyon hoped his son would follow him into the clergy, young Kenyon was intent on practicing law, a profession well suited for the cool, analytical intellect he demonstrated early on. Admitted to the bar in 1891 at age twenty-two, Kenyon began practicing in Fort Dodge, about 150 miles north of Lucas County, where Lewis cut his teeth as a union leader. By the time he was thirty-eight, in 1907, he had caught the eye of the Illinois Central Railroad, which recruited him to be its general counsel.

He might have finished out his days as a prosperous corporate lawyer, had not William Howard Taft's Justice Department, bent on cracking down on big trusts, lured Kenyon away to serve as point man. Kenyon led a crusade that brought nearly double the antitrust prosecutions in four years than Taft's predecessor Theodore Roosevelt had launched in eight, targets that included the likes of Standard Oil, American Tobacco and U.S. Steel.

By now Kenyon's star was shining brightly in the Iowa political firmament. In 1911, when death created a U.S. Senate vacancy, the Iowa legislature selected Kenyon, who gained re-election by the legislature in 1912 and, after the ratification of the 17th amendment in 1913, by the general electorate in 1918.

In the Senate, Kenyon lived up to his reformist reputation; he backed tariff reductions and Federal taxes on personal incomes and corporate profits. He also sought aid for the debt-ridden farmers of the Midwest and helped to organize what over the years would become known as the Farm Bloc.

But the union could not depend on the Senator to fight its battles. Even in the Senate, Kenyon maintained a lawyerly bearing and friends knew that in his heart he yearned for a judicial position. Indeed soon after the hearings concluded, Harding would appoint him to the Federal Court of Appeals. In the meantime Kenyon seemed to impose his judicial temperament as a restraint on his progressive convictions, a tendency that would diminish his value to the mine workers union as they carried their struggle for survival to Capitol Hill.

It was clear from the start of the hearings that there would be no restraint on the mine owners' side. During the 1913 investigation, the operators had been on the defensive in the face of charges of treating their workers unjustly. They came away from those hearings, and from subsequent skirmishes with the UMW, convinced that the union and its backers were, as one coal operator put it, "the greatest publicists on earth." But the mine owners had learned a lesson over the years. Now they were on the attack.

They made their first target the controversial change in the Mine Workers constitution in 1912, which asserted that the miners were entitled not merely to "an equitable share of the fruits of their labor" but rather to "the full social value of their product." That revision, L. Tailor Vinson, the chief spokesman for the operators charged, transformed the UMW from an ordinary labor union into "an organized band of robbers. They boldly claim, boldly announce that what they propose is to keep on making demands for increases until they finally take over all the mines in North America, including Canada," Vinson declared. "Every single solitary disturbance, every murder, every assassination that has been committed in the coal industry in West Virginia is traceable directly to this announced policy of this organization to unionize first and then to own the property themselves."

The miners also were handicapped by the detached attitude of the senators, who seemed to view the life-and-death struggle in West Virginia as just another item among the sundry and varied matters that filled their legislative lives. When the union's spokesmen tried to counter Vinson's attack by arguing that the excesses of the coal companies had violated their constitutional rights, that claim seemed to take the committee by surprise. "What constitutional rights—I suppose that is what this committee should investigate—what constitutional rights under the Federal constitution do you feel you have been denied?" Chairman Kenyon asked, his offhand manner seeming to minimize the importance of the issue.

But Fred Mooney was ready for him. "We are denied a republican form of government; we are denied public assemblage; we are denied the right to belong to a labor union—that is also the law of the state," District 17's secretary treasurer told the committee.

Yet constitutional rights seemed too abstract an issue to engage the attention of the senators. They were more caught up by the charges of violence made against the union. Asked about the alleged shooting of a state trooper by the miners, Mooney put the matter in a different perspective: "The state policeman that was killed went to a moonshine still and got some of that whisky and refused to pay for it," he explained. "And the fellow he had skinned out of the whisky shot him in the back after he started to leave."

Senator Kenneth McKellar of Tennessee, serving his first Senate term after six years in the House, paid more attention to what he regarded as a slur against his home state than the injustices inflicted upon the miners. When Vinson charged that the union had imported hundreds of "gun men," mainly from Tennessee, McKellar spoke up for the first time in the proceedings. "How do you know they are from Tennessee?" he demanded.

"That is the information that has come to us from the military authorities," Vinson told him. The fifty-three-year-old McKellar, a case-hardened Memphis lawyer with a populist streak, had concluded that in Tennessee he could gain more votes by baiting the coal companies than denouncing the union. "My information is that Tennessee is about as law abiding a state as we have in the union and we are not having any trouble like they are having in West Virginia," he told Vinson. "I am going to insist strenuously that we know where these men from Tennessee come from."

Mooney was of course delighted to find any senator challenging the coal companies, whatever the grounds. "A statement like that is almost unworthy of an answer," Mooney told McKellar about the charge that the union had imported gunmen from his state. If there were any gunmen brought into the state, Mooney said, it was the operators who had done the importing. The only men brought in by the union were organizers, Mooney added, and most of these were now employed distributing relief checks to the strikers and their families.

By this time Vinson was in full retreat. He hastened to correct his earlier statement. "Our list does not show that anybody came from your state, Senator," the abashed lawyer said.

Vinson created another opportunity for self-embarrassment by claiming that miners could earn as much as $400 to $700 a month. That got the attention of Republican Samuel Shortridge of California.

"You mean individual miners?" He asked.

"Yes, sir," Vinson replied.

"You mean working with a pick and shovel?"

"I think I will resign and become a miner," Shortridge chortled.

This was too much for Mooney. The highest average income for skilled miners in West Virginia, during the peak of the World War boom was only $1,066 a year, he pointed out. The top scale for miners was $4.52 a day, and the average number of days a year was only 217.

There is quite a difference between $1,000 a year and $700 a month, Kenyon observed drily.

But such tactical triumphs were few and far between for the union as the operators pressed their assault, arguing that the operators would not and indeed could not deal with the union because the union's position was inherently unreasonable. Even when it appeared to offer a compromise, its fundamental position remained unyielding in its determination to control the mines. S. B. Avis, whom Mooney viewed as the "most venomous and malignant" of the coal company lawyers, artfully set a trap for Mooney to help make that argument. Suppose the mine operators accepted the union's latest compromise proposal but had no room to take back the union men on strike. Would the union continue the strike?

"Yes," Mooney replied.

That was of course just what Avis wanted him to say. "That means then that if they have got all the men they need they must discharge some of these men and replace them with your men, does it not?" Avis asked, driving the point home.

There would be plenty of room for the strikers, Mooney insisted.

"But if there is not room for them, then you are going to continue this strike, are you not?"

"You have not any right to dwell on suppositions," Mooney answered lamely. But Avis had made his case with Mooney's help.

The union hoped to repair some of the damage suffered in the opening day of the testimony when District 17's president Frank Keeney took the stand on Friday July 15. Powerfully built, with large facial features and an open countenance, Keeney commonly wore a broad grin. But the friendly demeanor cloaked an iron will and a quick mind, and a far more supple intelligence than that of most of his colleagues. He could be equally convincing in a blustery harangue to the rank and file or in a sophisticated argument across the bargaining table from the mine owners. But on this day in the Senate hearing room, Keeney soon ran into difficulty as Avis resumed the mine owners' efforts to depict the union as the enemy of law and order. "Is it not a fact that it is the policy of your organization to defend any member of your organization from any crime with which he is charged during labor troubles?" Avis asked.

Keeney fought back. "I say that we have the same right to protect our members as the coal operators have to protect the Baldwin-Felts guards," he replied. "You do not suppose that we will permit our members to be annihilated because someone presumes them guilty of some crime?"

Stymied, Avis tried another approach. He asked Keeney to explain why the number of casualties in the Mingo County violence had been far greater among the mine guards and other forces supporting the operators than among the miners.

Keeney paused for effect and then answered: "I can explain that in this way," he said. "When a real mountaineer of Mingo County

shoots twice and don't hit a man you know he is not shooting at
you. And the men they imported in there to do the shooting could
not equal them; that is all." Keeney's braggadocio echoed his
remarks to Washington reporters the previous winter when he re-
butted charges that the miners had been shooting at state troopers
by saying that the miners were such crack shots that "if they ever
shot at a trooper more than twice he wouldn't be alive."

If Keeney was pleased with his response to Avis, so was Avis. "In
other words," Avis said, reiterating Keeney's point, "the men you
had were better shots than the men on the other side." Whatever
satisfaction Keeney might have gotten from his riposte, Avis was
only too content to underline the impression left by Keeney of a
union official bragging that the men on his side were expert killers.

But Avis's grilling of Mooney and Keeney was just a rehearsal
for the main act in the drama, the appearance on July 16, the third
day of the hearings, of the union's star witness, the hero of Matewan and champion of the West Virginia mine workers, Sid Hatfield. While the press and spectators who jammed the hearing
room craned their necks for a better look at the constable's sharp
features, "Smilin' Sid," as his admirers now liked to call him, gave
his version of the shoot-out, in a voice so low that Kenyon twice
had to urge him to speak up. In his flat mountain twang Hatfield
recounted the arrival of the detectives, their eviction of the miners
and then their first encounter with Testerman and Hatfield at the
scene of the evictions. The detectives came back to Matewan, to
catch their train back to Bluefield, Hatfield explained, leading
to their second confrontation with Hatfield and Testerman, which
ultimately exploded in violence and bloodshed.

"I went up and told Mr. Felts that I would have to arrest him,"
Hatfield recalled. "He said he would turn the compliment on me,
that he had a warrant for me." It was after Testerman demanded to
see the warrant, and pronounced it bogus, Hatfield said, that Felts
shot the mayor. "Then the shooting started in general."

That was about as far as he was prepared to go. When the senators began to probe for details, Hatfield's answers seemed to be-

come hazy. "How many men did you have with you?" Senator Kenyon asked.

"Well I did not have any men with me at the time they had me arrested," Hatfield said. "It was train time and a whole lot of people would meet the train."

"Did not the people come in to help you arrest them?" Kenyon wanted to know.

"No sir," Hatfield replied without wavering.

"Were you all alone?" Kenyon pressed.

"I didn't ask for any help," Hatfield replied, ignoring the fact of the dozen or so special deputies who had been sworn in to meet the challenge of Albert Felts and his men.

Now it was Avis's turn, and he could hardly wait.

"How many shots did Albert Felts fire?" he demanded.

"Well, I didn't have time to count them," Hatfield replied. "If you had been there I don't think you could have counted them."

But Avis had a contradiction he wanted to expose. During Hatfield's trial, defense witnesses had claimed that Felts had fired twice. Hatfield himself did not testify at his trial. But in his prior testimony to the grand jury he had sworn that Felts had fired only one shot. Before Avis could pursue this discrepancy, Harold Houston, the UMW attorney, hurried to object. The trial prosecutor, Houston said, had turned over a transcript of the grand jury testimony to the counsel for the coal operators, but none to the miners. His client still faced charges of killing the six other Baldwin-Felts detectives who had died along with Albert Felts in the Matewan shoot-out. Under the circumstances he was not going to allow Avis to lead Hatfield down a road toward a possible perjury charge.

Chairman Kenyon let Hatfield off the hook. "The appearance of Mr. Hatfield is voluntary and we are not forcing him to give any testimony and we do not want to do anything one way or another that might affect his case," the senator declared. "I will not ask him to answer that question."

Now Avis went after Hatfield hammer and tongs, determined to confront him with every instance of misconduct in his checkered background, real or alleged. The lawyer had no shortage of ammunition. But Hatfield remained impassive in front of the barrage, admitting nothing, denying almost everything.

First there was the matter of the widow Testerman.

"Mr. Hatfield, did you not within less than two weeks after Mayor Testerman was killed marry his widow?"

"I did."

"And are you not now running his place of business."

"I am."

"Don't you know Mr. Hatfield that a number of witnesses who testified before the grand jury, one of whom also testified against you in the last trial, have been assassinated?"

"I do not know that," Hatfield replied flatly.

Avis brought up the murder of Harry Staton, the former justice of the peace who had testified against Hatfield during the murder trial.

"I have been informed that one of the operators killed him," Hatfield said.

"One of your codefendants is under indictment for doing that, is he not?," Avis asked, referring to Calvin McCoy.

"Not that I heard of," Hatfield replied.

Finally Avis found a crime that Hatfield would acknowledge being connected with.

"Are you not under indictment for killing Anse Hatfield?" Avis asked.

"Yes sir."

It was easy enough for Hatfield to deal with questions about the charges he faced that he already knew about. But suddenly Avis asked him about a charge he had not heard of before—a McDowell County indictment for conspiring to blow up a tipple in August of 1920.

Caught off guard, the witness replied, honestly enough, "This is the first I heard of it."

To Harold Houston, it sounded like a phony charge, and he leaned over to his client to joke about it.

Avis caught him and snapped: "Don't smile, Mr. Houston, because that is true."

"That is made up like the rest," Hatfield told him.

But he was wrong about that. The McDowell County indictment, as Hatfield would soon find out, would turn out to be all too real, and its consequences would prove to be tragic both for Hatfield and for the union cause.

But for the time being, Hatfield had his hands full dealing with Avis's questions. "I will ask you Mr. Hatfield, if you did not pose for the newspapers as a gunman, with pistols in your hand," the lawyer next queried.

"No sir, I did not pose to be a gunman."

But Avis had in his hand a widely circulated photo that showed Hatfield, a gun in each hand, standing on a Matewan street grinning broadly, which he eagerly distributed to members of the committee. At this point, Tennessee's McKellar, who had become more sympathetic to the union cause as the hearing progressed, intervened and asked Hatfield to explain the photo.

"The paper man came to my store and he come in and made himself acquainted," the witness said. "He said that he wanted a picture of my gun and I took the guns and stepped out on the street and he made my picture."

"So it was simply a matter of him coming into your place and he wanted to make your picture for the newspaper after the killing?" McKellar prompted.

"Yes sir."

Continuing his efforts on Hatfield's behalf, the senator asked the witness if he had ever been involved "in other difficulties or shootings of any sort." Hatfield recalled his shooting of the mine foreman, five years earlier, but said he had given himself up and had been cleared on grounds of self-defense.

"And that is the only previous difficulty you had for which you have been tried?" McKellar asked. "It is all I had anywhere," Hatfield responded more or less truthfully. He had been in plenty of other trouble, but had never been put on trial till the murder charges resulting from the Matewan shootings.

Now it was lawyer Houston's term to help defend Hatfield's reputation. "Mr. Hatfield, have you ever used intoxicating liquors in any form?"

"Not for years," said the police chief.

At this point, the operators' lawyer, Vinson, lost patience with the rehabilitation effort.

"Why is this material?" he asked. "I would like to inquire if Mr. Hatfield's character is at issue in this case."

No, it was not, Senator Kenyon replied.

But the chairman was wrong about that. Hatfield had become the national symbol of the union's struggle. And by being forced to acknowledge his disreputable past during his testimony, the last to be offered on behalf of the union, "Smilin' Sid" had done his enemies and the foes of the UMW a considerable service.

Hoping to exploit the advantage they had already gained when they presented their side as the hearings began their second week, the mine owners inflicted almost as much damage on their case as the UMW had done to itself. Their first witness, Harry Olmstead, the spokesman for the Williamson Operators, to make clear the nature of the forces against whom he was contending, submitted a list of more than 125 incidents of violence, "assaults, burnings, killings and explosions," all perpetrated by the union, Olmstead claimed in furtherance of its quest for power.

As to union claims of violence, Olmstead dismissed them as part of the organizing strategy of the union. "Lurid tales" are published, Olmstead testified, to the effect that the "brutal mine guards" have been guilty of assaulting men, women and children. "Wholly false," said Olmstead of such charges, "and not supported by any proof whatever."

Kenyon, who had developed a skepticism for the testimony of both sides, was not satisfied. If the companies did not employ Baldwin-Felts men as mine guards, he inquired, did they employ them in any capacity at all?

As a matter of fact, yes, Olmstead conceded. "We employed these Baldwin-Felts men in secret service," but for no other purpose. "We have had 12 to 15 of these men throughout the field, whose daily reports were relied on to head off the violent machinations of the union." And these men had been used for no other purpose, he told the committee. But then he was quickly obliged to remind himself of an exception, the contingent that had been dispatched by Tom Felt to Matewan on May 19 to evict the union miners, setting off the year-long struggle in the mountains.

But Kenyon was not through with him yet. Did the fifty-six coal companies in the Williamson field employ and pay any sheriff's deputies?

"There have been," he said, and then hastened to qualify his answer. "In the latter part of September and first of October, after those days that the riot was very close on," Olmstead said, "I mean after the threatened riot at Williamson and on the public streets, a conference was held in the governor's office in Charleston."

Kenyon had a considerable store of patience, but Olmstead had managed to exhaust it. "Please just answer my question," he told Olmstead.

"That is the only way I can answer it," Olmstead persisted.

"You do not have to go into all that detail to answer that question do you?" Kenyon said firmly.

Finally Olmstead gave in. As a result of an agreement with the governor and Mingo County, the mine owners for about a month did indeed pay the salary of eight to ten sheriff's deputies, he conceded, amounting to about $1,800. The payments were made, Olmstead claimed, "with the understanding that the money would be returned when they had it available to pay back."

The senators were clearly upset. "Do you believe that it is a good principle, namely, that police officers should be paid by any particular interest?" Republican Senator Thomas Sterling of South Dakota asked Olmstead.

"No it would be very much better if the county would pay it itself," Olmstead said, "and we would be very glad if they did, Senator."

At this point, counselor Houston, who had been listening to this colloquy with far more satisfaction than he could have felt during the earlier sessions, added another point about the payments. Not only were they inappropriate, he contended, they were illegal under the laws of West Virginia.

For his part, Olmstead professed to be unaware of such a law and quickly withdrew from the witness table.

Despite such awkward moments, the coal companies seemed increasingly confident of their ability to dominate the proceedings and blacken the name of the United Mine Workers. This self-assurance made them insensitive to how some of their anti-union activities might appear to the senators, when exposed in the cold light of the hearings. But this lesson was driven home to them by the testimony of Charles Lively, the labor spy.

By calling Lively on Wednesday, July 20, the sixth day of hearings, the operators hoped to impress the senators with the inside information that the union men had supposedly confided in him. Instead, the senators seemed far more disturbed with Lively's devious tactics, during his ten years as a paid informer for the Baldwin-Felts agency while posing as loyal union activist than in what he had learned. After listening to Lively's description of his hoodwinking of his supposed comrades, even winning election as a union officer and also as delegate to the 1913 UMW state convention in West Virginia, Senator Kenyon broke in with a pointed question: "Were your expenses paid by the miners when you went to the convention or did the Baldwin-Felts agency pay your expenses?"

"Well the miners paid my expenses there to that Charleston convention; yes," Lively replied. "I felt that it was necessary that I leave them pay them in order to keep off suspicion."

"Did the Baldwin-Felts people pay your expenses, too?" Kenyon wanted to know.

"No," Lively said; he was, after all, not without scruples, he stressed. "Because that was one thing I always made a practice of—never to charge anything I was not out of."

Here McKellar picked up the thread of the questioning, probing further into the detective's ethical standards. "You felt in the way you were working, you were doing entirely what was right and proper?"

"Yes sir."

"You saw nothing wrong in that?" McKellar persisted.

"I saw nothing wrong about it, nothing illegitimate or illegal," Lively insisted.

Kenyon was still curious about how Lively handled his expenses in his dual role. On some days, he would have expenses incurred on behalf of both the UMW and Baldwin-Felts, would he not?

"Yes sir," Lively affirmed.

"What did you do then, how did you keep your books?" Kenyon asked .

"When I made any expense of that kind I would kind of divide it up."

"You wanted to be very careful that both sides did not pay your expenses?" Kenyon asked.

"Yes, sir," Lively said.

"I see you have a delicate sense of right and wrong," Kenyon drily observed.

The sarcasm seemed to have been lost on Lively, who now had to contend again with McKellar. "If you had disclosed your connection with the detective agency, do you suppose the miners would have let you in there at all?" he challenged Lively.

"I think they would have turned me over to the undertaker," Lively replied.

McKellar was now like a boxer who had maneuvered his opponent against the ropes. "At the same time, while you were accepting money from the miners as their representative and employer, you were really, as you have just said, in truth and in fact, the paid agent of the company that you knew was opposed to the miners?" he asked. "That is true is it not?"

"Well I was in the pay of the detective agency," Lively said, pay that amounted to $75 a month and expenses. This was in addition to money he earned working in the mines. Lively had also been paid by the Western Federation of Miners, for whom he had worked briefly as an organizer.

"And did you accept their money while you were in fact operating against them?" McKellar asked.

"I accepted their money, and I done exactly what the man over me told me to do. He told me what to do, and I had to carry out his instructions."

"And did you think that was right?" McKellar continued. "Now while you are testifying do you think that was the right action on your part?"

"Yes," Lively replied.

At this point, Avis rushed to the support of his witness and the undercover tactics. "He has that right," the lawyer said. "That is the method practiced by the Department of Justice." When McKellar expressed disbelief, Avis added: "I think that it is practiced in every department at Washington."

"I do not believe it," McKellar insisted.

"But the destruction of Molly McGuires in Pennsylvania was done exactly as this was done."

McKellar was adamant. "I will say that it violated every idea of right that I ever had. I never would have believed that a thing like this would happen, and I am not surprised that you are having trouble down there in Mingo County."

"Senator," Avis started to explain, "with all these murders and depredations being committed . . . "

But McKellar cut him off. "Well, let us go on with the examination of the witness. I am frank to say that I cannot approve of that conduct."

The memory of McKellar's condemnation persisted after Lively's two hours of testimony, and even after the hearings recessed two days later, until mid-September. Still, while the revelations of Lively's duplicity and the other excesses committed in the effort to break the strike tarnished the public's view of the coal companies, these disclosures had been offset at least in part by the airing of the union's own dirty linen. Particularly troublesome for the union was the focus on its involvement with violence, as dramatized by the appearance of Sid Hatfield.

The net result of the hearings was at best a standoff, causing most Americans and their leaders who had paid attention to throw up their hands and turn away from the struggle in Mingo County. For the mine owners, who were having their own way and crushing the strike, this was entirely satisfactory. But for the union, which had been fighting a losing battle in Mingo County and hoped for public outrage to reverse the tide, the hearings amounted to a tragic failure. Now in the wake of their frustration on Capitol Hill, the union and its supporters would face new disasters at home.

Sid Hatfield 1919.

Boss detective Tom Felts: He sought revenge for his slain brothers—and got it. Credit: West Virginia University Library/ West Virginia Regional History Collection.

Defendants in the Matewan shoot-out trial: Sid Hatfield is standing 5th from left, Ed Chambers is 3rd from right. Credit: West Virginia University Library/West Virginia Regional History Collection. Source: H. B. Lee.

"The most dangerous woman in America": Mother Jones with Mingo County organizers in 1920, Sid Hatfield on her left. Credit: West Virginia University Library/West Virginia Regional History Collection.

Hatfield's lighter side: "Smilin' Sid" clowns for a photographer.
Credit: West Virginia University Library/West Virginia Regional
History Collection. Source: H. B. Lee.

"It was Uncle Sam that did it": U.S. troops guard the streets of Matewan.
Credit: West Virginia University Library/West Virginia Regional History
Collection. Source: H. B. Lee.

Don Chafin: Top Gun in
Logan County. Credit: West
Virginia University Library/
West Virginia Regional History
Collection. Source: H. B. Lee.

First line of defense: State police and mine guards manning the
trenches on Blair Mountain. Credit: West Virginia University
Library/West Virginia Regional History Collection. Source: H. B. Lee.

Ready for trouble: Mingo County's volunteer militia rallied
against the union march. Credit: West Virginia University
Library/West Virginia Regional History Collection. Source: H. B. Lee.

A farewell to arms: After the battle, U.S. soldiers stacked arms and ammunition of both sides. Credit: West Virginia University Library/West Virginia Regional History Collection.

8

"Even the Heavens Weep"

FROM THE ONSET of the struggle in Mingo County, with the shoot-out at Matewan Station, the fate of Sid Hatfield had been intertwined with the destiny of the mine workers union. It was Hatfield who, by gunning down Albert and Lee Felts, had turned the labor conflict into a blood feud. It was Hatfield who had sparked the union resistance to the use of strikebreakers during the violent months that followed the Matewan confrontation. And it was Hatfield's acquittal in the murder trial in Williamson and his defiant testimony in the Senate hearings that had sustained the miners' spirits. So it was only natural that as the conflict in southern West Virginia neared its climax, it was again Hatfield who would serve as a catalyst for the denouement.

The first hint of how events would unfold had come during his Senate testimony, when S. B. Avis, the coal company lawyer, had confronted him about a criminal conspiracy indictment in Mc-Dowell County, linked to one of the previous summer's numerous violent outbreaks. Caught unawares, Hatfield had tried to laugh the matter off. But when he got back to his room in the Harrington Hotel, a few blocks from the White House, a telephone message confirmed that Avis had known what he was talking about. Hatfield and more than thirty others, most of them Mingo miners, had been indicted for raiding the mining camp at Mohawk and blowing up the coal tipple. Hatfield had of course been in and out of trouble with the law before. Ordinarily another criminal charge would not necessarily have been cause for concern.

But certain aspects of this indictment seemed suspicious on their face. First, the timing. The Mohawk raid had come the previous August, nearly a full year earlier. It was not the custom of the mine companies and their allies in law enforcement to wait so long to seek punishment for a crime allegedly committed by union men or their allies. Then there was the place. McDowell County, under Sheriff William Hatfield, was a coal company stronghold, and along with Don Chafin's Logan County a center of resistance to the union drive. There the coal companies and their Baldwin-Felts allies could rest assured that they could do by and large whatever they wanted and get away with it.

Hatfield made no secret of his misgivings as he and his union comrades talked in the lobby of the Harrington. If he went to McDowell County, there was a good chance he would never come back, he said. But Sam Montgomery, the union's erstwhile gubernatorial candidate, who had served as counsel at the Kenyon hearings, had a different perspective. As a leading member of the West Virginia legal and political establishment, Montgomery found it hard to believe that the system in which he had labored and put his faith could be so corrupted as to condone murder in cold blood. Go to McDowell County, Montgomery advised Hatfield. But leave your guns at home. Behave like a law-abiding citizen and you will be treated that way. As an extra precaution, sitting in the lobby with Hatfield, Mooney and Keeney dictated a letter to McDowell County Judge James French Strother, who would preside over Hatfield's trial, to advise him of Hatfield's fears for his safety. Judge Strother would see to it that the rule of law would prevail in McDowell County, Montgomery told Hatfield.

Satisfied with his lawyer's advice, on Thursday July 28, only twelve days after he had testified before the Kenyon committee, Hatfield peacefully submitted to arrest on the Mohawk mine charge. Clearly this was no routine matter. Wary of what might happen in Mingo County, where support for the union was strong,

McDowell Sheriff William Hatfield came to Matewan to personally take Sid Hatfield into custody, bringing with him Welch police
chief Harry Chafin. They took the suspect and his wife Jessie with
them on the next train to Welch, where Hatfield was booked and
jailed and held overnight.

Jessie Hatfield stayed at the Carter Hotel, across from the depot, and the next day posted $2,000 bond, sufficient to free her
husband and allow him to return with her to Matewan. Sheriff
Hatfield promised the wife of his prisoner that her husband would
be safe when he returned for trial, and offered the same assurance
to reporters who called. "There isn't going to be any trouble," the
sheriff told one and all. "We'll see to that."

But Sam Montgomery was not so sure. The more he thought
about the situation and the more he heard rumors of what awaited
Sid Hatfield in Welsh, the more anxious he became. It was too late
now for Hatfield to refuse to go, if that had ever been much of an
option. But Montgomery no longer felt satisfied that he could rely
on Judge Strother to protect Hatfield. He tried another tack, calling the *Wheeling Intelligencer* to say pointedly: "I am very anxious
about Hatfield's case." Hatfield's friends, he said, "feared that if
he submitted himself to be taken into McDowell County that he
would be killed." The newspaper dutifully reported Montgomery's
remarks on its front page. The lawyer now could only hope that
his words would serve as a warning to Hatfield's foes and thus as a
deterrent to keep his worst fears from coming true.

He would have had even more reason for concern if he had
known that McDowell County Sheriff William Hatfield, who had
promised to guarantee Hatfield's safety, had already left the county
to "take the waters" at Craig Healing Springs in Virginia. On Monday August 1, two days after Montgomery made his somber assessment, Sid Hatfield and Jessie got up before dawn to take the 5:15
train to Welch. The Norfolk and Western, which had brought the
Felts-Baldwin detectives to Matewan in May of 1920, now would
take Sid Hatfield to meet his fate. Along with the Hatfields came
Hatfield's closest friend, Ed Chambers, who intended to testify on

Hatfield's behalf, Chambers's wife Sallie, and Jim Kirkpatrick, a Hatfield friend and also a Mingo County deputy, who had volunteered to serve as bodyguard. Kirkpatrick's presence was evidence that Hatfield and his friends knew the police chief was in danger. But it was a measure of how gravely they underestimated the threat that they relied for protection in the heart of McDowell County on one man. In reality, as would soon become all too clear, they needed not a single deputy but at least a dozen, all armed and ready.

It was nearly 8 A.M. when their train paused on its winding passage to stop at the little town of Iaeger, about fifteen miles outside of Welch, where the boarding passengers included a personage all too familiar to the Hatfields—Charles E. Lively. A man not easily fazed by situations that would disturb most people, Lively offered the Hatfield party a perfunctory greeting and then calmly took a seat next to Kirkpatrick, where he remained in silence for the forty-five additional minutes it took for the train to get to Welch.

With the trial's start still about two hours off, the visitors from Matewan tried unsuccessfully to get a room at the booked-up Carter Hotel, then stopped for breakfast at a restaurant near the depot. They could hardly avoid noticing the presence there, as on the train, of the ubiquitous Charles Lively. After breakfast C. J. Van Fleet, the union lawyer who had been assigned to Hatfield's defense and who had come in the night before, invited them to use his room at the Carter until they could get one of their own.

The trial would not start until the arrival of the 10:30 train, bearing witnesses and some of Hatfield's codefendants. When Hatfield and his companions heard the train whistle they should come across the street to the courthouse, Van Fleet told them. The lawyer had high hopes for a motion for change of venue, which he had already filed and which he planned to argue before Judge Strother. But in any case, as the lawyer explained before leaving for the courthouse, Hatfield would have to appear in court until the judge ruled on the motion.

As they waited in the hotel room, the bodyguard, Kirkpatrick, looked out the window and saw a familiar figure on the courthouse lawn. "There is Charlie Lively," he said. "He's keeping pretty close track of us this morning, isn't he?"

Hatfield went to the window and looked out himself but said nothing. To pass the time Hatfield showed Kirkpatrick the two guns he had brought in his wife's traveling case. He had decided not to bring the guns to trial and cause another commotion like the furor he had touched off at his trial in Williamson. Kirkpatrick admired one of Hatfield's weapons, a large army-issue revolver. A big gun like that could come in handy, he said. Hatfield readily swapped the military weapon for one of Kirkpatrick's service pistols. Soon after, they heard the whistle of the 10:30 train and the five of them headed for the court.

Kirkpatrick had the pistol he had traded for with Hatfield, but both Hatfield and Chambers were unarmed. The day was sunny, but there was the threat of rain and Sallie Chambers clutched an umbrella. Just ahead was the McDowell County courthouse, an ivy-covered Victorian structure sitting atop a hill, behind an eight-foot-high stone wall. Above the wall the lawn sloped upward toward the building. Two sets of stone steps, running toward each other from the street, led to a common landing at the top of the wall. From there another flight of steps led to the courthouse entrance.

Unnoticed by Hatfield or his companions as they headed out of the hotel toward the courthouse, a group of Baldwin-Felts detectives watched them from the top of the steps. In charge of the group were Lively and two other veterans of the mine wars, Bill Salter, who had survived the Matewan shoot-out by hiding in a trash can, and George "Buster" Pence, renowned for the tactic he used to escape prosecution for killing union men: "Shoot 'em with one gun and hand 'em another one," was the way Pence put it.

Climbing the steps, Ed and Sallie Chambers were in the lead, followed by Hatfield and his wife. Kirkpatrick was in the rear. Inside the courthouse, at just about this very moment, Van Fleet, the lawyer for Hatfield and Chambers, was shaking hands with the Mc-Dowell Country prosecutor, G. C. Counts, on an agreement to change the venue of the trial to the less perilous surroundings of

Greenbrier County. But it was a victory that came too late for Van Fleet's client.

As he got to the landing Hatfield caught sight of a group of his fellow defendants coming up the opposing stairs, waved his hands and shouted a greeting. It was his last conscious act.

As if Hatfield's gesture had been a signal, the Baldwin-Felts agents opened fire. As the bullets burst around her, to Jessie Hatfield it seemed as if thirteen men were shooting. Sallie Chambers guessed six or eight. But it was the trio of Lively, Salter and Pence who did all that was necessary for the execution.

While they were blasting away at Hatfield and Chambers, another detective, Hughey Lucas, fired a volley of shots from his own gun against the stone wall of the courthouse. His purpose was to create an alibi for the assailants by making it seem as if Hatfield and Chambers had shot first but missed.

Hit four times, Hatfield fell dead. Meanwhile Lively had raced down the steps to confront Ed and Sallie Chambers, reached across in front of Sallie Chambers and shot her husband in the neck. As Chambers rolled down the steps Lively kept firing. And when Chambers's body came to rest on the steps, Lively ran over to him, gun in hand. Sallie Chambers cried out, begging him not to shoot anymore. But Lively ignored her and shot Chambers again, behind his right ear.

As for deputy Kirkpatrick, whom Hatfield had relied on as a bodyguard, he turned out to be a slender reed. No sooner had the shooting started than he ducked behind a stone wall. Before their protector could get his gun out, Hatfield and Chambers were dead, and Kirkpatrick fled.

"He was poor protection, he couldn't do anything," Jessie Hatfield said later without bitterness. "There were too many men for him, he had to run."

Jessie Hatfield ran, too, straight to the sheriff's office, where the week before Sheriff Hatfield had assured her that he would safeguard her husband. But on this day the sheriff was nowhere to be found, and his deputies ignored her pleas to arrest the men who had shot her husband.

Sallie Chambers was made of sterner stuff. She stayed at the scene and in her grief and fury, began to beat Lively with her umbrella. Lively swore at her and tore the umbrella out of her hands. Overcome by shock and grief, she threw herself on her husband's body, rubbing his hands and face and trying to open his pockets to show that he had no weapons. Lively ordered her taken away.

As she was being dragged off, the newly widowed woman noticed Salter, one of her husband's assassins, and shouted:

"Why did you do all this for? We didn't come up here for this."

Salter was unmoved. "Well that is all right," he said.

"We didn't come down to Matewan on the 19th of May for this either."

The Baldwin-Felts agents had good reason to remove Sallie Chambers from the scene. They had work to do. Buster Pence, true to his formula of "kill 'em with one gun and hand 'em another one," saw to it that pistols were placed in the lifeless hands of Hatfield and Chambers. It was another piece of evidence, along with the bullets Hughey Lucas had fired into the wall, to bolster the claim of self-defense for Lively and his accomplices. Immediately after the shooting, G. L. Counts, the McDowell County prosecutor, ordered the arrest of Lively, Pence and Salter and told reporters that the evidence against them was "absolute." But the McDowell County jury that tried the killers evidently felt differently because their claim of self-defense won them acquittal in the same county courtroom to which Hatfield and Chambers were headed when they were assassinated.

Only a few months earlier, on March 21, 1921, Sid Hatfield had returned to Matewan in triumph after his acquittal in the Williamson murder trial to receive the cheers of the largest crowd Matewan had ever seen. Now just before dawn on Tuesday August 2 Hatfield returned again, this time in a coffin along with his slain comrade Ed Chambers to an even larger crowd. But this time there was no cheering, simply silence broken only by the sobbing of the mourners.

Some 2,000 persons lined Mate Street or plodded along the thoroughfare made muddy by an intermittent summer shower, following the coffins onto the swinging wire footbridge across the rain-swollen Tug. As the coffins and the huge crowd moved across the river the flimsy bridge swayed and sagged under the extra weight. Hatfield's casket came first, with his widow walking close behind, followed by Chambers's coffin, and his widow. Earlier that day hundreds of miners came with their families and filed into the homes of Hatfield and Chambers for one final look into the caskets of their two heroes. In Huntington, 2,000 union men laid down their tools for an hour and sent a committee bearing wreaths to the graves. The UMW closed its headquarters in Charleston and placed a placard on the door that asked a pointed question: "Shall the government live of the people, for the people and by the people in West Virginia or be destroyed by the Baldwin-Felts detective agency?" In many of the nation's newspapers, the coverage of the funeral overshadowed the news that the unforgettable tenor of Enrico Caruso would be heard no more, the world's most celebrated opera star having died of pneumonia in Naples the day after Hatfield and Chambers were slain.

State police and armed militia patrolled the streets on the lookout for new violence. But no shots were fired. All that could be heard above the rain was the keening of the two widows and the steady low murmur from the crowd, anger mixed with grief.

By the time the procession reached the cemetery, on a point in the mountains overlooking the Tug and the Kentucky shore, the rain was pouring down in sheets. The Reverend J. C. Holbrook of the Methodist Episcopal Church saw to it that the caskets were hastily closed as he conducted the brief graveside ceremony. Few in the crowd had umbrellas, but most stayed, listening in silence to Holbrook's reading from the Scripture. "And now abideth faith, hope and charity," the clergyman intoned. "These three, but the greatest of these is charity."

But charity was not what was foremost in the minds and hearts of the mourners. It was Sam Montgomery, delivering the eulogy, who best captured the moment in a bitter impassioned speech. It was not only the friends of Sid Hatfield and Ed Chambers but also the great mass of Americans whose attention had been captured by the bloodshed on the courthouse steps, to whom his words were addressed.

He did not let the occasion go to waste. "We have gathered here today to perform the last sad rites for these two boys who fell victims to one of the most contemptible systems that has ever been known to exist in the history of the so-called civilized world," Montgomery began. And who was to blame? Montgomery focused his outrage not on the gunmen but rather on the higher-ups who gave them their orders and their reward. "Sleek, dignified church-going gentlemen, who would rather pay fabulous sums to their hired gunmen, to kill and slay men for joining a union than to pay like or less amounts to the men who delve into the subterranean depths of the earth and produce their wealth for them."

The Reverend Holbrook had spoken of faith, hope and charity, but Montgomery saw little opportunity for any of these virtues to flower in the bloody soil of the Mountain State. "There can be no peace in West Virginia," he declared, "until the enforcement of the laws is removed from the hands of private detective agencies and from those of deputy sheriffs who are paid, not by the state but by the great corporations, most of them owned by non-residents who have no interest in West Virginia's tomorrow." As he neared his peroration, Montgomery looked around at the rain-soaked audience and took inspiration from the circumstances of the day. Earlier in his talk he had thundered his indignation. But now, as he concluded, his voice fell low, just loud enough to be heard over the rain in the silence of the graveyard. "Even the heavens weep with the grief-stricken relatives and bereaved friends of these two boys," he said.

The miners though had no time for tears. The story of Hatfield's slaying swept through the coalfields, as did the words of Montgomery's impassioned funeral oration. But the miners hardly needed a call to arms. Events spoke for themselves.

Sid Hatfield, the hero of Matewan and defender of the union cause, shot to death with his wife by his side. His killers free on bond advanced by the mine owners and certain in the view of the union men to escape punishment for their deed. Meanwhile in Mingo County hundreds of union men remained in jail without any formal charge and without benefit of bond. The *Wheeling Intelligencer* pronounced the shooting on the courthouse steps "the most glaring and outrageous expression of contempt for law that has ever stained the history of West Virginia." The *UMW Journal* declared: "Probably never in the history of the country did a cold blooded murder ever create as much indignation." Around the country labor groups adopted resolutions that blended sympathy, outrage and the demand for revenge.

In the midst of this backlash, Charles Lively called a press conference from the safety of Welch, where he explained the killings as "a case of self-defense, pure and simple." As Lively told the story Hatfield caught his eye as he was ascending the stairs to the courthouse. "I could see Sid's jaws set like a steel trap," he said. Both Chambers and Hatfield pulled out their weapons and after Hatfield fired, Lively fired back. To buttress Lively's account, Mitchell, the Welch police chief, stated that after the shootings he found a still warm pistol lying beside Chambers's body and also found a pistol in Hatfield's trouser pocket.

Those statements only added to the fury of the union and its supporters, since it lent credence to their belief that Lively and his confederates would escape punishment. Meanwhile, in the midst of this crisis for their union, its leaders were hamstrung. The week before Keeney had announced plans to send large groups of organizers into Mingo County with the idea of having them arrested and thus overcrowd the jails in the southern part of the state. Sam Montgomery had hinted broadly at the strategy in his interview with the *Intelligencer.* "There are about 40,000 idle coal miners in West Virginia and a good big percent of them would just as soon spend a vacation in Mingo County as anywhere else," he said.

But in the wake of the McDowell County murders, all bets were off. Keeney called off the invasion of Mingo. "My men are willing to go to jail, but I am not willing to have them killed," he said. He and Mooney were unable even to leave Charleston to attend the funeral of Hatfield and Chambers because of the strictures of martial law. But the anger among union rank and file was hard to contain. Several hundred miners trooped to union headquarters where they descended on Montgomery, fresh from his funeral oration. The lawyer spoke to them for a few minutes, counseled patience, then sent them on their way.

But many union men had lost patience. Something had to be done, they believed. But what? It was at this point that Mother Jones reappeared on the scene. Though the old warrior had remained in West Virginia since her fiery "Clean Up West Virginia" speech in Williamson the previous June, she had been relatively silent. The years had taken their toll on "The Most Dangerous Woman in America," as her foes branded her, slowing her down physically and throwing her off balance. Her typically free-form oratory became even more rambling than usual, and often lacked coherence. "The boys are good to me," she wrote a friend of her UMW comrades. "They don't overwork me, the fact of the matter is they let me come and go as I want to."

But one reason she was not being called upon was apparently because she was no longer considered dependable. Her behavior was so irregular that some rank-and-file members suspected her of being in the pay of the operators or of having come under the influence of Governor Morgan, an accusation for which it would later turn out there was some basis.

Still no one could predict how she might react on any given occasion. In the wake of Sid Hatfield's slaying, she took it upon herself to call on Keeney and Mooney at union headquarters in Charleston and demand they convene a mass meeting somewhere in Kanawha County. Keeney and Mooney refused. Any such gathering in the heat of outrage, and in the midst of martial law, could lead only to arrests and bloodshed that would cost the miners more than their foes. Furious, Mother Jones staged a protest meeting of her own. With twenty-five or thirty miners who had gathered at union headquarters on Summers Street as her audience, she berated Keeney and Mooney as if they were scabs. "Keeney and Mooney have lost their nerve," she announced. "They are spineless and someone must do something to protect the miners."

A few days later, on Sunday August 7, under pressure from Mother Jones and others, Keeney and Mooney did call a meeting on the grounds of the state capitol in Charleston, across the street from the governor's mansion, with about 500 miners in attendance. Governor Morgan could hear them plainly from his porch, though he could not make out what they were saying. "They were pretty noisy," he recalled later. "I didn't regard it as a menace, but I did think at the time in all probability it had for its object a certain amount of intimidation."

If that was indeed the purpose of the demonstration it failed. Morgan, a tall, husky figure of a man, whose brown hair was just turning grey, after all had been hardened by service in the First West Virginia Infantry during the war with Spain and was stolid in temperament. He went about his Sabbath routine as usual, teaching Sunday school in the morning, dining with his family at noon and afterward going for an afternoon drive in the country. Told the demonstration leaders wanted to meet with him, he went to his office, where Mooney and Keeney presented a petition asking for a broad range of demands—chiefly for a joint commission of management and labor to adjust wages and mediate disputes, but also for an eight-hour day and the election of checkweighmen at the mines. For good measure the petition also included a statement from the 1920 Republican Party platform pledging "to correct the abuses that have grown up under the so-called private guard or detective system," a promise the Republican-controlled legislature had notably failed to keep.

Morgan concluded the thirty-minute conference by agreeing to take the union proposals under consideration. But no one in the group that met with him was hopeful he would react positively. Afterward Keeney returned to say a final word to the demonstrators. "We are going to organize Mingo and Logan County," he vowed, "or fill the jails so full they won't be able to feed them." Then he told the miners to go back home and await their marching orders.

It was ten days later, August 17, when Morgan responded to the petition by flatly rejecting all the union demands. Prior to his election as governor Morgan had run for no other office but that of Marion County judge. Unlike Cornwell he had not even been exposed to the limited give and take of the state legislature, and nothing in his background as a normal school graduate and country lawyer inclined him to consider unions as having a legitimate role to play in the coal economy. Thus he would not appoint the joint commission the miners wanted because, in his view, that would imply official recognition of the UMW as representing the union. This was something the coal operators had refused to do, a position that Morgan believed under Supreme Court rulings they had a perfect right to maintain. Morgan saw things exactly as the operators did. "There is no fight in West Virginia between the operator and the union miners," as he explained to a friend, since the union had no status under the law, and thus might as well not exist. By the same line of reasoning there was no dispute between the operators and their employees. "All the trouble that has arisen is the result of some agitators and organizers representing the United Mine Workers not resident in the unorganized fields, desiring to organize same."

What the governor's legalisms did not take into account was the steadily mounting anger among the miners. While Morgan was drafting his response to the UMW petition, many union miners began to arm themselves, and talk spread of a new protest march, like the abortive uprising of 1919. With groups of armed miners patrolling the roads, Logan County sheriff Don Chafin became increasingly nervous and called for help from the state police. The result was a tragi-comedy of errors. On Friday August 12 a squad of five troopers galloped into the little town of Clothier, about ten miles north and east of Logan and put on a show of force. One of the five rode his horse right into a parked car. The horse stumbled and fell to the ground and his rider was thrown to the ground.

Feeling foolish and frustrated, the troopers vented their anger at the owner of the parked car, pulling him from the vehicle, abusing him and chasing him home. A group of armed miners rushed to the scene, bent on revenge. Mistaking an auto driven by a railroad worker for a police car, the miners opened fire and put six bullet holes in the vehicle. When a state police car sped to the scene, the miners stopped that car, pulled the officers out into the road, took away their weapons and chased them home. By nightfall armed miners in groups of five to ten patrolled all the roads into Clothier, determined to keep the state police at bay. They cut all phone and telegraph wires and in effect took control of the area.

The following week, with news of Morgan's rejection of the union demands, the contagion of rebellion spread. Morgan's dismissal of the UMW petition presented to him after the August 7 demonstration fed resentment. So did a state supreme court ruling denying freedom to scores of union men jailed in Mingo for union activity and upholding the governor's authority under martial law as recast after the court's June ruling in the Lavinder case. Armed miners began assembling just outside of Charleston, near the town of Marmet, which had been the rallying point for the 1919 march.

By August 20, some 600 were camping out in a hollow a mile away from Marmet station, and hundreds more were on the way. They brought with them a menacing assortment of weaponry—from .22 caliber bird guns to double-barreled shotguns and the Springfield rifles that many had carried in France along with every variety of pistol, revolver and other handgun. Their guards patrolled the roads and shooed away strangers. A journalist who made his way past them was apprehended and escorted from the encampment by two rifle-bearing miners. The miners were circumspect about their intentions, only talking vaguely of "making a demonstration" against Mingo County, as the newspapers reported. But among themselves they spoke freely of marching on Mingo County, freeing the union organizers held in Williamson jail and bringing an effective end to martial law. To get to Mingo they would have to cross Logan County and challenge the power of Sheriff Chafin, and if he got in their way, so be it. But no one was sure how they could accomplish these objectives or if they should even be attempted. For guidance they naturally looked to Keeney and Mooney, but the two officers of District 17 were having difficulty charting a course. Disappointed by the lack of reaction to the Senate hearings and frustrated by the legal system, they had devised a strategy inevitably marked by ambivalence. Their idea was to stage a demonstration that would be strong enough to gain them public sympathy and support yet would avoid bringing down the full force of the political and economic power structure against them and their union. They were operating at great risk and under severe handicaps. "We were worn out," Mooney said later, "caught between the restlessness of the miners and the insistence of the coal operators that we keep the mines in operation."

So far as the outside world was concerned, Keeney and Mooney decided that it would be best for themselves and for the miners if they kept their distance from the protest. Asked about a flier summoning the miners to assemble at Marmet bearing his name and Mooney's, Keeney called that manifesto a forgery and repeatedly denied that he or any of the other District officials had any connection with the assemblage. "I wash my hands of the whole affair," Keeney told the *New York Times* on August 19, as the preparations for the march moved forward. "I've interfered time and again to stop such enterprises. I seem to have halted them only temporarily. This time they can march to Mingo, so far as I am concerned."

For the benefit of the press, Keeney expressed grave doubts about the ability of the miners, however angry they were, to overcome the physical hardships involved in a cross-country trek of more than fifty miles over rutted roads and mountainous terrain.

Not to mention the ferocious opposition of Don Chafin. Asked about reports of the imminent march of the union men, the sheriff had vowed firmly: "No armed mob will cross the Logan County line."

Journalists trying to trace the roots of the demonstration were frustrated. After "careful inquiry" failed to identify a leader for the march, one reporter pronounced the issue "a mystery." But to anyone who understood the mine workers union in West Virginia, the origins of the march were not such a mystery. For years the union leadership had learned to operate much of the time on a sub rosa basis, for the sake of the survival of the union, and of themselves. But the lack of a formal communications structure was more than made up for by a powerful grapevine, guided by the leadership, which spread the word among the rank and file as to when to picket and when to strike, when to work and when to march. After the failed 1919 march, John Spivak, the ACLU's emissary to the West Virginia UMW, scoffed at the notion that "several thousand miners from dozens of communities had spontaneously taken their guns and marched to a specific spot." As he pointedly remarked to Keeney and Mooney after they had helped disperse that rebellious gathering: "What I was thinking about is that there is a helluva lot of mental telepathy in these hills." Both men guffawed and then Mooney threw his arm around Spivak and said: "Yeah, there sure must be." The same form of telepathy was operating two years later, as the miners once again massed at Marmet, or so Keeney and Mooney wanted the world to believe.

To be sure the telepathy had its guiding instruments, among the most active of them being Savoy Holt, a glib and fiercely aggressive young organizer from Cabin Creek who had been on the committee that met with Morgan at the August 7 demonstration at the Capitol. Holt now traveled the state from one local to another, rousing the men to action. In Ward, in Kanawha County, he told the 700 members of the union local of the demonstration forming at Marmet and called upon them "to gather across the river." The local voted to give $1,500 to buy supplies for the march and the members themselves chipped in another $1,500. About 250 soon left for Marmet, many of them armed. Race was no bar to participation. If "white people had guns they should not be backward, they ought to get one, too," Scott Reese, a black official of the local, advised his brothers.

To the east in the town of Boomer, in Fayette County, "Brother Holt from Cabin Creek," as he was introduced to a union meeting, was forthright and firm. He and others had gone to see "Eph Morgan" and asked that martial law be revoked. The governor had refused. "Now it's up to us." Miners were on their way to Marmet, he said. "If you are men you will be there, prepared as instructed."

J. S. McKeaver, a mine superintendent on good terms with the union, urged the men not to heed Holt, warning they would be crushed by the state of West Virginia and the Federal government if necessary and that their union would be hurt. But afterward, McKeaver saw the miners, about 500 of them, arming themselves and then heading out toward Marmet.

It was the same story all over the state as locals sent money and men to back the demonstration. In Mammouth in Boone County local 404 members raised $200 to buy provisions and then headed out to Marmet. In the mining camp of Edwhite in Raleigh County, local 4823 sent eighty men to the demonstration, contributed nearly $600 for provisions and spent another $130 on two high-powered rifles and ammunition. Some wore their old uniforms from the Great War. But most took to wearing blue bib overalls and tying around their necks a red bandanna, which soon became the hallmark of the insurgent army, leading both friends and foes to refer to them as "rednecks," a term that had not yet achieved its latter-day wide currency as a regional slur.

For Keeney and Mooney to remain in the background while the buildup of the union forces at Marmet continued would have been difficult in any case, but this task was made even harder when a new problem presented itself in the person of Mother Jones. On Wednesday August 24, with the number of miners under arms nearing 10,000, the doyenne of UMW organizers sent word to Mooney and Keeney that she wanted to speak to the miners about a telegram she had received from President Harding.

Keeney and Mooney were immediately suspicious. If the president of the United States wanted to make a statement about the troubles in West Virginia, why would he choose Mother Jones of all people as his instrument for communication? Her recent erratic behavior was cause enough to make them uneasy about what she might say now in this tense situation.

They had better reason than they then knew to be suspicious. As the union would later learn, Mother Jones had been in frequent touch with Governor Morgan, who had managed to convince her that she should persuade the miners to turn back to avoid a bloody and losing battle. Jones's friendship with Morgan, whom she considered "a good Christian man," was typical of her contacts with powerful men such as John D. Rockefeller and former UMW President John Mitchell, whom she sought to manipulate but to whose flattery she was susceptible. At any rate Keeney and Mooney had little choice except to arrange for her to address the miners as she asked. Mounting an impromptu platform, Mother Jones read from a piece of paper that she claimed to be the message from Harding. She quoted the president as urging the miners to abandon the march in return for which he purportedly promised "that my good offices will be used to forever eliminate the gunmen system from the state of West Virginia."

Keeney and Mooney were openly skeptical. The "telegram" and its message seemed too pat and convenient. They asked to see the telegram. "Go to hell," Mother Jones told them. "It's none of your damn business."

But of course it *was* their business. The miners dispatched, Keeney and Mooney went back to union headquarters in Charleston to establish whether Harding's message was authentic. That took only a few hours. A telegram to the White House from Mooney soon brought a response from Harding's secretary, George B. Christian: "President out of city. No such wire sent by him."

Viewed in retrospect, Mother Jones's position was not unreasonable. It was a case that she might well have argued to the miners in a straightforward fashion. But her deceit smacked of arrogance and betrayal. The miners were furious with Jones and spoke of her as a "sellout" and "traitor," and her ill-advised gambit would mark her last involvement with the UMW's cause in West Virginia. More important for the present, the net result of the fake telegram was to make the miners even more determined to go on with the march.

No sooner had the miners begun to mobilize at Marmet than Sheriff Chafin started to ready his own defenses. Though he was only thirty-four years old, and short and stocky in build, Chafin had long been a towering figure in Logan County, as accustomed to power and its uses as if it were his birthright. It was easy to understand why he would feel that way. When he was seven years old, in 1894, his father was elected county sheriff and that office, along with just about every other public position of consequence in Logan County, had been exclusively occupied either by Chafin family members or their business cronies ever since. Chafin himself had spent most of his adult life in office—four years as county assessor, four years as sheriff, then four years as county clerk while his brother-in-law, Frank P. Hearst, held down the post of sheriff, who, under West Virginia law, could not succeed himself. In 1920 Hearst found another position while Chafin persuaded the voters to return him to his family's customary habitat in the sheriff's office.

During his first campaign for sheriff in 1912, Chafin had promised to rid the county of the mine guards who were much despised throughout the state as a result of the Paint Creek–Cabin Creek strike already raging in full fury. He was as good as his word to outward appearances. But in actuality, what Chafin did was to replace the old mine guard system with an ingenious scheme that proved to be just as insidious. Under the arrangement devised by Chafin, the coal companies no longer had to pay the Baldwin-Felts agency to protect them against the union; they simply paid Sheriff Don Chafin's deputies. According to the inquiry conducted by Governor Cornwell after the failed 1919 miners' march, payments to Chafin were based on production and ranged from half a cent to one cent a ton. This amounted to significant money in those times and parts—$46,630 in 1920, and in the first nine months of 1921, a period marked by unending labor unrest, another $61,500.

No one in county government audited Chafin's books. But it was widely understood that Chafin collected a certain amount for each deputy, paid the deputies from that amount and held something back for his own future. This arrangement apparently worked very well for Chafin. The office of sheriff paid only $3,500 a year and he had earned comparable sums in the other county positions he had held. Yet by 1921 he owned up to Senator Kenyon's committee investigating conditions in West Virginia that his net worth was about $350,000.

No one doubted that the coal companies got their money's worth. Chafin expanded his reach by having justices of the peace appoint scores of "special constables," to whom he duly issued badges and guns. Together with the regular deputies, who at times numbered more than 300, Chafin's "Standing Army of Logan," as the miners called it, maintained a tight cordon around his county. He deployed his troops at the depot in the town of Logan where they met every train and screened the arriving passengers. Those who gave any reason to suspect they might be in Chafin's town on UMW business were given a choice of leaving on the next train or spending the night in jail.

Sometimes Chafin's border patrol displayed more zeal than common sense. When J. L. Heiser, the clerk of the State Department of Mines, who happened also to be grand chancellor of the West Virginia Knights of Pythias, arrived in town to conduct the initiation of new members of that fraternal order, the deputies who greeted him somehow became convinced that he was really a union organizer. That night he was hauled out of his room, shoved into a car and soundly beaten. Word of this outrage got out, leading to newspaper editorials denouncing Chafin's oligarchical rule and a storm of other unfavorable publicity. Chafin was discomfited enough to send an emissary with an apology and a check to cover Heiser's hospital bill. But he did not loosen his grip on Logan.

Like many men of his age and station, Chafin was known to take a drink. On one occasion, in September of 1919 when he evidently had one or so too many, he sauntered into UMW headquarters in Charleston, brandishing a pistol and claiming he had a Logan County warrant for a union staffer. Though Chafin was then simply the county clerk, not the sheriff, brother-in-law Hearst had thoughtfully appointed him a deputy. Still he was outside his bailiwick in Kanawha County, where he had no authority to arrest anyone.

This was barely two weeks since the forced disbandment of the miners' army that had massed at Marmet to march on Chafin's fiefdom, and feelings toward Chafin in the union's offices were not cordial. Chafin's bellicosity did not improve the atmosphere. One word led to many more, and William Petry, vice president of District 17, ordered Chafin to leave. In response Chafin waved his revolver in the air, whereupon Petry shot him through the chest with his 22-caliber pistol. Chafin recovered, and Petry, who was cleared when the local authorities accepted his claim of self-defense, said his only regret was that he had not used a larger-caliber gun.

But that was two years past. Now Chafin was cold sober and determined to back up his boast that no "armed mob" would cross into Logan County. He got on the phone to the governor, who complained that he was handicapped because he had not time to muster the state militia, and asked Chafin to step into the breach. Do what you can to protect the county, Morgan told the sheriff.

The "best information" Chafin could get was that the miners' army was now 9,000 strong, and growing. Drastic measures seemed required. Chafin called for volunteers, and scores of Logan's solid citizens responded, just as the law-and-order vigilantes had answered the call to arms in Mingo County the previous May. "Lawyers, bankers, preachers, doctors and farmers" was the way the sheriff described them. To bolster their ranks, Chafin's deputies descended upon the camps of strikebreakers. "Anyone who doesn't come fight is fired," was the rallying cry. Those inured to the threat of losing their jobs were warned they faced jail. Hundreds were pressed into service, bringing the total strength of the defenders to nearly 3,000. To equip his forces, Chafin stripped the county armory and local hardware stories clean of weaponry, turning Logan into a sort of arsenal of free enterprise, which boasted not only machine guns and rifles but also a squadron of three biplanes parked on Logan's baseball field. Wasting no time, under the direction of the deputies, the volunteers felled trees and hauled lumber to erect breastworks and dug trenches and blocked roads.

The perimeter Chafin established was in a sense two years in the making, its origins going back to the miners' march of 1919, when Chafin had first begun to plan to beat back a union assault. The defense lines extended for about fifteen miles along the Spruce Fork Ridge, near the border of Logan and Boone Counties, which marked the rough separation of union from non-union territory. Chafin's idea was to shield the town of Logan from attack both from the northeast, in Boone County where the main union force was assembled, and the southeast, where miners advancing from Raleigh County posed another threat. Defenders massed their forces at gaps along the ridge, particularly Blair Mountain Gap, a pass between the two 1,800-foot peaks that make up Blair Mountain. A dirt road ran through the pass, providing a natural avenue to the town of Logan. But defenders positioned on the crest of the mountain peaks could command the approaches to the pass and the mountain, and make any invading force pay a heavy price.

Chafin's army would not lack for transport. A fleet of privately owned cars would carry his troops to the front when the time came. And as with the vigilante army that had assembled in Williamson the previous summer, a fire alarm would call the volunteers to action.

Chafin's preparations however were by no means sufficient to relieve Governor Morgan's anxiety, which increased with each new report of the progress of the union army. The governor had already sounded the alarm earlier in the week, on Tuesday August 23, by appealing to Secretary of War John W. Weeks, as he had done the previous spring. But he got much the same reaction.

Once again General Read sent his intelligence chief, Major Charles Thompson, to Charleston to gauge the extent of the emergency. And once again, in Thompson's view, the problem in West Virginia still seemed to be a problem West Virginia could handle.

That certainly did not satisfy Morgan. On Thursday August 25, as the *New York Times* reported that an "army of malcontents, among whom were union miners, radical organizers and not a few ex servicemen," was marching on Mingo, the governor appealed directly to Harding, asking for 1,000 men, and military aircraft, armed with machine guns. To underline the urgency of his state's predicament, Morgan issued a public statement declaring that the miners had been "inflamed and irritated by speeches of radical officers and leaders."

As Morgan intended, that increased the pressure on Washington to act. If the Harding Administration was not yet ready to give all the help Morgan sought, at least it was ready to do more than it had been doing. On Friday August 26, Secretary Weeks dispatched Brigadier General Harry Bandholtz, who had been General Pershing's provost marshal general in the AEF, to Charleston. Summoning Bandholtz to his office, Weeks gave him his orders, which, he made clear, came directly from the president himself: Make the miners go home.

If anyone in the U.S. Army high command could be said to be suited for such an assignment, it was probably Harry Hill Bandholtz. In distinguishing himself in both wars that his country had waged against foreign foes during his lifetime, Bandholtz had displayed a notable combination of soldierly courage and discipline with diplomatic tact and negotiating skill. Born in Michigan the year before the Civil War ended, he gained his commission at West Point in 1890. Major Bandholtz won the Silver Star leading troops against the Spanish in Cuba in 1898 and spent the next few years in the Philippines as a colonel, first battling Aguinaldo's guerrillas then as a provincial governor and ultimately as head of the Philippine Constabulary. Appointed a brigadier general at the onset of World War I, he led troops against the Kaiser's army in the Meuse-Argonne before Pershing promoted him to provost marshal. His performance in that post earned him the Distinguished Service Medal and impressed Army brass enough so that Bandholtz was dispatched to Hungary as U.S. commissioner, in effect ambassador, to that defeated former enemy nation. His main responsibility was to protect Hungarians from the excesses of the Rumanian army of occupation and oversee the departure of this troublesome force. He earned the lasting gratitude of the Hungarians when, armed only with a riding crop, he drove away a mob of Rumanian troopers intent on looting the national museum of its Transylvanian treasures and sealed its entrance. The Magyars came to regard the American mission as "a Mecca for suffering Hungarian pilgrims" and after Bandholtz left erected a statue of him in the park facing the embassy with his own parting words inscribed in English: "I simply carried out the instructions of my Government as I understood them, as an officer and a gentleman."

That was much the same dictum Bandholtz sought to follow in West Virginia, though dealing with the mine operators and the miners must at times have made him yearn to be back in Budapest. Arriving in Charleston from Washington about 3 A.M. on Saturday August 27, Bandholtz and his aide Colonel Stanley Ford immediately headed for the state capitol, where Major Thompson briefed them on what he had learned. Bandholtz then sent for Morgan, who responded eagerly, repeating to the officers what he had said in his telegram to Weeks.

Had Morgan done all he could to resolve the problem? Bandholtz asked.

Yes indeed, he had, Morgan insisted, as he had been insisting for days. The only answer was Federal troops, he told Bandholtz, a response that did not surprise Bandholtz.

Before sending for troops, Bandholtz said, he wanted to talk to the union leaders. Did Morgan want to be present at that meeting?

No, the governor would pass on that opportunity. He thought the meeting would go better if he were not there, was the way he put it to Bandholtz.

It was close to 5 A.M. Bandholtz called Keeney and Mooney, rousting them both out of bed, and ordered them to meet him at the governor's office. They did not dally, pausing only to phone their lawyer, Harold Houston, to get him to accompany them. Bandholtz went directly to the point. According to a statement issued by War Secretary Weeks, the labor leaders were "briefly and courteously informed" that the condition was due "to the action of members" of the district miners union, "that leadership entailed responsibility as well as prerogatives" and that in the event the president proclaimed a state of Federal martial law, the leaders would be held strictly accountable.

In Mooney's account of the story, Bandholtz was even blunter. "You two are the officers of this organization and these are your people," the general told Mooney and Keeney. "I am going to give you a chance to save them, and if you cannot turn them back we are going to snuff this out just like that." For emphasis, he snapped his fingers right in Mooney's face. Much of the country was suffering through hard times, as Bandholtz and the union leaders well knew. The general was concerned that given this widespread adversity, the disorder in West Virginia might spread. "This will never do," he told the union leaders. "There are several million unemployed in this country now and this thing might assume proportions that would be difficult to handle."

Mooney and Keeney did not argue the merits of Bandholtz's case with the general. They simply told him that they did not think they could do the job, but they agreed to try. When they asked Bandholtz for a statement they could use to convince the miners to give up their effort, Bandholtz at first refused. But when the two union leaders, remembering the episode of Mother Jones's phony telegram, insisted they would be unable to accomplish anything without some endorsement from him, Bandholtz yielded and gave them a brief memo confirming he had dispatched them to bring the march to an end. Afterwards he wired Washington: "I told the union leaders that a crisis had now arisen in the state of affairs, that they as leaders must be considered responsible to a great extent for the present situation and that in any event I should be reluctantly obliged to hold them responsible in case it might become necessary to resort to the drastic extreme required by my instructions."

In the capital, as soon as Bandholtz's telegram arrived, Major General James G. Harbord, the deputy chief of staff, and Acting Secretary of War Joseph Wainright hurried to the White House to inform Harding, then sent word back to Bandholtz praising him for his handling of the union leaders.

That same day Harding would hear from John L. Lewis, urging him to call a conference of Mingo County mine workers and operators to settle the trouble in West Virginia. But this was a step the president had no interest in taking.

Mother Jones also added her thoughts to the mix. The venerable organizer rushed over to the War Department offices in the War and State Building next to the White House to lobby Wainright against dispatching Federal troops. "Everything will come out all right without soldiers being sent," she claimed.

But Wainright and Harbord had doubts about that. They decided not to rely entirely on Keeney and Mooney carrying off their peacemaking mission. Get Morgan to redo the request for troops he had sent to Washington the day before, Harbord instructed Bandholtz. But this time, Harbord urged, Morgan should include the steps he would take to assume state responsibility including expediting mobilization of the National Guard. The West Virginia legislature that year had approved reestablishment of the national guard, effective July 1, but here it was late August and no follow-up action had been taken except to appoint an adjutant general, John Charnock, as guard commander.

In this same precautionary mode, Harbord ordered General Read to have a detachment at Camp Sherman in instant readiness. He also instructed Major General Charles T. Menoher, chief of the Army Air Service, to arrange for Kanawha Field, outside of Charleston, to serve as a base for air operations, either reconnaissance or tactical air support. That was all it took to bring Brigadier General William Mitchell, commander of the First Provisional Air Brigade, to the scene.

By the time he arrived at Kanawha Field, Billy Mitchell was forty-two years old, had been in the Army twenty-three years and had a well-earned reputation for making headlines and enemies. The son of U.S. Senator John Lendrum Mitchell from Wisconsin, he enlisted as a private at the start of the war with Spain, rose rapidly through the ranks and in 1912, at age thirty-three, became the youngest officer ever named to the general staff. Early on he saw the potential of aviation, and in 1916 he took private flying lessons.

No sooner did the United States enter the Great War than Mitchell managed to get himself seconded to France, where he worked closely with French and British air commanders and soon was established as the premier American military aviator in Europe. Correctly assessing the European War as "only the kindergarten of aviation," Mitchell's chief concern after the Allied victory was that unless the United States established a dominant air force when the next war came, "we would start out again by making terrible mistakes and perhaps be defeated before we began."

On his return to the United States he was named deputy chief of the Air Service and soon became embroiled in bitter feuds with his superiors, who failed to agree with him on the immediate importance of developing airpower. To drive his point home, and win public support, Mitchell staged a series of dramatic experiments in which his aircraft sank various warships, starting with submarines then working their way up to a destroyer and ultimately to capital ships. Each such test, as Mitchell foresaw, attracted public attention but also antagonized senior officers in both the Army and the Navy. In July 1921, when he hastened to West Virginia, he had just successfully completed the latest of his demonstrations by sinking the battleship *Ostfriesland,* a relic of the Imperial German Navy, off the Virginia Capes, thus arousing even more irritation in the upper echelons of the military. His life was further complicated by the fact that his wealthy wife, Caroline, had left him in the midst of his experiments, confirming widespread Washington gossip about his marital difficulties and threatening a major scandal.

But none of this could diminish Mitchell's enthusiasm for the opportunity that he saw offered him by the miners' uprising in Appalachia. Only a few hours after Bandholtz had arrived in Charleston, Mitchell was strutting around the Kanawha Field wearing a pistol, spurs and his row of combat ribbons, and discoursing on how air power could be a potent weapon for suppressing civil disturbances.

"All this could be left to the air service," he told a reporter. "If I get orders I can move in the necessary forces in three hours."

How would Mitchell handle masses of men under cover in gullies, a reporter wanted to know.

"Gas," said the general, perhaps recalling Allied plans that had been made but never fulfilled for a 1919 offensive against Germans, which would have relied on airplanes using poison gas. "You understand we wouldn't try to kill people at first. We'd drop gas all over the place. If they refused to disperse then we'd open up with artillery preparation and everything."

While Mitchell, anticipating World War II tactics by eighteen years, ruminated on the uses of airpower, Keeney and Mooney were struggling to carry out Bandholtz's orders to make peace. Fully conscious of their burden after being lectured by the general, they left the state house, picked up another union official, hired a taxi and headed south toward Marmet and the rebellion.

On the way they passed several groups of miners encamped for the night or moving up to join the main body. But they did not stop till they reached Hernshaw, about four miles below Marmet, where they met up with a group of about eighty miners, carrying small arms but no rifles. They paused long enough to relay the message from Bandholtz. The miners did not respond directly, but they did not seem favorably impressed; as the leaders left, the miners fired several hundred shots in the air.

Discouraged but still determined, Keeney and Mooney drove on nearly half a mile when they spotted a truckload of provisions standing on the road, with no driver or passengers in sight. Mooney suspected that trouble waited. He shouted out his own name and Keeney's into the early morning air. Whereupon a dozen men came out from behind trees and rocks, letting down the hammers of their rifles. "Boys, boys," one of them shouted in relief. "In two more seconds we would have fired on you."

The union leaders pressed on until they encountered the main body of the insurgent force. Several hundred of the marchers were strung out along a stream called Drawdy Creek, organized in companies each under the direction of an ex-soldier. Most were veterans of the Great War, but there were some who had served in the war against Spain, too. Many wore regular Army uniforms, and some even carried gas masks. A miner named Harvey Dillon, who lived in Winifrede, in Boone County, recognized the union leaders and ordered his troops to make a path for them to pass, then walked to the cab.

"What are you fellows doing here?" he demanded.

Mooney read Bandholtz's note to him and explained their mission. After the fiasco of Mother Jones and the fake telegram Dillon was skeptical. "Are you telling us straight?" he asked.

Mooney handed over the memo. History is riddled with coincidences large and small, and this encounter would now provide another example. Two decades earlier the rebel Dillon had been an American soldier battling other rebels in the Philippines, where he had served as an orderly to then-Colonel Bandholtz. Glancing at the memo, Dillon was immediately convinced of its credibility.

"That's his signature," he declared. "I served under him in the Philippines and would know it anywhere. Boys, we can't fight Uncle Sam, you know that as well as I do," he told the union leaders. "What do we do now?" he asked. "Turn back from here?"

Mooney advised them to head north about ten miles to Danville, a rail junction in Boone County, about halfway between Marmet, their rallying point, and Logan, their destination, and to wait there until special trains could be arranged to take them out. For Dillon and his comrades this was not an easy order to carry out. As Dillon talked to the union leaders and his men he was fighting back tears and many of his men were weeping openly.

Mooney and Keeney went on their way, carrying out their mission to each group of miners they encountered. Everywhere the reaction was much the same as it had been with Dillon's brigade—first skepticism and resistance, followed by reluctant compliance.

By early afternoon Mooney and Keeney had herded most of the miners' army into a ballpark at Danville. They were a rebellious lot still, many of them vowing to go on with their mission, and some denouncing their leaders whom they now suspected of betraying their cause.

Sweltering in the bright sunshine, the rebels, several hundred strong, listened intently while Mooney once more read Bandholtz's message and the grumbling lessened. Keeney, as he had earlier, warned the miners that they would be foolhardy to continue the march. Bandholtz was not in West Virginia on a personal whim. He was acting on the orders of the president of the United States. If the miners ignored his command they would be facing the full power of the Federal government.

But still the leaders were not sure enough of their ground to put the issue to a vote. "We're not going to call for a vote," Keeney declared. "We are just going to ask you to take our advice and let us lead you out of here."

Their final orders were for the miners to wait while the leaders arranged for special trains to take them away from Blair Mountain, Logan County and Don Chafin's eager defenders. Mooney and Keeney sent word back of what they had accomplished to Bandholtz, who all day long had been receiving encouraging reports that the miners, in response to the pleas of their leaders, were turning back and abandoning their march.

Early on the afternoon of Saturday, August 27, Bandholtz, Ford and Thompson set out to see for themselves. They drove all the way to Marmet, about fifteen miles, and everywhere they went they saw miners headed back. And at the railroad towns they encountered groups of miners waiting for the special trains, which Governor Morgan had supposedly agreed to get the railroad to send, that would take them back to their homes.

Bandholtz sent the good news back to Washington. As near as he could tell, he informed the War Department, the troops would not be needed. But he urged that they be kept in readiness. And even as he boarded the train back to Washington, Bandholtz could not stop worrying. He now trusted Mooney and Keeney to keep their word. His anxiety had more to do with the other side in the conflict. As he had warned the War Department, he had little confidence in Morgan's ability to keep order, adding that "the state had made only a feeble attempt to check the growth of the insurgent movement or to keep reasonable touch with its progress." Events would soon make clear how well founded were these concerns and how fragile was the hastily made peace in West Virginia.

9

"I Come Creeping"

THE MAIN PROBLEM that faced Bandholtz in West Virginia was that too many of the people he had left behind in the state did not really want to make peace. Indeed trouble started, though Bandholtz was unaware of it, even before he left for Washington, on Friday evening, August 26, when a miner known as "Bad Lewis" White led a group of armed miners into a pool hall at Clothier, the same town where the mounted state troopers had caused trouble two weeks earlier. The union leaders had always felt uneasy about the loyalty of Bad Lewis—for one thing his brother was a Logan County sheriff, working under Don Chafin. On this Saturday night his actions would give them more reason for suspicion.

In the pool hall White and his gang found Charles O. Medley, a Norfolk and Western engineer, whose train was laid over for the night in the depot, and whom he then escorted at gunpoint to the train depot. Medley's brakeman and firemen were already there, having been rounded up by other miners. White gave the crew their orders: Fire up the engine, and head north to Danville, and keep the running lights out. In Danville, White told Medley to unhitch the engine and turn it around so it would push the cars for the return trip they intended to take—back to Blair Mountain and then on to Logan.

Wearing two Smith and Wesson revolvers and riding a veloci-
pede, White then set out to recruit miners to board his train. He
had not gone very far when he encountered Mooney and Keeney.

"What the hell do you fellas mean by stopping these marchers?"
he demanded.

The two leaders explained that they were simply trying to save
the miners from being wiped out by the U.S. Army.

White was not impressed.

"Oh hell," he said. "What you two need is a bullet between
each of your eyes."

By this time, Mooney and Keeney were convinced that White
was an agent provocateur, working for Chafin and the mine operators in an effort to sow confusion among the union men and bring
down the wrath of Bandholtz against them. It must have taken all
the self-restraint they could muster to resist the temptation to give
White a dose of the medicine he had prescribed for them.

Instead they let him be and went to the ballpark, where the
miners were still waiting for the trains promised to take them
home, which, due either to Governor Morgan's inefficiency or duplicity, had yet to arrive. White took advantage of the delay to harangue the miners with fearful stories of the mine owners' thugs
firing at helpless women and children at Blair. "To hell with
Keeney," Lewis shouted. "They are killing women and children up
at Blair."

White managed to get a score or so miners to board the train.
Then he headed south toward Blair, stopping at every town along
the way where White repeated his tirade about the violence being
done against innocents in Blair. By the time the train arrived just
outside Blair about 300 armed miners were aboard, ready to re-
sume the mission of storming Don Chafin's redoubt in Logan.

Whether White was, as Mooney suspected, working in cahoots
with Chafin or whether he was simply driven by his surpassing hatred of the coal operators, his actions fit in with the sheriff's overall
strategy: to force the arrival of Federal troops whose presence he
hoped would crush District 17 hopes of organizing southern West

Virginia once and for all. White's hijacked train was a step in that direction because it provided Chafin with reason enough to once again mobilize his own forces. Earlier on that Friday when the report came from Bandholtz that the miners were disbanding, he had sent word to members of his defense army to stand down. By midnight most were in their homes or on their way there and Chafin had left his office. He was not quite out the door of the building when he heard his phone ring and ran back to take the call. It was Walter Hallinan, the state tax commissioner, phoning from Charleston to tell Chafin of the arrival of White's contingent in Blair. Chafin ordered Logan's fire siren to sound again, and by dawn on Saturday August 27 some 800 of his defenders were back at the barricades.

Meanwhile Governor Morgan and his aides were displaying the same lassitude they brought to every task in connection with the labor unrest except when the chance came to appeal for Federal troops. All through Friday night, August 26, while White fulminated and Chafin swung into action, Mooney and Keeney fretted about the failure of the promised trains to come through.

The best they could find out was that the governor's office, instead of expediting matters as it had pledged, was dragging its feet. In desperation they turned for help to the Associated Press correspondent who was with them. He called the AP bureau in Pittsburgh, and that led to pointed questions being asked in Washington and finally Charleston. By 5 A.M. the trains had arrived, several thousand miners had boarded and the revolution appeared once and for all to be over.

But Chafin was not through stirring the pot. He had an even higher card to play than Bad Lewis White. At about 3 A.M. that Saturday morning Chafin had called Major Davis in Williamson who was in overall charge of enforcing the martial law edict and asked for help to meet the threat to Logan from Lewis White. Davis sent a contingent of state police to Logan headed by Captain Brockus, who had played such a catalytic role in the Three Days' Battle in May. Brockus arrived there Saturday afternoon, not long after Bandholtz returned to Washington. No sooner did Brockus appear in Logan than Chafin dispatched him and his men to Clothier on what amounted to a mission of revenge. Brockus's assignment was to arrest the thirty or forty miners who had disarmed and embarrassed the state police on August 12. Later, when asked why he had chosen that particularly inauspicious time to make these arrests, on warrants that had been issued a week or so before, Chafin's only explanation was that Brockus "was very anxious to get hold of the ones that had disarmed his men." But it was Chafin's responsibility to decide when the warrants would be served. Only a fool would not have realized that the decision he made was certain to threaten the shaky truce that had been created in West Virginia only hours before. And whatever else people might think of Chafin, no one considered him a fool.

Whatever Chafin's motives, he saw to it that Brockus did not lack for manpower to handle the job. He sent 200 sheriff's deputies to join the ninety troopers under Brockus's command. They soon found themselves on dangerous ground. The area surrounding Clothier was closely patrolled by union miners, who had ordered local residents to keep their lights out at night, to make it difficult for the mine owners' "thugs" to find their way. In the gathering darkness, Brockus's force encountered a group of armed miners and ordered them to give up their weapons. Five miners were arrested and placed at the head of Brockus's column as the march continued.

As Brockus's men reached the town of Sharples, just a couple of miles below Clothier, they encountered three more miners in a Model T whom they also disarmed, arrested and ordered to march alongside the other prisoners in the front of the column. By now Brockus has eight captives shielding his column, but this turned out not to be enough to ward off trouble.

Suddenly they were confronted with five miners with rifles lining the road. "Who are you?" Brockus shouted.

"By God that is our business," the answer came back in the night.

"What are you doing here?" another miner shouted at Brockus.

"We've come after you Goddamn miners," someone in Brockus's contingent cried out.

That started the shooting. The miners fired from the doorways and windows of their homes, turning on all the lights in their cabins and in the mine itself. The road on which Brockus's detachment marched was now bathed in light, like a firing range. As the miners and police fired at each other at point-blank range, Brockus's men dove for cover in a ravine beside the road. His captives also tried to flee. But three of them were shot in the first volley. William Greer, a Matewan miner, was killed immediately. Another miner was seriously wounded and soon died. Another was shot three times but survived.

With bullets bursting throughout the hills and gullies, even Brockus finally realized that prudence demanded retreat. His men headed back toward Logan, taking with them five prisoners.

But four of the deputies in Brockus's force lost their way and followed a route that took them into union territory. One of the men, Fulton Mitchell, led them to the cabin of a man known to be vehemently opposed to the union and a great admirer of Sheriff Chafin, who invited them to stay for lunch. Lulled into complacency they stacked their arms on the front porch, where the rifles did not go unnoticed by neighbors who did not share their host's sympathy for Chafin and the mine owners. Before Mitchell and his comrades finished their meal they found themselves prisoners of the miners who marched them away and held them in secret location safely out of Chafin's reach.

On Sunday, August 28, news of Brockus's incursion spread rapidly through southern West Virginia. What had happened was bad enough, but reports of the encounter soon made things seem worse. By some accounts scores of men and women had been killed by Brockus's forces. James Blount, a miner from Ward, a town near Marmet, was told that "they were shooting the women and children and they needed men over there to help stop it." Along with other members of his local he got his gun and headed for Marmet.

That Sunday evening Governor Morgan sent his new adjutant general, John Charnock, the commander of the still nonexistent West Virginia National Guard, along with a UMW official, A. C. Porter, to the scene of the previous night's battle at Sharples to investigate. Charnock called a meeting of union leaders and other townsfolk at which Porter read a letter from Keeney urging them to lay down their arms. The miners were not swayed. In the past, they pointed out, they had been able to avoid harassment by Chafin's deputies as long as they stayed out of Chafin's stronghold of Logan. But now, the union men complained, Chafin's men were invading the union's own home ground, bringing violence and even death. The discussion became heated, until finally some of the miners threatened to blow up the train that had brought their visitors.

Charnock and Porter realized they were talking to deaf ears. They rushed back to alert Morgan. Echoing the metaphor used by the ACLU's Jonathan Spivak a year before, Porter likened the Blair area to Belgium at the start of the Great War, describing it as "a monster powder keg awaiting only the smallest of sparks to launch one of the bloodiest industrial wars in the history of the world." As hyperbolic as that seemed, the signs of an imminent explosion were real enough as the weekend truce negotiated by Bandholtz collapsed and the miners once again were marching to battle.

On their way they looted coal company stores, walking off with guns, ammunition and supplies. In the town of Gallagher, on Cabin Creek, the miners stole a 111 shot Gatling gun from the company. In Fayette County, miners hauled out a machine gun with 10,000 rounds they had pilfered from the Willis Branch mine months before and stored for safekeeping ever since. The miners stopped trucks, autos and trains, took them over at the point of a gun, loaded them with guns and provisions and climbed aboard. If a car or truck broke down, and could not be easily repaired, it was shoved off the side of the road while its passengers waited for another vehicle.

Some who joined the insurgency complained later that they were bullied into it. Burrell Miller, a farmer who lived in Marmet, was confronted by a group of miners who demanded he haul provisions for them.

Miller refused at first. But one miner, a black man, pointed a gun at him and said: "Throw the harness on and come on." Miller obeyed.

John Brown, a miner who lived near Blair, was taken from his home late at night by a group of armed men.

"I told them I would not fight," Brown later testified.

One of his captors offered him a grim choice: "Fight, guard or die."

Brown chose to stand guard duty watching a bridge leading into the insurgent camp.

But there were plenty who were eager to join the march. Most of the rebels hailed from the Upper Kanawha Valley, near Paint Creek and Cabin Creek, where the union had fought and won the great battles of a decade ago. But others were from mining towns all around West Virginia, from along the Big Coal River in Boone County, the New River Field in Fayette County and the Winding Gulf Field in Raleigh County. A small number made longer journeys—from northern West Virginia, and a handful from the states of the central competitive field—Ohio, Indiana and Illinois. Some came by car and truck, but most reached Marmet by train. The early arrivals bought tickets on regular passenger trains. But when Morgan ordered the Norfolk and Western to shut down, the miners commandeered trains and crews. Many arrived on flat cars that had been used for hauling logs, with no sides on them, just large standards to hold the logs.

Ed Reynolds, the president of local 404 in Raleigh County, led about 600 miners aboard one such "outlaw train," with a switch engine and eight flat cars bound from Racine in Boone County. They had not gone far when the engineer stopped because the track signals were against them. Reynolds sent two miners with guns to confront the engineer, who finally agreed to take the miners as far as Madison, about fifteen miles from Blair Mountain.

There was no written blueprint for the march, but to the men who joined, their objectives were clear, drawn from the demands they had made on Governor Morgan earlier in the month, and now they made no secret of them. "Some would say they were going to Logan to organize, some would say to kill the sheriff—hang him," recalled W. F. Harliss, a Clothier physician who watched about 5,000 of the marchers pass through on their way to Blair Mountain, the gateway to Logan. "Some would say they were going to Mingo to do away with martial law and release the prisoners in Mingo jail."

As they marched many chanted: "We'll hang Don Chafin to a sour apple tree," chorusing the words to the tune of the Battle Hymn of the Republic.

Others sang a more poignant ballad:

> *Every little river must go down to the sea*
> *All the slaving miners and our union will be free*
> *Going to march to Blair Mountain*
> *Going to whip the company*
> *And I don't want you to weep after me.*

All this was too much for Morgan. At midnight on Monday, August 29, the governor once again wired Secretary of War Weeks for help, citing the gun battle with Brockus's contingent, the capture of the four Logan deputies by the miners and the growing threat from the advancing miners' army. The forces assembled by Chafin "will be utterly unable to repel the attack," Morgan warned. To complicate matters for Morgan, Sheriff Chafin called to warn him that unless the miners released the four deputies held captive, Chafin would lead a force to free the men. The miners offered to release their prisoners if Chafin would turn loose ten union men held in Logan County jail for each deputy, a proposition that Chafin scorned. When Secretary Weeks continued to insist, relying on Bandholtz's advice, that West Virginia had not done enough on its own to control the situation, Morgan sent another telegram on Tuesday August 30 sounding an even louder alarm. "Danger of attack on Logan County by armed insurrections is so imminent that legislature cannot be assembled in time to eliminate probability of clash and bloodshed," he declared. "Number of insurrections constantly growing and immediate action in my opinion is vital."

In the face of Morgan's mounting alarm, Harding took counsel with his advisers. Twice on that Tuesday he conferred with Weeks at the White House, Weeks bringing with him on his second visit a delegation of West Virginians headed by Senator Howard Sutherland and including some of the state's most prominent bankers and businessmen, who urged the immediate dispatch of troops. Harding still resisted yielding to the governor's appeal for Federal armed intervention, but recognized that he had to do something. What he finally did late on Tuesday afternoon was issue a proclamation taking note of Morgan's assertion that his state was gripped by violence that he could not control and ordered "all persons engaged in said unlawful and insurrectionary proceedings to disperse and retire peaceably" by noon on Thursday September 1. It was the first such presidential proclamation issued since the United States entered the Great War.

The president then sent Bandholtz back to West Virginia to judge whether the miners would obey the proclamation. If they did not meet his deadline, it was now clear that Harding would send troops. But if the troops did come, Weeks made clear in a letter to Morgan, that their mission would be limited, simply "to restore peace and order in the most effective and prompt way" and that their role would *not* be to help solve Morgan's problems with the United Mine Workers. "The problem will be regarded by the military authorities purely as a tactical one," the secretary said.

Harding had given the miners two days to abandon their insurgency. As ultimatums go, this seemed reasonable on its face. But given circumstances in West Virginia, the president might have granted the miners two weeks, and still nothing would have come of it. Indeed, even while Harding and Weeks allowed themselves to hope that order could be maintained in West Virginia events were moving swiftly in a direction to dictate otherwise.

On the evening of Tuesday August 30, a few hours after Harding issued his proclamation, a group of about seventy-five miners, led by the Reverend John Wilburn, pastor of the Baptist Church in Blair, heedless of the president's action, and without giving notice to anyone on either side, began advancing on Blair Mountain. Before they set out, Wilburn, who supplemented his meager clerical pay by working in the mines, gave his men a sort of combination briefing and pep talk. "Come on boys, we will eat dinner in Logan tomorrow," he told them as they left. He also instructed them not to take prisoners.

Wilburn marched his men up a narrow hollow behind the Blair schoolhouse and after climbing a mile and half reached the ridge of the mountain where they bivouacked for the night. Next morning, Wednesday August 31, as Wilburn's men were waking up and preparing to break camp, John Gore, Chafin's chief deputy, and two of his men, John Colfago and Jim Munsie, headed up Blair Mountain from Logan on the other side, in a Model T. They were delayed by a blow-out, greatly irritating Gore. Sipping on a quart of moonshine, while Colfago and Munsie fixed the flat, he told a ten-year-old boy who helped with the task that he intended "to show those redneck SOBs something." The repair work done, the deputies resumed their journey and soon heard gunshots. They stopped their car and got out to look around.

Wilburn, camped nearby, heard the same shots, organized a patrol to investigate and ordered the rest of his men to follow.

Wilburn's patrol soon came into sight of the three deputies, who demanded to know who they were. Wilburn replied with the same question and also demanded the password. The deputies in unison shouted out "amen," the password of defending forces. It was the wrong answer, as both sides realized, and the shooting started.

The three deputies fell. Gore and Colfago died almost immediately and Munsie, who was seriously wounded, was finished off by one of Wilburn's men, who cried "That's for Sid." One of Wilburn's men, a black miner named Eli Kemp, was seriously wounded and taken to a doctor's office in Blair, where he eventually died.

It would be some time before news of this bloodshed became general knowledge. But even so, forces on both sides had already been gearing up for what they believed would be the forthcoming battle. On August 30 Governor Morgan had appointed Colonel William Eubanks, a National Guard officer, to take command of the volunteer army Chafin had mobilized. Though West Virginia's National Guard still existed only on paper, Eubanks's appointment gave Chafin's troops at least the aura of state authority. Along with his official connection to state government, Eubanks brought with him 250 American Legionnaires, volunteers from Welch, the site of Sid Hatfield's murder. Indeed, volunteers poured in from all over. More than 600 came from McDowell County in two special trains, led by Sheriff William Hatfield, the man who had conveniently absented himself from Welch on the day Hatfield was slain. Another 200 AEF vets, organized by the American Legion, arrived from Bluefield. And from Williamson came 130 veterans of the Mingo Legion, which had seen service that spring. The representation from Charleston, a union stronghold, was understandably one of the smallest—only about thirty volunteers, and that included ROTC cadets from Charleston High School. Huntington's former police chief Sam Davis recruited a contingent of twenty-five men described as "prominent" citizens and fifty veterans of the Great War, led by two former officers, ex-captains Ivan G. Hollingsworth and H. L. McNulty. They did not come empty-handed. They brought with them fifty-five high-powered rifles, a machine gun and ammunition. The defenders' arsenal was bolstered by contributions from Kentucky Governor Edwin P. Morrow, as dedicated a foe of the UMW as was Morgan himself, who sent 40,000 rounds of ammunition, 400 rifles, two machine guns and three airplanes, which Eubanks would soon put to use.

Those among the defenders who wanted to wear a uniform dressed themselves in khaki and, when they could find them, wore broad-brimmed campaign hats like the state police. The rest wore white armbands, in juxtaposition to the red bandannas worn by the union men, and called themselves "whites." Their passwords were "Holden," the name of a so-called model company town near Logan, along with "amen," the fatal word spoken by John Gore and his deputies when they encountered Wilburn's force on Blair Mountain.

Headquarters, initially set up in the Logan County courthouse, was moved to more commodious quarters on the fourth floor of the Aracoma Hotel, named for the daughter of a slain 18th-century American Indian chief. The Aracoma served as a combination barracks and mess hall. In its lobby Logan County matrons dispensed hot food and coffee to up to 500 volunteers at a time.

Trucks were loaded with provisions—clothing, sandwiches, soft drinks, cigarettes and chewing tobacco—and sent off to those manning the breastworks and the trenches. Schoolhouses and company stores near the front were set up as supply stations and bivouacs. From the defense bastion on Blair Mountain, phone wire was strung to the nearby George's Creek Company store, where a phone provided contact with headquarters in Logan. The state police set up their own headquarters in another company store.

As for the miners' army, they had the natural advantage of the built-in organizational structure provided by their union.

Each local formed its own contingent, generally headed up by the local leaders who served as field commanders. They established two sets of passwords: For one the challenge was "Where are you going?" and the required response was "To Mingo"; for the other the challenge was "How are you coming?" and the response: "I come creeping." Wives and daughters, wearing the insignia of UMW locals on their nurse's caps, marched along with the men to tend to the wounded.

Early on they suffered a blow when their leaders, Mooney and Keeney, fled the state. On Wednesday night, August 31, a carload of miners came to Mooney's home and told him they were determined to march through to Logan, regardless of what Bandholtz said or Mooney and Keeney told them. "The best thing for you two to do is to clear out and stay out until we get through here," one of his visitors told Mooney, who immediately drove to Keeney's home to decide what to do.

The two men had already been talking about leaving, and for good reason. Two days earlier a Mingo County grand jury had indicted them both in connection with two killings during the Three Days' Battle the previous May. Even more ominously they had learned earlier that day that they were about to be indicted in Logan County on five counts ranging from misdemeanor to murder in connection with the killings of Gore, Colfago and Munsie. They remembered all too well Sid Hatfield's fate when he appeared to answer charges in McDowell County, another stronghold of the coal operators, and decided, as Mooney later put it, "to clear out for a few days." Just after midnight on September 1 they left Charleston and crossed the Ohio River to Point Pleasant in Ohio. There they were met by a local UMW organizer who took them to Columbus, the state capital and headquarters city for the Ohio UMW, where they were for the time being at least out of reach of the mine owners.

With their departure, the marching miners' were left without an acknowledged leader. But with Mooney and Keeney gone, the man who more than any other made decisions and took charge was Bill Blizzard, the head of a District 17 subdistrict, a man regarded by Mooney "as all fire and dynamite, hot headed and irresponsible." As troublesome as he was for the coal operators because of his aggressiveness, he often also got under the skin of his fellow union officials. Indeed he spent much of the time watching these colleagues at their office at Charleston "so they can't put anything over on us," as he liked to tell his secretary.

Together with Ed Reynolds, who had commanded the "outlaw train" from Racine, Blizzard developed the march's strategy of enveloping Logan in a classic pincers movement. The northern arm would assemble at Jeffrey in Boone County and push west and south up Hewett Creek and across Spruce Fork ridge. The southern arm would start at Blair in Logan County and head due west up and over Blair Mountain. If all went well, they would meet in Logan and dance on Don Chafin's grave.

But in keeping with the ruling principle of warfare, few things went according to plan. Leaders of individual units made up their own minds about when to advance, or retreat, and in what direction and in what force. Moreover the confusion inherent in combat was intensified in the battle for Blair Mountain for both armies by their lack of formal discipline and training and their impromptu organization.

For all the combat experience in French trenches of which many in the miners' army could boast, it was common sense and the instinct for survival that dictated their tactics. One of the inherent drawbacks in trying to seize a mountain is that the defenders hold the high ground. So it was at the siege of Blair Mountain. Well-armed defenders on the twin crests of the mountain could look down on the graded road following the pass between the crests as it turned sharply west then ran along the face of the north side of the mountain for about a quarter of a mile before dropping down toward Blair. A frontal assault under those conditions would be akin to suicide, as the miners quickly realized. A better prospect was to outflank the defenders by using the thick underbrush along the steep sides of the mountain as cover.

This was the course followed by several groups of miners who made up the southern arm of the pincers anchored in Blair. Starting on Wednesday August 31, they began inching their way up the side of the mountain, slipping behind rocks and trees as they made their way on a route that would eventually take them to Logan. But the going was slow, the defense fire was unrelenting and they made little headway.

More promising was the assault staged from their base in Jeffrey by the miners making up the northern arm of the pincers, who launched a major attack on Crooked Creek Gap, marching along the hollow from Hewett Creek. They advanced about five miles to the Baldwin Fork, where Hewett Creek split, with Baldwin Fork itself flowing westward toward Logan while the other branch of

Hewett Creek meandered south to Crooked Creek Gap. There a narrow trail would take them to Crooked Creek and then on to Logan.

The defending force on the northern front had two main strong points. At Mill Creek, which runs into the Guyandotte River west of Baldwin Fork, Sheriff Bill Hatfield commanded 600 McDowell County volunteers, supplemented by 300 Logan Deputies. At Crooked Creek Gap, the erstwhile AEF captain Ivan Hollingsworth headed a force of 300 Logan Deputies, backed up by two machine guns. One of these was operated by "Tough Tony" Gaujot, who had fired the same gun in the Paint Creek–Cabin Creek violence. The miners at first made little headway at Mill Creek, where the defenders were too many and too well armed. But then they found a more promising target along a branch of the Mill Creek called Craddock Fork. On the morning of Thursday, September 1, about 500 miners led by Ed Reynolds, pulling the Gatling gun they had taken from the Gallagher company store, assaulted Hollingsworth's forces along Craddock Fork. After three hours of battle, Tony Gaujot's machine gun jammed and the miners broke through, advancing as far as the left fork of Crooked Creek, less than four miles from Logan itself.

It was Hollingsworth who staved off disaster for the defenders. He pulled back about half a mile, had his men put up new breastworks and mounted the one operating machine gun overlooking the approach trail. The miners pressed on, but the going was slow and bloody. "Time and again they tried to accomplish their purpose, but at each attempt machine gun and rifle fire drove them back," an Associated Press reporter who looked down on the battlefield from a defense observation post reported. He saw two of the attackers fall, and others try to rescue them. Machine gun slugs, which clipped the dust in front and behind, forced them back. At one point about fifty miners charged straight ahead, attempting to overrun the ridge. But heavy fire drove them back, carrying five of their wounded comrades.

Though the attackers appeared to have been stalled, their closeness to Logan triggered near panic in Chafin's stronghold.

That afternoon Walter R. Thurmond, president of the Logan Coal Operators Association, wired Congressman Goodykoontz that "Unless troops sent by midnight tonight the Town of Logan will be attacked by an army of from four to eight thousand Reds and great loss of life and property sustained." Goodykoontz reacted by telegraphing Harding, "Your proclamation is being contemptuously ignored," and appealing for Federal troops.

While they waited for Harding to act, Chafin and Eubanks did not rest. They dispatched deputies, machine guns and munitions in a convoy of trucks up Crooked Creek to reinforce the beleaguered Hollingsworth.

But Chafin did not limit himself to ground warfare. He had earlier rented three biplanes supposedly only for reconnaissance. On Wednesday August 31 the planes had dropped copies of Harding's proclamation ordering the miners' army to disperse. The next day, Thursday, September 1, though, they took off with a more menacing cargo—tear gas and pipe bombs. The gas cylinders were dropped at Blair and at Bald Knob in Boone County, where the miners were believed to be massing for another attack, but fell wide of the mark and had no discernible effect. One of the pipe bombs, about six inches long and filled with black powder, nuts and bolts, exploded near a miners' command post house, leaving a small crater but causing no other harm. Another dropped above the miners' encampment at Jeffrey, landed near two women washing clothes, but turned out to be a dud.

Morgan, who on August 31 had sent yet another telegram to Harding, warning that armed men were "commandeering automobiles and conveying dynamite and other explosives up Lens Creek to the trouble zone," on that same day took a more constructive step in his own interest. He finally re-established West Virginia's National Guard. Following Morgan's orders, Adjutant General Charnock issued a call for volunteers for temporary duty with the Guard and began organizing the first companies.

While Morgan waited for Harding to act, Harding waited for word from Bandholtz, who had returned to Charleston on the afternoon of September 1. By the time he arrived, private airplanes had dropped copies of Harding's proclamation all through the Sharples area. Harding's words seemed to matter little because the noon deadline he had set expired with little response. Nevertheless, Bandholtz decided to make one final effort to bring peace without Federal troops. He sent Colonel Ford and Major Thompson to the Sharples area to see what hope, if any, there was of the miners giving up the fight. To aid their case, they had a letter from Morgan promising the miners that they "would not be molested by state or county authorities while making a sincere effort to return to their homes in compliance with the proclamation of the President."

Not surprisingly, as the officers learned, Morgan's assurances carried little weight with the union folks, for whom the memories of the Sharples raid were still fresh. During their visit, Bandholtz's emissaries encountered Philip Murray, vice president of the UMW and years later president of the CIO, who had been dispatched by John L. Lewis on a peacekeeping mission of his own. Colonel Ford talked to Murray, who was accompanied by a UMW organizer, David Fowler, but found that the union official had made little progress. In his desperation, Murray had sought the advice of William Wiley, general manager of the Boone County Coal Corp., to ask his assessment.

By Wiley's later account, Murray seemed to have little heart for the venture. "Suppose I am asked to do the impossible and go out and stop these men now: Do you think I can do it?"

Wiley thought not. "It would be like sweeping the Atlantic Ocean with a broom," he told the union leader.

"Don't you believe, if I did go out and try to stop this I would lose my life?" Murray asked the mine manager.

"Yes sir, I do believe it," Wiley told him.

That was enough for Murray. He gave up and returned to Charleston. By midnight on September 1, twelve hours after Harding's deadline, Bandholtz, having heard the glum news from Thompson, also abandoned his peacemaking efforts. It was after midnight when he sent for Governor Morgan and told him he believed he had no choice but to send for troops. Bandholtz, clad in his pajamas, summoned reporters and gave them the news. Immensely relieved, Morgan left Bandholtz's hotel room and told reporters: "I have nothing to say. I am through."

Bandholtz wired Major General Harbord in the chief of staff's office in Washington: "The invaders have not obeyed the President's proclamation and there is no apparent intention to do so. It is therefore recommended that the troops now held in readiness be sent to West Virginia, without delay."

And so the orders went out from Major General Harbord in the nation's capital to Camp Sherman and Columbus Barracks, Ohio, home of two crack infantry regiments—the 19th and the 10th, to Camp Knox, Kentucky, base of the 40th infantry, and to Camp Dix, New Jersey, where the 26th infantry was stationed. From Edgewood Arsenal in Maryland, Harbord summoned a Chemical Warfare unit equipped with "a large quantity" of 150-pound teargas bombs, "guaranteed to incapacitate any person within 300 yards," according to the Army. Harbord also ordered Major General Charles T. Menoher, chief of the Army Air Service, to send twenty-one aircraft from the 88th Aero Squadron to Kanawha Field. This was Billy Mitchell's outfit. But Harbord and the Army evidently had had enough of Mitchell's cowboy rhetoric in West Virginia. Harbord's orders were clear. Mitchell's planes were to go. Mitchell was to stay home. Major Davenport Johnson would command the squadron when it arrived in West Virginia.

Even as the orders went out, and the deployment began, Bandholtz offered his explanation to Washington. While Governor Morgan, the mine owners and their allies in West Virginia placed the onus strictly on the union, Bandholtz saw things differently:

"It is believed that the withdrawal of the invaders as promised by Keeney and Mooney would have been satisfactorily accomplished but for the tardy sending of trains," and he added pointedly, "and particularly but for the ill-advised and ill-timed advance movement of State constabulary on the night of August 27, resulting in bloodshed."

But Bandholtz's reproach, as pointed as it was, did nothing to alter the realities that faced the union rebels. Time was running out on their uprising. Mindful that Federal troops were on the way, on Thursday September 1 the miners launched one last desperate effort to break through the defenders' lines and reach Logan. In preparation for their attack, the insurgents dispatched a patrol to destroy a railroad bridge on the Guyandotte line of the Norfolk and Western, hoping to keep reinforcements from reaching the defenders' positions. The bridge was set on fire, but a sentry who extinguished the blaze discovered a charge of dynamite and saved it from being blown up. But the miners went ahead with their planned assault anyway that same morning.

The attack began with a feint at the center of the defense lines at Blair Mountain. The miners opened up on an outpost manned by the "Bluefield Boys," a volunteer contingent from that town, with machine-gun and rifle fire. Having gained the attention of the defenders, the miners sent their main force against the left and right flanks of the defenders. "Attack was pushed desperately," reported one local journalist from his vantage point in a machine-gun nest on the defense ramparts. "The enemy seemed to have no sense of fear whatever and advanced over the crest of the hill in the face of machine gun and rifle fire." But in reality the defenders gave as good as they got. "We couldn't fire a shot but what they would rake our line from top to bottom," one of the miners told reporters. To this beleaguered insurgent the defenders seemed able to volley back 100 rounds for every shot fired at them.

And when it came to devious tactics, the defenders were at least a match for the attackers. At one point the defenders in the first line of trenches abandoned their posts, seemingly driven off by the force of the attack. The advancing miners promptly occupied the trench, exulting in the ground they had gained. But they had little time to celebrate. A hidden machine gun located barely fifty yards away raked the position and drove them back. Another machine-gun nest, protected by a rock cliff and barricades of timber and stones, kept up a steady fire. Fortunately for the miners it could only fire in one direction, but it was enough to help repel several assaults.

For the miners it was their last gasp of rebellion. By the time the Blair Mountain force of insurgents had abandoned their assault and fallen back on their own lines, the U.S. military presence had arrived in the form of the Army Air Service. By late Thursday afternoon September 1, fourteen twin-engined De Haviland and Martin bombers had landed at Kanawha field. Though the planes were fully armed for combat, they would perform only a limited mission. "You will under no circumstances drop any bombs or fire any machine guns," Bandholtz instructed squadron commander Johnson. Eager to avoid spilling blood unnecessarily, Bandholtz wanted the planes to scout the two opposing armies, thus providing him with his own source of intelligence.

But the Federal force that mattered most were the infantry units that began arriving Friday night September 2, some 2,100 strong. Now Bandholtz set about his appointed task. Washington had given him as much leeway as any commander could want, or expect under the circumstances. To be sure some restraints were imposed in keeping with the fundamental resolve of the president and his secretary of war to keep the Federal involvement as limited as possible. Accordingly, Harding and Weeks had both decided against declaring Federal martial law, in keeping with the Supreme Court's landmark ruling in *ex parte Milligan*, handed down in 1866. In that case the high court reversed the court martial conviction of an Indiana civilian, Landon Milligan, accused of aiding the Confederate cause and sentenced to death. Even though the United States was at war, the justices held that Milligan's constitutional rights had been violated. "The constitution . . . is a law for rulers and people, equally in war and in peace," Justice David Davis wrote in a long-remembered opinion. Its provisions, he added, cannot "be suspended during any of the great exigencies of government. . . . Martial law can never exist where the courts are open." That meant that in order to declare martial law, Harding would need to ask Morgan to close the West Virginia courts, a step this president, so devoted to establishing normalcy, wanted at all costs to avoid.

To the contrary Bandholtz was instructed to act with caution and restraint, to support civil authority and not to impede its functioning. On the other hand he was told that he had the authority to do what was necessary to carry out his mission and to "make such dispensations as appear proper with respect to those who commit or may be about to commit physical violence."

If civil authorities were unwilling or unable to act, Bandholtz could arrest and imprison any person whose behavior "impedes the accomplishment of your purpose."

For all of its difficulties, Bandholtz's task offered one positive aspect. Each side eagerly welcomed the troops as helpful to its cause. Obviously they both could not be correct in their assessments, and it was the union leaders who turned out to be grievously mistaken. The union and its supporters viewed the arrival of the troops as a chance for vindication. Now they believed, very naïvely as it turned out, that their cause would get the attention they sought. "The only way we can be assured of a square deal is by the presence of federal troops," a miner identified only as a leader of the march told a local reporter. On Saturday September 3, as they waited for the troops, union leaders sent out word that "not a single shot will be fired on Federal troops coming up from the rear of the miners' line." William Petry, Chafin's erstwhile antagonist, said the union forces had promised "they would submit without objection to rules and regulations that might be laid down by Federal authorities."

But whatever benefits the union thought to reap from the arrival of the troops, Governor Morgan and his allies, the coal mine owners, expected that the Army's intervention would mean the beginning of the end of their troubles with the union. Accordingly Morgan sent out word to all state officials civilian and military to cooperate with the troops and to "obey the direction" of Bandholtz and his aides.

In Washington, for the first time in a month, Federal officials could get through the day without facing a fresh crisis in West

Virginia. Taking advantage of the lull, and of the Labor Day holiday, President Harding and the First Lady left for a three-day cruise on the presidential yacht, the *Mayflower*. Elsewhere the observation of the holiday was dimmed by the parlous economic conditions to which Bandholtz had adverted in his initial meeting with Keeney and Mooney. In New York the Central Trades and Labor Council called off the traditional Labor Day parade because unions had been spending so much on aid to their unemployed members that there was not enough left over to pay for marching bands and uniforms.

In West Virginia, there was still plenty of work to do. On Saturday September 3 Bandholtz decreed an immediate ceasefire and then gave orders to his troops to stage a broad enveloping movement, surrounding both armies. He sent the 19th infantry, from Camp Sherman along with some units of the 26th, from Fort Dix, east by train along the Coal River, moving to the rear of the miners' army. The 40th infantry moved into positions behind the forces commanded by Chafin on Blair Mountain.

The 19th, two companies of combat veterans under the command of Captain John Wilson, boarded a train that took them through the Coal River valley from St. Albans, just outside of Charleston, to Madison, in the heart of the Kanawha Valley. In Madison, Wilson soon encountered William Blizzard, the supposed commander of the rebel army. Renowned for his cantankerousness, Blizzard in this case promised to cooperate with the captain, though in their dealings he never let down his guard. He agreed to Wilson's request to try to persuade the miners to come down out of the hills, if Wilson would assign a squad of soldiers to accompany him.

A potential problem developed when Wilson searched Blizzard and found a pistol. But he also had a Kanawha County permit to carry it, and Wilson allowed him to keep the weapon. Blizzard eyed Wilson warily.

"Does this mean you are going to allow only men with permits to keep their guns?" Blizzard asked, according to Boyden Sparkes, a correspondent for the *New York Tribune* and *Leslie's Weekly* who accompanied the 19th on its mission.

Those were his orders, Wilson replied.

What about the men on the other side, would they be allowed to keep their guns?

"If they have permits, yes," Wilson said.

Blizzard was not pleased. "You know what that means?" he asked Wilson. "Our boys'll be unarmed and those Baldwin-Felts thugs will just shoot 'em down whenever they please." Blizzard set out for the hills and did what he had to do.

A few hours later, just before daybreak, another troop train arrived, bringing more men from the 19th, horses, howitzers and the regimental commander Colonel C. A. Martin. By this time Blizzard had returned to Madison and reported that the miners had pulled out and were on their way home. Soon after both trains rolled on toward Jeffrey, about five miles from Blair Mountain. On their way they encountered scores of miners headed back, "simply a swarm of stubbly faced men getting out of the hills and back to their homes as fast and as quickly as flivvers could take them," Sparkes reported. What was notable about these retreating miners was they had no guns.

About that, Blizzard told Martin and Wilson what they had already surmised. When he spread the word among the miners to call off their insurrection, he also warned them that the Army would only take the guns from men who had no permits—the miners— but not from the members of Chafin's army. "That's why you don't see the guns," Blizzard told Martin candidly enough. "When we need 'em again, we'll know where to look for 'em."

Not all the miners were so quick to give up. In two areas Federal troops were slow to reach, Crooked Creek Gap and Blair Mountain, the Red Bandanna warriors continued their assault even into the weekend. Defenders at one point had only thirty-three bullets left for their Springfield rifles and dispatched a plane to Charleston, which returned with 30,000 rounds.

There was enough shooting so that Boyden Sparkes, and three other correspondents, decided to see the action firsthand and hired a car to take them to the front. When their car could go no further on the primitive rural roads, they set out on foot. Within fifty feet of the summit of Blair Mountain, they came under fire from state police. Sparkes was hit twice: One bullet went through his right leg, another creased his scalp. All in the party threw themselves to the ground. As the shooting continued, they shouted, "friends" and "unarmed" in the direction of the gunfire.

"Stick up your hands if you're unarmed," they were told.

They obeyed and scrambled up the hillside, where they were taken into custody.

One of the state troopers later told a reporter: "We believe in shooting first and challenging afterward."

Back in Logan the reporters were first taken to the county jail, then released once they had established their identity. When Sparkes, whose wounds turned out not to be serious, sought to write about his experience, Colonel Eubanks allowed him to use an office typewriter, but to the correspondent's indignation insisted that he submit his copy for censorship. "I was amazed by this frank announcement of an intention to nullify an article of the Constitution," Sparkes wrote later.

His indignation only increased when he had to deal with the censor. He turned out to be "Tough Tony" Gaujot, who held the rank of major in Eubanks's defense forces. Glancing at Sparkes's story, he quickly crossed out a line describing the Army's arriving that read, "Gaunt faced women, barefooted and expressionless watched the troops pass. Some of them waved half-heartedly."

"Cut that out," Gaujot snapped. "No sob stuff for those red necks."

Noting that Gaujot was a winner of the Congressional Medal of Honor, Sparkes added: "But I should never give him any medals for his qualities as a censor."

While the 19th Infantry was preoccupied disarming the miners, the 40th undertook what was presumed to be the easier task of dealing with Chafin's defenders. The first train of its troops pulled into Logan on Saturday afternoon September 3 in the midst of a rainstorm. If in Madison the troops were greeted by the union miners with a mixture of anxiety and relief, in beleaguered Logan, the stronghold of Don Chafin's and of the anti-union forces, the mood was downright joyous.

Even the drenching rain did not prevent a crowd of residents from flocking to the station to cheer the arriving troops. And when the first elements entered the Aracoma Hotel, the women and ministers broke off from their duties as food servers to applaud.

Despite the warmth of this greeting, Colonel C. F. Thompson commanding the troops soon encountered a problem—Colonel Eubanks, the National Guard Officer whom Morgan had put in command of the defense forces, and most of his staff were several sheets to the wind. This was not entirely a surprise to Thompson, whose previous conversations with Eubanks had led him to conclude that the Guard officer resorted to the bottle to ease the tensions of his job.

As it was, Thompson found Eubanks and his aides "so unmistakably under the influence of liquor as to render them unfit in our opinion for an orderly transaction of business."

Indeed, given the confused state of the leadership of the defensive army, Thompson concluded that "there had been dissension among the leaders, lack of a carefully organized plan of defense and that the state of intoxication found upon our arrival had endured for at least most of the proceeding 24 hours." Many persons joined the defenders in search of adventure and then disappeared, Thompson noted. Boys in their early teens manned positions with high-powered rifles. Many fired their weapons for no apparent reason.

Despite this disarray, Thompson carried out his assignment. In the early hours of Sunday morning, his men awakened the defenders at their barricades and trenches and sent them back to Logan, while the soldiers, traveling by car, by mule and on foot moved into positions on Blair Mountain and Crooked Creek. These movements went without mishap, except for a volunteer who shot himself in the foot in the lobby of the Aracoma Hotel, the place he chose to unload his rifle.

By Sunday afternoon, September 4, little more than twenty-four hours after the troops had arrived, it was clear the war was over. Miners and their families strolled through the streets of their towns. About 1,000 miners had surrendered formally. Thousands more simply drifted away and disappeared. All told only 400 guns were turned in.

Those who surrendered were taken by train to St. Albans, just outside of Charleston, loaded onto street-car trains and shuttled through the capital. While thousands of curious citizens lined the streets, the once defiant rebels leaned out the windows, laughing and shouting at the crowd, some waving American flags. Many seemed to take satisfaction that they had not yielded to the coal operators and their local allies, but instead the Federal government had intervened to put down their rebellion. "It was Uncle Sam that did it," one shouted.

Once the shooting stopped, the search for casualties began.

Mindful of stories that scores had been killed, their bodies still lying in the woods, Colonel Martin sent a company of troops with miners and guides and stretcher bearers to search the area but found no corpses. Reporters covering the battle were told that the miners "carried their dead and wounded away with them." But no one has ever proved or disproved this contention. The precise death toll was never established, but estimates range from fewer than twenty to more than fifty. In any case this was a much lower figure than was feared would be produced by the size of the forces involved. Chafin had been informed at one point that the miners' army numbered 9,000; his own forces he put at about 2,500. Other estimates went even higher. The official Army history of the Federal role in domestic disorders put the total on both sides between 10,000 to 20,000.

Both the miners and the defenders were well armed and had plenty of ammunition, which they fired freely. The roar of the guns became a steady pounding in the ears of men on both sides. "You could hear it, it seemed like for miles along the river," Ira Wilson, one of the miners, testified later. "It would echo and roll around so much sometimes you would think they was right down in Blair. Machine guns cracked up there so you would think the whole place was coming down on you."

The casualty figures seemed to belie the reputation of West Virginians for marksmanship. But combatants had to reckon with the thick late summer underbrush that clogged the hills and hollows that made up the battlefield. Many often fired without knowing exactly what they were shooting at. As one Bluefield volunteer described it to his local paper: "Someone spies the dark shadow of an armed man stealing along the road and lets go at it."

But even in conventional military engagements, the number of dead and wounded on each side is not necessarily the best gauge of their results. This was particularly true of the Battle of Blair Mountain. Its real significance is best reckoned not by the blood shed by the opposing forces but rather by its economic and political consequences. By these measurements it soon became clear that the union miners of West Virginia had suffered a staggering defeat.

10

Requiem for a Rebellion

A MONTH AFTER the miners' rebellion collapsed, UMW Vice President Philip Murray gave the union's national convention a firsthand report on the Battle of Blair Mountain. If the Army had not arrived when it did, Murray claimed, "there would have been very little cause for further complaint from anyone about further activities of Baldwin-Felts mine guards in the state of West Virginia. It was self evident to any casual observer," Murray added, "that the outcome was inevitable as the citizens army was making a steady advance into the camp of the enemy." But this was a case not proven. The miners did not overwhelm Chafin's defenders, and even if they had, it was not clear what they might have gained from such a tactical success. Given what actually had happened in southern West Virginia, the future looked bleak for the union, as Murray tacitly conceded. The Federal troops had restored order, Murray told the UMW convention. But they were bound to withdraw before long, and when they did leave, Murray said, "they are going to leave behind them the source of all this evil. It must become evident to all that a determined effort should be put forward by the labor unions of this country to remove this menacing evil from the lives of our people." But Murray was just whistling into the wind, a wind that was blowing with gale force against the mine workers in West Virginia and against organized labor throughout the country.

Ever since the Matewan shootout had triggered the crisis in West Virginia, UMW leaders looked for succor to the Federal government in Washington, to the Congress and then to the White House, first when Wilson was in the Oval Office and then when Harding replaced him. And their entreaties continued after the Battle of Blair Mountain, supported by others on the left. In the immediate aftermath of the miners' surrender, *The Nation* noted that "the miners have yielded not only to the superior force of the Federal Government, but also apparently to some confidence in its purpose and ability to do justice," and urged the Kenyon committee to pay heed to the miners' grievances when the committee resumed its work on September 19, two weeks after the West Virginia uprising's collapse.

But as it turned out, the Kenyon committee's three months of labors, which included a visit to the sites of the struggle in West Virginia, produced only a mouse. Unable to get his colleagues to agree on a report that could have pointed the way to the sort of remedies the union had sought, Chairman Kenyon had to settle for a brief statement of his own "personal views." This did little more than portray the battle in West Virginia as a conflict between "two determined bodies trying to enforce what they believe are rights, which rights are diametrically opposed to one another, and we have the situation of an irresistible force meeting an immovable body. In such case there can be nothing but trouble." Not surprisingly Congress took no action.

As for the executive branch, while Harding and his advisers had been reluctant to respond to the appeals for Federal troops from the state house in Charleston, their impatience with Governor Morgan was no measure of their sympathy for the union cause.

John L. Lewis, who had taken pains to cultivate his ties to the new Republican administration, sought out Harding's labor secretary, James J. Davis, himself a West Virginian, asking for help. His hope, Lewis told reporters, was that the Federal government would use its troops to disarm agents of the coal operators as well as the miners and then extend the miners the right to bargain collectively. Davis, a glad hander whose main role, a cabinet colleague observed, was to "keep labor quiet," was solicitous but unmoved. In Washington Samuel Gompers called at the White House to ask President Harding to consider convening a conference of miners and operators to deal with the crisis in West Virginia. Harding listened with "keen interest and sympathy," Gompers claimed. But sympathy was all that he had to give. His only obligation as president, Harding told Gompers, was to restore law and order in West Virginia, and that had already been done by fiat of General Bandholtz.

Far from helping the union, the Federal government was actively considering action against it. Called upon by Morgan to arrest miners on behalf of Logan County authorities, Bandholtz refused, pointing out that Federal troops cannot act against alleged violators of state laws. But when the governor appealed for action against the miners for violating Federal laws, he found a more supportive listener in Colonel Walter A. Bethel, the legal specialist whom Bandholtz had brought to Charleston to serve as his judge advocate. In a memorandum to the Department of Justice arguing for prosecution, the colonel pointed out that the deadline in Harding's proclamation, ordering the miners' army to disband by noon on September 1, had been ignored. Therefore, ipso facto, the miners, by disobeying the president, were guilty of insurrection. Bethel's view found support within the Department of Justice, where criminal division lawyers recommended a Federal indictment. But President Harding ultimately opposed prosecution, and Attorney General Harry Daugherty let the matter drop. The Justice Department never offered an explanation, but it was evident to one and all that any Federal investigation into the miners' uprising would inevitably focus public attention on the close ties between the coal operators and the state and local governments, and this was a can of worms that no one in Warren Harding's government wanted to open. As one assistant attorney general put it: "We are of the opinion that no steps should be taken by the Federal government at this time for it may embarrass the state officials."

Anyhow, any Federal prosecution would have been a redundancy, because the state of West Virginia was coming down on the union rebels with all its might and main. It was a vengeful Governor Morgan who signaled the state's purpose hard upon the miners' surrender. Even Morgan conceded that it would be unreasonable to punish all who participated in the uprising, because some, he noted, had been dragooned into insurrection, against their wills. But, the governor stated, "every effort will be made to punish the guilty leaders, who after inciting their followers to take up arms, sought to escape just punishment and the dangers of conflict by remaining a safe distance from the actual scene of warfare."

Morgan's attitude was no surprise to the UMW leaders.

Anticipating legal trouble, even before he and Frank Keeney fled to Ohio, Fred Mooney had helped to establish the Mingo County Defense League to defray costs of those rebels facing criminal charges. Circulars were sent the world around to solicit funds. When the miners' army gave up the fight, Mooney and Keeney, realizing they faced extradition, returned to Charleston. But they remained in hiding until union officials could work out a plan for them to surrender directly to Governor Morgan. On September 18, 1921, they appeared at Morgan's office, were taken into custody by Kanawha County deputies and brought to Williamson to face the Mingo County murder charges.

Even with the governor's involvement, union officials continued to worry about the safety of the two District 17 leaders, and John L. Lewis wired Morgan, asking for his personal assurances that no harm would come to the defendants.

If Lewis believed that the end of the uprising would have led Morgan to a more conciliatory attitude, he was soon disabused of that notion. Morgan responded with a bitter telegram linking the UMW leadership to the Bolsheviks ruling the Kremlin and accusing Lewis himself of complicity in the uprising. "Your silent encouragement of unlawful acts would indicate that Lenin and Trotsky are not without sincere followers in your organization," the governor declared. "It is a matter of record that you have not lifted your voice in protest against this violence."

Regardless of Morgan's accusations, Keeney and Mooney were well looked after by the authorities in Williamson, where they were among Mingo County friends. They ultimately posted bail, pending trial. But by this time they faced even more legal trouble. Along with twenty other miners they were charged with treason against the state of West Virginia. The state might have indicted the miners' leaders for any one of a number of felonies tied to the insurrection, and certainly would have had an easier time making its case. But instead it chose the charge of treason, a particularly detestable crime, the better to portray the miners the way the coal companies and their allies wanted them seen, as men beyond the pale, outcasts in their own state.

Much as prosecutors would have liked to convict Mooney and Keeney, their absence from the state when the uprising was at its height would have made the case against them hard to make. The state decided it had a better chance against William Blizzard, the so-called field marshal of the insurgents. But making the charge of treason was much easier than making it stick. The treason provision in the West Virginia constitution is narrowly drawn and identical to the language of the Federal constitution as set forth in article three, section three. "Treason against the State shall consist only in levying war against it, or in adhering to its enemies, giving them aid and comfort." Moreover, to make the charge harder to prove, West Virginia's constitution, like its Federal model, adds the restrictive clause that "No person shall be convicted of treason unless on the Testimony of two Witnesses to the same overt act, or on confession in open court."

No one could deny that the insurgents had committed violent acts and rejected lawful authority. But the claim that they were trying to make war against the state distorted reality. Indeed, before the march started, the miners sought the intervention of the state, in the person of Governor Morgan, with whom they pleaded to help find a peaceful solution to their problems. If the miners saw themselves as making war against anyone, it would have been against the mine owners, or the Logan County sheriff's office, a point that drew criticism from observers outside the state. "In

West Virginia indictments for treason seem to be thrown about as carelessly as if they were indictments for the larceny of a chicken," the *New York Times* declared. Closer to home, John T. Porterfield, prosecutor for Jefferson County, where the trial was to be held, recused himself from the case, contending that the charge treason was improper, adding that he regarded the trials as "a waste of scarce resources and mean-spirited vendettas." That left the chief counsel for the coal operators association, Anthony M. Belcher, in charge of prosecuting the case for which the companies later billed the state $125,000. UMW District 17 lawyer Harold W. Houston headed the defense team, roughly replicating the order of battle for the Matewan shoot-out trial in Williamson the year before.

Union lawyers had sought the shift of the trial to Jefferson County, in West Virginia's eastern panhandle, to avoid the hostile atmosphere of Don Chafin's Logan. The change also made for a striking historical coincidence. Only sixty-three years before, the same courthouse in Jefferson's county seat of Charles Town, where Blizzard's fate was to be decided, had served as the stage for another dramatic legal confrontation with profound political overtones. This was the trial of treason defendant John Brown, the abolitionist zealot whose raid on the Federal arsenal at nearby Harper's Ferry was one of the sparks that ignited the Civil War.

But the prosecution's chances of repeating Brown's conviction were dimmed by Judge John Mitchell Wood's charge to the jury, which exposed the holes in the state's case.

"Every violent opposition to the execution of the laws of the state, every resistance by force and violence to the officers of the state in the performance of their duties is not treason," Wood declared. Rioters might conspire to commit unlawful acts, and with intent to use violence, and yet, that would not necessarily be treason. But unlawful acts committed by an assemblage of individuals would not amount to treason "unless their purpose is by force and violence to commit some act or some acts, which if successful will subvert the government in whole or in part." To Blizzard's jury, whatever the union rebels had done, or intended to do, none of it seemed intended to subvert the government. They voted for acquittal on May 25, 1922.

Public sentiment among the citizens of Charles Town had all along favored Blizzard, and some of his more ardent backers reacted to the verdict by parading through town, carrying the alleged traitor on their shoulders. Their jubilation was premature. The state was not yet prepared to give up. Blizzard was then charged with murder, in the killing of Gore and his deputies, but was freed when the jury could not reach a verdict. When the jurors were released, they stood ten to two for acquittal.

Blizzard's escape from punishment was a bitter pill for the mine operators, one they refused to swallow without a fight. They still wanted a treason conviction. If they could not get one against Blizzard, they would settle for another rebel miner, by the name of Walter Allen. He was such a minor figure in the rebel army that even the prosecution's witnesses could testify to nothing more damaging than that he had been seen "with the armed forces" in Logan County, had carried a gun and distributed ammunition. But by this time the legal tide had turned against Allen and the miners. Judge Wood again presided, as he had in the Blizzard trial, but his handling of this case suggested that the mine operators and their allies had made clear to him that they had lost patience with his independence.

The change was evident during the *voir dire*. When the defense challenged jurors who admitted to a bias against unions, as it had done successfully in the Blizzard trial, Judge Wood overruled it until eventually the defense gave up on challenging. When the defense asked for instructions to the jury that would make clear how limited Allen's involvement was, Judge Wood rejected their motions and instead told the jurors that if they believed Allen was part of the miners' army, "the said Walter Allen was guilty of treason."

After the jury brought in the guilty verdict that seemed inevitable under the circumstances, Wood gave the defense one concession by agreeing to release Allen on bail pending appeal. Allen disappeared and all efforts by local authorities to track him down were in vain. The state dropped charges against the other twenty men charged with treason. Also abandoned was the murder charge against Mooney. The murder prosecution against Keeney went forward but the trial resulted in his acquittal.

Not satisfied with their legal assault, the coal operators sought to blacken the reputation of the mine workers union by importing the celebrated evangelist Billy Sunday to lambaste labor organizers.

Sunday employed a picturesque rhetoric whose extravagance recalled the tirades of Mother Jones, though of course from the opposite side. Of union organizers he said, "I'd rather be in hell with Cleopatra, John Wilkes Booth and Charles Guiteau, than to live on earth with such human lice." Shedding his coat and tie and rolling up his sleeves, he added, "If I were the Lord for about fifteen minutes," the evangelist declared, "I'd smack the bunch so hard that there would be nothing left for the devil to levy on but a bunch of whiskers and a bad smell."

These insults only added to the injuries the union had suffered in the state's legal system. The net result of the rebellion and the legal sequel was to inflict a devastating blow on the UMW in West Virginia. The West Virginia local's treasury was drained as a result of the heavy spending to support the strike and wage the subsequent legal battles. Nor was there much hope of help from national headquarters because the UMW landscape everywhere else was almost as gloomy.

The fundamental problem was that the artificial demand for coal stimulated by the Great War had vanished, but new mines that had opened to meet that demand still remained. John L. Lewis picked the moment to stage a new nationwide strike. Circumstances could hardly have been worse. Coal supplies were abundant, which meant that the strike would cause no hardship to the public and thus no pressure on the operators from the government to give ground to the union.

Under these circumstances, the best Lewis could do was to wring an agreement from major producers to continue existing pay scales. But even that was too generous for the producers of

West Virginia. They demanded that the union agree to give back the most recent $1.50-a-day pay increase, if they were to continue to recognize the union. Keeney and Mooney were willing to go along, however reluctantly, in the interest of "the perpetuation of the union."

They took the offer to Lewis, who during the dark days of the Blair Mountain march and the legal struggles that followed had been a steadfast ally of District 17, even briefly taking a seat at the defense table during Blizzard's treason trial. But now with the UMW in serious trouble, and with his own hold on its presidency in danger, Lewis proclaimed a draconian strategy not to yield any of the recent hard-fought gains the UMW had won. "No backward step," was Lewis's motto and under that rubric there was no room for the bargain Mooney and Keeney proposed.

As Mooney later bitterly wrote: "No backward step was taken but the ground lost by the union became a landslide into the gutter for the union." In West Virginia the miners signed contracts for tonnage rates far below the prewar levels, membership tumbled from 50,000 to a few hundred while nationally the UMW's membership declined from about 600,000 to fewer than 100,000 by the end of the decade. It was a ghastly time for organized labor on every front. Spurred by a postwar economic slump, corporations mounted a nationwide drive for the open shop, under the rubric the "American plan," which set unions back on their heels and thinned their ranks. From 1920 to 1923 the AFL lost two million workers, or nearly 25 percent of its total membership. And courts seemed to be ready to issue strikebreaking injunctions almost for the asking.

Meanwhile Mooney and Keeney were forced out of the union by Lewis, bitter at their attempted mutiny. Keeney soldiered on for the cause, leaving the state to plunge into the nascent drive for industrial unionism and returning there at the onset of the Great Depression to make one last stab at organizing the miners. After that failed he finished his life as a parking lot attendant in Charleston, discredited by the union to which he had devoted his life.

The years were even less kind to Keeney's comrade-in-arms, Fred Mooney. He briefly entered politics, losing two races for the state legislature, on the Republican ticket in 1922 and 1924, then divorced his wife, and with his three sons moved to New Mexico, where he worked as a carpenter. The next years were spent drifting in the Southwest and the Far West. In 1934 he returned to West Virginia and found work in the mines as a superintendent and section foreman. In 1952, following a period of severe depression, he killed himself with a shotgun blast.

As his memorial he left behind the manuscript of a biography, *Struggle in the Coal Fields*, which was ultimately published by the University of West Virginia.

It took the Great Depression and Franklin Roosevelt to rescue Lewis's union and the rest of the American labor movement from near oblivion. Lewis abandoned his caution of the 1920s to break with the AFL and find in industrial unionism and the CIO a more aggressive and effective template for the labor movement in the turbulent 1930s. He helped break new ground for labor by vigorously supporting the auto workers' union sit-down strike against General Motors. It was the boldest venture for American organized labor since the miners' march on Blair Mountain. When the auto workers occupied GM's huge complex in Flint, Michigan, police assaulted the buildings but were driven back by a barrage of auto parts dropped from second-story windows. The sit-downs were enormously successful, too much so to suit the middle-class ethos. As Lewis's CIO swept to new victories against the steel and auto industries, many Americans recoiled. "Property minded citizens were scared," notes New Deal historian William Leuchtenberg.

So was Roosevelt, for whom Lewis had forsaken his lifelong Republicanism, and to whose 1936 victory Lewis's CIO had made a massive contribution. "A plague o' both your houses," FDR famously said of both the CIO and its big business adversaries.

Lewis responded with majestic scorn. "It ill behooves one who has supped at labor's table and has been sheltered in labor's house to curse with equal fervor and fine impartiality both labor and its adversaries when they become locked in deadly embrace," Lewis retorted.

It was a scathing put-down, but it did Lewis and labor little good. The success of the sit-down strikes was not to be repeated. The New Deal succeeded in enacting only one more piece of pro-labor legislation, the Wages and Hours Act of 1938, a measure so riddled with compromises and exceptions that one Congressional critic offered a facetious amendment requiring the secretary of labor to report to Congress "whether anyone is subject to this bill."

In sum, both the aftermath of the miners' march in West Virginia and the auto workers' sit-downs in Michigan served to remind trade unions that in the land of the free, working-class gains can be made only by playing by middle-class rules, rules that demand respect for property and profit. But the larger truth is that these rules were generally accepted by workers, with the qualification that they were understood to be part of a larger compact with their country governing their rights as citizens of the United States. It was this compact, with its balance of responsibilities and protections, requiring the respect for law and property in return for fair treatment and equal opportunity, including the right to organize, which had been betrayed by the coal operators of West Virginia and the auto makers of Michigan. The mine workers' allegiance to this compact not only inspired the great armed uprising in the West Virginia coalfields but also restricted it and contributed to its failure.

No sooner had the armed miners begun their ill-fated march on Blair Mountain in the violent summer of 1920 than apparatchiks of the newly formed Communist Party of the United States sprang into action, grinding out leaflets with a call to arms. "Help your struggling brothers in the mines of West Virginia," the broadsides urged. "To your task! All as one in the name of working class solidarity! The miners' fight for a union must be made the fight of all organized labor and all workers of America."

It was easy to understand why the Communists had been galvanized. Every day front-page headlines in newspapers across the country shouted the astounding story of this huge uprising, on a scale that dwarfed other insurrections. Class warfare in America, long only a metaphor and daydream for Marxists had at last been transformed into reality, etched in blood and bullets. The time had come for American workers to rush to the barricades.

Or so it seemed. But only for an instant in history.

Then suddenly, before the ink had hardly dried on the Communist summons to the barricades, the revolution was over. It was not crushed; rather it simply expired. Once the Federal troops arrived, the miners laid down their arms, without a shot being fired in anger. It was not only the strength of the Federal intervention but what it represented that sapped the fervor and the fury from the rebels. "We wouldn't revolt against the national guv'ment," one miner told General Bandholtz when he arrived in strife-torn West Virginia.

A look back at the Battle of Blair Mountain, and the long months of violence that led up to it, illuminates the economic and political struggle that shaped the power structure of modern America. The mine owners used their wealth to dominate West Virginia's political and legal system, a pattern that corporate America continues to follow, though rarely as blatantly or as successfully. Just as important, the resistance of the miners was tempered. They were denounced as traitors and Bolsheviks. But rather than seeking to betray or overthrow the American system, the miners were striving to make the system work for them.

The Blair Mountain uprising demonstrates that, middle-class mythology to the contrary, class conflict does exist in America.

But it also illustrates the limitations of that conflict in this country. Standing between the miners of West Virginia and an outright working-class revolution against the Federal government was their hope for their country based on its promise of opportunity, individual freedom and fairness under the law. This optimism, which flourished from the nation's earliest years, helped to erode the class consciousness that prevailed abroad and confronted the American workers with a fundamental dilemma: Their patriotism and allegiance to the American dream, feelings shared with the middle class, conflicted with the recognition that to assure themselves and their families of economic security and dignity, they had to challenge the corporate power structure, upon which the middle class depended for its well-being.

Nowhere was this tension more clearly demonstrated than among the West Virginia miners as they battled the coal operators in the years right after the Great War. For a long time past, the miners had endured exploitation and brutality at the hands of the mine owners and their minions, and it was against these nemeses that the miners staged their march. But it did not occur to them to hold responsible the national government nor the economic and political system on which that government was based. In the end the West Virginia miners accepted that system and the middle-class ethos undergirding it because they believed in the rule of law and the promise of the democratic process. That was why they turned away from revolting against the government, and why many of them waved American flags as they marched off after their defeat.

In the immediate aftermath of the miners' failed rebellion, Federal investigators began looking high and low for signs of Communist influence, evidence that would have lent credence to the great bugaboo of the times. They turned up next to nothing, except for a few IWW and Communist fliers, like the one calling workers to the barricades in support "of your struggling brothers in the mines of West Virginia." As Fred Mooney later learned, "two communists had ensconced their hides (as they always do) safely behind the walls of the Washington Hotel in Charleston, got circulars printed and got some marchers to carry them into the lines." But an Army intelligence officer reported that he could find no trace of any organization linked to the march, except, of course, for the United Mine Workers.

Efforts to depict the rebellion as being inspired by alien influences also contravened the facts. Keeney, Mooney and most of their fellow union activists were all home-grown West Virginians, as were the vast majority of union members. Indeed the 1920 census figures showed that more than 93 percent of the population of Logan County and 97 percent of Mingo County was native born. At any rate the union did what it could to encourage its foreign-born members to become citizens. "There were no aliens or communists there," Jonathan Spivak, the ACLU's emissary to the West Virginia UMW, said of the union battleground in the state.

By the time they reached the leadership of District 17, Mooney and Keeney had rejected the ideologies of the left both in theory and practice. Mooney's wide range of reading as a young man included Voltaire, Plato, Herbert Spencer and interpretations of Marx by Engels and others. But Marx himself, he conceded, "I could not absorb." As for Keeney, though he had once joined the Socialist Party, after his experiences in dealing with socialists in the Paint Creek–Cabin Creek Strike, he came to regard them as ineffective and unreliable allies. By 1919 he was admonishing the members of District 17 that it was their duty "to eliminate from their organization any group that is preaching their different 'isms'."

Asked during his Kenyon committee testimony about the meaning of the provocative phrase in the UMW constitution asserting that miners were entitled to "the full social value of their product," Keeney denied that this was a call for a takeover of private property. That language did mean, Keeney acknowledged, that a miner should receive "all the wealth he creates." But he believed it allowed for some exceptions, including "running expenses, transportation" and "a fair return upon the investment to the man who owns the tools of production." Keeney's service in the trenches of West Virginia's labor wars had made him class conscious with a militant edge. "I haven't left the class I was born into and I hope I never will," he told a journalist. Still he was willing to work within the system. During the Great War, he had urged miners to produce all the coal they could, even when at times it meant ignoring rights and protections won at the bargaining table. It was Keeney, together with Mooney, who at Governor Cornwell's behest had rushed to the scene at Marmet in September 1919 and persuaded the armed miners to give up their march and go home. And the two had carried out the same mission in August 1921 before Captain Brockus's raid destroyed their peace mission.

In the struggle in West Virginia's coalfields, miners, mine owners and independent observers all accepted one truth—unionism was at the heart of the battle. But as David Corbin points out in his incisive analysis of West Virginia's long ordeal, the miners' drive to organize was inextricably linked with their view of themselves as American citizens. As Americans, they believed they had a right to organize and join a union. And the union in turn would help them redeem the American promise of economic and social justice.

It was no accident that the bedrock of the miners' claim to the right to organize was the Federal Constitution. "We propose to stand by and support those men that want to belong to the organization of the United Mine Workers of America and their only desire is to exercise their constitutional rights," Fred Mooney told the Kenyon Committee at the outset of the hearings.

Senator Kenyon pressed the issue: "What constitutional rights do you feel you have been denied?" he asked. With his state under martial law, Mooney had no trouble finding an answer: "We are denied a Republican form of government; we are denied the right of public assemblage; we are denied the right to belong to a labor union." Mooney of course knew that there is not a word in the Constitution about labor unions. But he believed that right was inherent in the rights that were enumerated by the Framers.

The Constitution created a system under which the miners enjoyed the protection of these rights as a matter of law, peacefully, at least in theory. But if the reality of their lives contradicted that principle, the miners were prepared, if necessary, to salvage those rights at the point of a gun. In 1919, when the West Virginia legislature, like others around the country, caught up in the Red Scare, was in the process of enacting a so-called Red Flag law curbing free speech, a union local in the Coal River area adopted a protest resolution serving notice on "the ruling class of this state" that "As a final arbiter of the rights of public assembly, free speech and a free and uncensored press we will not for a single moment hesitate to meet our enemies upon the battle fields. And there amid the roar of the cannon and the groans of the dying and the crash of systems purchase again our birthright of blood bought freedom." Alarmed that this fiery manifesto would become a weapon in the hands of the UMW's enemies, Keeney moved swiftly to get the resolution revoked. But the spirit behind it could not be extinguished, as the march on Blair Mountain demonstrated.

"Going to march to Blair Mountain, going to whip the company," the Red Bandanna Army sang as they marched. They failed to keep that promise, but they did stake out a claim on history.

Within a generation, the hopes of the rebellious miners had been largely fulfilled as their government finally redeemed its part of the compact with its citizens who happened to be workers. Today's workers have been spared the fear and desperation that haunted the miners who marched on Blair Mountain. They do not have to face eviction or jail, or the threat of violent death. And no one talks of rising up in arms.

But if much has changed, much remains the same. With all the gains made under the New Deal reforms, workers in post-industrial America have not come close to keeping pace with soaring corporate profits while the maldistribution of wealth accelerates. In the 21st century, as in the 20th, labor's leaders are still on the defensive, battling to forestall further losses of political power and protections for their members. The bosses still hold all the high cards.

In these not-so-benign circumstances, the courage and commitment to their cause, and to each other, of the West Virginia miners, and the women who marched along with them to Blair Mountain, deserves wide recognition and respect. For the significance of the Blair Mountain march extends beyond "every mine and mill where workers strike and organize," the domain of Joe Hill's ghost, to Americans in all walks of life.

The saga of the West Virginia uprising seems freighted with extra salience these angst-ridden days because their rebellion capped a period of violence and turbulence with striking parallels to the Amert left the United States confronting new dangers, real and apparent. Then, as now, threats at home and abroad haunted the Republic. Fearing an imminent worldwide Bolshevist revolution and plagued by labor unrest and disorder in their own country, many citizens blamed the record number of strikes on the plottings of Lenin and Trotsky. Explosions wrecked prominent landmarks. In lower Manhattan a blast at the corner of Wall and Broad gutted the House of Morgan and killed forty passersby. And conspirators used the mails to spread terror. Apocalyptic visions gripped the nation's leaders, moving Warren Harding, only a year or so before he gained the presidency, to warn that the nation was facing "a desperate situation." And then, as now, leaders of government and business argued for the need to restrict civil liberties and stifle dissent to protect the nation's security. It was this sentiment that undercut the efforts of mine workers of West Virginia to gain the public attention and support they needed in their struggle against an entrenched political and economic oligarchy.

The danger of terrorism dramatized by the tragedies of 9/11 remains very real today. But if we concentrate on it to the exclusion of other concerns, we ignore other threats to our welfare. Many of our workplaces are breeding growing dissatisfaction and insecurity, our economy is producing increasing inequality and the labor laws put into place in the 1930s to prevent recurrences of what happened in Mingo County and many other places are no longer working very well to protect workers. There are no signs of bandanna armies forming, of course. But grievances of workers are real and profound, and we run a risk as a nation and society if we overlook them.

"Defender of the rights of working people" reads the inscription under the likeness of Sid Hatfield carved on his headstone overlooking the Tug River. "We will never forget." For all his flaws, Hatfield deserves to be remembered. But it is even more important to remember the men and the cause "The Terror of the Tug" championed.

The rebellion of the West Virginia miners was defeated. But the example they set should help sustain all citizens, in and out of the labor movement, who believe that the principles the Red Bandanna Army fought for, economic fairness, political justice and human dignity, will, as Faulkner famously said of the spirit of mankind, not only endure but prevail.

Reference Notes

Chapter One: Matewan Station

1   "Can be relied on": Tom Felts to Albert Felts, May 18, 1920, *WVCF*, p. 214.

1   Opening up the region: Lambie, pp. 125–30; Cohen, pp. 1–10.

3   Breathtaking in its scope: Wolfe.

3   More than four million workers: Dubofsky, *The State and Labor in Modern America*, pp. 76–77.

5   To cut out the boil: Geiger and Carroll.

5   Mooney recalled: Mooney, p. 70.

5   "In violation of every law": Ibid., pp. 66–70.

6   Wood informed Baker: Laurie and Cole, p. 309; Laurie.

6   Background of Mooney and Keeney: Corbin, "Frank Keeney Is Our Leader"; Phillips, Cabell.

7   "Drunkards and crooks": Mooney, p. 38.

7   "Keeney and Mooney agreed": Mooney, p. 51.

7   Agreed to disband: *NYT*, Sept. 7, 1919; Bailey, pp. 454–55.

8   "False reports": *NYT*, Sept. 7, 1919.

8   "That would be too slow": *NYT*, Sept. 22, 1919.

8   "To protect their Constitutional rights": Bailey, p. 407, citing John L. Lewis to John J. Cornwell, Sept. 11, 1919.

8   Endorsed nationalization: Johnson, p. 101.

9   Troops were withdrawn: *NYT*, Nov. 5, 1919.

9   Promise of arbitration: Murray, pp. 158, 162–63.

9   "The most happy and contented": Bailey, p. 411.

9   Skyrocketing profits: Ibid., p. 412.

10 Sparsely populated: Corbin, p. 1.

10 "They drank and fought": Ibid., p. 27.

11 Made him notorious: Bailey, pp. 347–48.

11 Lewis's announcement: *Bluefield Daily Telegraph*, Jan. 31, 1920.

11 Mine owners' heavy-handedness: Bailey, p. 419, citing *Williamson Daily News*, Jan. 13, 1920, March 23, 1920 and March 25, 1920.

11 Declared itself the winner: Ibid., p. 422.

12 Builders leaped to their feet: *Bluefield Daily Telegraph*, Feb. 7, 1920.

12 They were pistol whipped: Testimony of Frank Ingham, *WVCF*, p. 29.

12 "We want this raise": Testimony of W. E. Hutchinson, *WVCF*, p. 80.

12 Hundreds of others did the same thing: Mooney, p. 71.

13 The organizing drive's progress: *NYT*, May 21, 1920.

13 Blankenship's background: Bailey, p. 255, citing *Williamson Daily News*, April 8, 1916.

13 "They can say what they please": Bailey, p. 438, citing *Williamson Daily News*, Jan. 30, 1920.

14 "Primitive scruples and dubious attainments": Phillips, Cabell.

14 Hatfield-McCoy feud: Jones, pp. 1–16.

14 Sid Hatfield's lineage: Felts MS, Savage, p. 11.

14 Sid Hatfield's days as a miner: Hunt et al., pp. 55–61; Savage, p. 11.

15 "A little shooting match": *WVCF*, p. 219.

15 Hatfield's scorn: Bailey, pp. 361–62, citing *Williamson Daily News*, Dec. 13, 1919.

16 He sobered up but ran with the boys: Savage, p. 13.

16 Sid Hatfield and Jessie Testerman: Felts MS; Savage, pp. 27–28.

16 "A question of master and servant": Testimony of W. E. Hutchinson, *WVCF*, p. 92.

16 Hauled Felts into court: Bailey, p. 427, citing *Williamson Daily News*, April 27, 1920.

17 Yellow-dog contracts upheld: Lunt, pp. 15–16.

17 "Obey the law": Mooney, p. 72.

17 A telegram of protest: *NYT*, May 20, 1920.

18 History of Baldwin-Felts agency: Hadsell and Coffee.

18 Violence in Colorado: Perlman and Taft, pp. 336–37.

18 Felts's denial: Testimony of Tom Felts, *WVCF*, p. 897.

19 Lively and Mooney: Mooney, pp. 71–72.

20 $1,000 offer to Testerman: Testimony of Charles E. Lively, HTT.
20 No machine guns: Mooney, p. 73.
21 Attention to Anse Hatfield: Memorandum, May 13, 1920, *WVCF*, p. 212.
21 Arrangements with Sid Hatfield: Ibid.
22 Confrontation at miners' cabins: Testimony of Sid Hatfield, *WVCF*, p. 206.
22 Testerman sent Harry Kelly: Testimony of Jesse Webb, HTT.
23 Deputies gather at depot: Testimony of Hugh Combs, HTT.
24 Versions of what happened next: Testimony of Sid Hatfield, pp. 205–12; Testimony of Charles E. Lively, pp. 383–86; Testimony of C. T. Blankenship, pp. 487–90; and Testimony of Thomas L. Felts, pp. 881–905, *WVCF*. Also Testimony of Charles E. Lively, Hugh Combs et al., HTT.
25 "Split the creek": Bailey, p. 447.
25 "I can't see why they shot me": Ibid., p. 448.
26 One train passed by: Ibid., p. 448, citing J. W. Wier to John J. Cornwell, 20 May 1920. Cornwell papers.

Chapter Two: "What Does Labor Want?"

27 "Many men do not hunt work": Zieger, p. 14.
27 Lewis's early life: *Dictionary of American Biography, Supplement 8:1966–70* (New York: American Council of Learned Societies, 1988).
28 "Our ship made port": Zieger, p. 19.
28 Without ever standing for election: Dubofsky and Van Tyne, p. 32.
29 Development of AFL's approach: Foner and Garraty, p. 629.
30 Gompers's early life: *Dictionary of American Biography*, pp. 369–70.
31 "What does labor want?": Lewis P. Eigen and Jonathan P. Siegel, *The Macmillan Dictionary of Political Quotations* (New York: Macmillan, 1993), p. 320.
32 Working conditions for coal miners: Zieger, p. 9.
33 Difficult to supervise: Dix.
33 Cheating the miners: Geiger and Carroll.
34 "The Company Town": Corbin, *Life Work and Rebellion*, p. 61.
34 One mine worker's ballad: Zieger, p. 11.
35 Mine owners provided the impetus: Taft, p. 167.

35   The 1897 strike: Corbin, pp. 44–45.
36   The Central Competitive Field Agreement: Taft, p. 171.
37   Growth of UMW: Ibid., p. 166.
37   One cloud remained: Ibid., p. 188.
37   Blaming U.S. Steel: Testimony of Frank P. Walsh, *WVCF*, p. 604.
37   Corporate connections: Testimony of Philip Murray, *WVCF*, pp. 540–45.
38   The UMW soon lost its foothold: Geiger and Carroll.
38   UMW support in 1912: Corbin, *Life, Work and Rebellion*, p. 81.
38   Mother Jones's origins: Capozzola.
39   The 1900 anthracite strike: Foner and Garraty, p. 603.
39   Her full range of demagoguery: Lee, pp. 26–27; Scholten.
40   The Bull Moose Special: Geiger and Carroll.
40   Hatfield takes charge: Ibid.
40   Rank and file reaction to settlement: Corbin, pp. 98–100.
41   "All fire and dynamite": Mooney, p. 46.
42   Mistrust on both sides: Corbin, pp. 100, 106.
43   Olmstead's warning: Ibid., p. 108.

Chapter Three: Seeing Red

46   "Another shocking outrage": *NYT*, May 21, 1920.
46   The ACLU joins the attack: Ibid.
46   Gompers adds to protest: *NYT*, May 23, 1921.
47   Wilson's eroded body: Smith, p. 101.
47   Thomas said bitterly: Ibid., p. 148.
48   Forging an alliance: Dubofsky, pp. 50–55.
49   Helping the rail unions: Cooper, pp. 201–2.
50   Pershing's praise: Corbin, pp. 177–78.
50   "These local boys died": Ibid., p. 181.
51   District 17 membership: Ibid., p. 184.
51   National UMW membership: Jordan.
51   "The big interests in the saddle": Cooper, p. 264.
51   War on the Wobblies: Foner and Garraty, p. 563; Dubofsky, p. 78.
52   Repressive laws: Cooper, pp. 298–99.
53   Really a Soviet plot: *NYT*, March 4, 1919.
53   *Atlantic Monthly* estimate and the bomb plots: Allen, pp. 40–43.
54   "Certain to make matters worse": Dubofsky, p. 78.

55 "A crime against civilization": Ibid.

55 "That the government would intervene": Ibid., pp. 78–79.

56 A hulking figure: Dubofsky and Van Tyne, p. 33.

56 "The captain of a mighty host": www.dol.gov/laborhalloffame.

56 Chanted a ditty: Blankenhorn.

56 "The law will be enforced": *NYT,* Oct. 19, 1921.

57 Palmer's early life: Murray, p. 191.

57 "Nipped in the bud": Daniels, p. 547.

58 The unfolding coal strike: Murray, pp. 157–63.

58 Labor Secretary Wilson threatens to quit: Daniels, p. 546.

60 Olmstead's Boast: Testimony of Harry Olmstead, *WVCF,* p. 255.

60 Hoover and the Palmer raids: Murray, pp. 207–9.

60 A limited role: Smith, p. 135.

61 His reasoning a mishmash: Murray, 201–2.

62 "Do not let the country see Red": Daniels, p. 546.

62 Plea to Tumulty: Quoted in telegram from Jonathan Spivak to Louis Budenz, American Civil Liberties Union, May 21, 1920, ACLU Archives.

62 "From out of me poured details": Spivak, pp. 75–79.

63 Wilson did not react: Lunt, p. 100, citing Justice Department files.

63 Congress should wait and see: *NYT,* May 29, 1921.

Chapter Four: "A Powder Keg Ready to Blow"

65 "A great rush for membership": *United Mine Workers Journal,* July 1, 1920.

65 "No gunman can meddle with me": Gorn, p. 270.

66 "Mingo nearly completed": Corbin, p. 202, citing Keeney to William Green, June 16, 1920, UMW archives.

67 "A powder keg ready to blow": John Spivak to Roger Baldwin, June 11, 1920. ACLU archives.

67 Ernst's response: Ernst to Keeney, June 28, 1920, *WVCF,* p. 116.

67 Help from the Labor Department: Testimony of Frank Keeney, *WVCF,* p. 106.

67 The best approach: Keeney exhibit 8, *WVCF,* p. 130.

67 "Are you in need of any miners?": Keeney exhibit 12, *WVCF,* p. 158.

68 Olmstead's complaint: Testimony of Harry Olmstead, *WVCF,* pp. 259ff.

68 Spent $14,000 on tickets: Testimony of Frank Keeney, *WVCF,* p. 158.

68 "Miners fired from ambush": *NYT,* Nov. 20, 1920.

69 Cornwell forced to rely on deputies: Cole, *State Police.*

69 Two miners and two union men wounded: *NYT,* July 5, July 6, 1920.

69 Burned to the ground: Bailey, pp. 454–55.

69 Shot from ambush: *NYT,* July 15, 1920.

69 A throwback to 17th century: Bailey, p. 454.

70 "They went after me": Testimony of George Blankenship, *WVCF,* pp. 259ff.

70 Very quiet: Lunt, p. 102, citing George Blankenship to John Cornwell, June 9, 1920, Cornwell papers, West Virginia collection.

71 A letter to all unions: Cole, "State Police."

71 "Is there no way?" Lunt, p. 103, citing William Ord to Cornwell, June 15, 1920, Cornwell papers.

71 Nothing could be done: Ibid., citing Cornwell to William Ord, June 17, 1920, Cornwell papers.

72 "That mountain dew": Testimony of Fred Mooney, *WVCF,* p. 19.

72 "As I deem proper": Lunt, p. 105, citing Jackson Arnold to James D. Francis, June 24, 1920, Cornwell papers.

72 "Please do not infer": Ibid., p. 105, citing J. J. Armentrout to Cornwell, July 16, 1920.

73 "Would require 500 men": Ibid., p. 105, citing Arnold to Cornwell, Aug. 27, 1920.

73 "Disorders and threatened disorders": *Charleston Gazette,* Aug. 29, 1920.

74 Read sent 500 men: Laurie and Cole, p. 311.

74 Damron's early involvement: *Charleston Gazette,* June 22, 1920.

75 Four detectives acquitted: Bailey, p. xxv, citing undated clip from *Bluefield Telegraph* in Eastern Regional Coal Archives.

75 Passed on his concerns to Cornwell: Lunt, pp. 107–08, citing James Damron to Cornwell, Sept. 2, Sept. 14, 1920, Cornwell papers.

76 Damron's guerrilla war: Bailey, pp. 197–99, 223.

76 Shot and wounded: Ibid., pp. 357–58.

77 Cornwell-Damron exchange: Lunt, pp. 109–10, citing Cornwell to Damron, Sept. 8 and Damron to Cornwell, Sept. 14, Cornwell papers.

77   Burkhardt had alarming reports: Corbin, p. 204, citing report of
     William Austin, camp inspector, to Commanding General, Camp
     Sherman, Ohio, Sept. 21, 1920, Secretary's Office, File 333.9,
     General Records of the Department of Justice.

78   "Extreme measures": Lunt, p. 109, citing Damron to Cornwell,
     Sept. 14, Cornwell papers.

78   Baker asked Cornwell: Laurie and Cole, p. 313.

79   "No such animal": Lunt, p. 114, citing William N. Cummins to
     Cornwell, Oct. 6, 1920, Cornwell papers.

79   "Served to intimidate": Laurie and Cole, p. 232.

79   "The saddest day": Daniels, p. 560.

80   Clashed four times: Mingo County File.

80   Cornwell once again appealed: *NYT,* Nov. 28, 1920.

80   Read deployed a battalion: Laurie and Cole, p. 312.

80   "Military control": *NYT,* Dec. 5, 1920.

80   Some 500 rifles and pistols: *NYT,* Dec. 3 ,1920.

80   "Vicious and disorderly characters": Lunt, p. 116, citing William
     N. Cummins to E. K. Beckner, Nov. 15, 1920, Cornwell papers.

81   80 percent of normal: *NYT,* Dec. 6, 1920.

81   To pay for groceries: Ibid.

81   "We are all Americans": *NYT,* Dec. 7, 1920.

81   "Appalling conditions": Burkinshaw.

82   "Excite the sympathy": *NYT*, Dec. 10, 1920.

82   "Failed miserably": *NYT,* Dec. 9, 1920.

83   "Political bankruptcy": Quoted in *Literary Digest,* Dec. 18, 1920.

83   "Law and order governor": *NYT,* Dec. 8, 1920.

84   Damron quits the bench: *Charleston Gazette,* Oct. 29, 1920.

Chapter Five: "It's Good to Have Friends"

87   "Barbarous warfare": *New York Call,* Jan. 21, 1921.

88   The UMW assessment: *NYT,* Jan. 10, 1921.

88   "The most tyrannical": *NYT,* Feb. 7, 1921.

88   Felts offered to pay: *Baltimore Sun,* Feb. 6, 1921.

89   Sid Hatfield's marriage: *Huntington Herald-Dispatch,* June 2, June 3,
     1920.

90   Anse Hatfield's testimony and murder: *NYT,* Aug. 16, 1920; Sav-
     age, p. 31.

91 He soon found himself charged: *New York World*, Feb. 1, 1921;
    Williamson Daily News, Aug. 28, 1920.
92 Baker turned Read down: Laurie and Cole, pp. 312–13.
92 Troops had been fired upon: *NYT*, Jan. 4, 1921.
92 Baker relented: Laurie and Cole, p. 313.
92 All it would take: *Washington Times*, Jan. 27, 1921.
93 A stern warning: *Baltimore Sun*, Feb. 6, 1921.
93 "Just a little free for all": *Washington Times*, Jan. 27, 1921.
93 "Not guilty," they shouted: *Washington Times*, Jan. 28, 1921.
94 Relative calm returned: Lee, p. 60.
94 Eliminating all union men: *New York Post*, Feb. 9, 1921.
94 Not a single juror selected: *NYT*, Feb. 6, 1921.
94 "The only hope": Ibid.
95 Bailey put an end to the idea: Savage, p. 40.
95 Undermining credibility: *New York Post*, Feb. 14, 1921.
96 "This here will get them": Testimony of Joe Jack, HTT.
97 "Mr. Hatfield sent me that word": *Washington Post*, March 3, 1921.
97 Asked to be introduced: Ibid.
98 A two fold incentive: *New York Post*, Feb. 23, 1921.
98 The double burden of guilt: *NYT*, Feb. 24, 1921; *New York Post*,
    Feb. 23, 1921.
99 Lively's five confessions: Testimony of Charles E. Lively, HTT.
104 The defense version: Testimony of Dan Chambers, HTT.
105 "I never heard Hatfield make such a statement": Testimony of
    Toney Webb, HTT.
105 Murderous intent: Ibid.
106 "It is ridiculous": *NYT*, March 20, 1921.
107 Until the mountains turned green again: Savage, p. 48.
107 A $10,000 bond: *New York Call*, March 21, 1921.
107 Greeted like heroes: *NYT*, March 22, 1921.

Chapter Six: "War, Insurrection and Riot"

110 They were not shy: Fisher.
111 The establishment backed Morgan: Bailey, p. 434.
111 Many in District 17 were jubilant: Spivak, p. 87.
111 A banner across Main Street: Savage, p. 34.
112 The 1920 election returns: Moore, p. 533.

112   Morgan's background: West Virginia Archives and History @www.wvculture.org/history/morgan.

112   "Miners are crack shots": *Baltimore Sun*, Feb. 3, 1921.

113   Morgan seemed shocked: *Washington Post*, March 1, 1921.

113   Hailing the verdict: *UMW Journal*, April 1, 1921.

113   *Smilin' Sid* on film: Savage, p. 50.

113   The new jury bill: Ibid., p. 51.

114   Doubling the state police: Cole, "State Police."

114   The violence escalated: Testimony of Frank Keeney, *WVCF*, pp. 171–73; Testimony of Capt. J. R. Brockus, *WVCF*, pp. 326–33; Cole, pp. 129–30; Laurie and Cole, p. 313; Ephraim Morgan to John Weeks, May 14, 1921; and Gen. George Read to Adjutant General, May 16, 1921, Mingo County File.

115   Brockus's background: WVCF, p. 323.

115   Heavy fire forced them to flee into the woods: Ibid., p. 329.

116   Brockus's report was grim: Ibid., p. 330.

116   Shootings on the railroad bridges: Ibid.

117   A flag of truce: Savage, p. 53.

117   "A shooting bee": *WVCF*, p. 117.

117   Morgan asks for troops: Laurie and Cole, pp. 313–14.

117   "No signs of relief": Rich, pp. 159–60.

118   Harding's early life: www.whitehouse.gov/history/presidents.

118   "Earnest and forceful": Russell, p. 143.

119   "The zenith of my political ambition": Ibid., pp. 250–52.

119   "Presidents don't run like assessors": Ibid., p. 333.

120   Deciding on whether to send troops: Memo, CofS., G2, Fifth Corps Area. For Read, 16 May 21, sub: Conditions in Mingo County, 13–15 May 1921, Mingo County File; Laurie and Cole, pp. 314–15; Rich, pp. 159–60; Berman, pp. 210–12.

121   Harding's telegram to Morgan: *NYT*, May 18, 1921; Rich, p. 160.

121   Transfer of authority: Cole, "Martial Law."

121   "There is now imminent danger": Testimony of Capt. J. R. Brockus, *WVCF*, p. 323.

121   A mass meeting: Huntington *Herald-Dispatch*, May 18, 1921; *NYT*, May 19, 1921; Cole, "Martial Law."

121   The "better citizens": Testimony of Capt. J. R. Brockus, *WVCF*, p. 339.

122   Singing "America": Savage, p. 55.

122 Carpenter's speech: Testimony of Capt. J. R. Brockus, *WVCF*, p. 344.

122 Brockus's arrival: *NYT*, May 20, 1921; *Charleston Gazette*, May 20, 1921.

123 Appointment of Major Davis: Proclamation of Governor Morgan, *WVCF*, p. 275.

123 Davis's career: Cole, "Martial Law."

126 Davis takes charge: Testimony of Capt. J. R. Brockus, *WVCF*, p. 338.

126 "Now it is out of reason": Ibid., p. 345.

126 Davis cracks down: *NYT*, May 22, 1921; *WVCF:* testimony of Blaine Maynard, p. 72; testimony of Capt. J. R. Brockus, p. 351; Cole, "Martial Law."

127 Habeas corpus petition: *NYT*, May 23, 24, 1921; Cole, "Martial Law."

127 Hatfield eludes pursuers: *NYT*, May 25, 1921.

128 A shipment of submachine guns: Cole, "Martial Law."

128 Hiram Johnson's career: www.sacbee.com/static/archive.

128 Johnson's resolution: *NYT*, May 25.

129 Brockus sent a posse: *NYT*, May 26, May 27, 1921; Cole, "Martial Law."

129 Reflecting Davis's attitude: *NYT*, May 27, 1921, cited in Cole, "Martial Law."

130 Memorial Day parade: Savage, p. 57.

130 Brockus and Pinson swept down: *NYT*, June 6, 1921.

131 The suspect opened fire: *NYT*, June 15, 1921; Testimony of Frank Keeney, p. 165; Testimony of Capt. J. R. Brockus, *WVCF*, pp. 332–34, 349; Cole, "Martial Law."

132 A wild scene: Testimony of Frank Keeney, pp. 165–67; testimony of Albert E. McComas, pp. 306–17; Testimony of Capt. J. R. Brockus, pp. 332–37, 349; Testimony of Howard Hanner, pp. 476–77; Testimony of Jackson Arnold, *WVCF*, pp. 995–97; Cole, "Martial Law."

132 Overturning martial law: *NYT*, June 15, 1921; Cole, "Martial Law," citing *Ex Parte A. D. Lavinder et al.*, 88. W.Va. 713 (1921).

133 Morgan issued an order: Proclamation of Ephraim Morgan, *WVCF*, pp. 266–67; *NYT*, June 29, 1921; Cole, "Martial Law."

133 "Never in our history": Text of Hiram Johnson's speech, *WVCF*, p. 304.

Chapter Seven: Mr. Hatfield Goes to Washington

135 Casualties of the heat: *NYT,* July 15, 1921.

136 96 percent of capacity: Statement of S. B. Avis, *WVCF,* p. 6.

136 As the union described it: Testimony of Fred Mooney, *WVCF,* pp. 20–22.

137 Kenyon's background: *Dictionary of American Biography* (New York: Scribner, 1956); *American National Biography,* Vol. XII (New York: Oxford, 1993); *Des Moines Tribune,* Sept. 9, 10, 1933.

137 Nearly double the prosecutions: Cooper, p. 149.

138 "Greatest publicists on earth": Testimony of William Wiley, *WVCF,* p. 512.

138 "The full social value": Statements by delegates to 23rd annual UMW convention, *WVCF,* p. 420.

138 "An organized band of robbers": Testimony of L. Taylor Vinson, *WVCF,* p. 9.

139 "Mooney was ready for him": Testimony of Fred Mooney, *WVCF,* p. 20.

139 McKellar-Vinson exchange: Ibid., pp. 13–14.

139 McKellar background: http://bioguide.congress.gov/scripts.

139 "Unworthy of an answer": Testimony of Fred Mooney, *WVCF,* p. 18.

140 Average income figures: Ibid., p. 24.

140 "Venomous and malignant": Mooney, p. 115.

141 "No right to dwell on suppositions": Testimony of Fred Mooney, *WVCF,* p. 57.

141 An iron will and a quick mind: Phillips, Cabell.

141 Keeney fought back: Testimony of Frank Keeney, *WVCF,* p. 176.

141 "When a real mountaineer shoots": Ibid., p. 184.

142 Hatfield's version: Ibid., pp. 205ff.

143 "I will not ask him": Ibid., p. 216.

144 "Don't smile, because that is true": Ibid., p. 217.

145 "I did not pose to be a gunman": Ibid., p. 218.

146 "Lurid tales" are published: Ibid., p. 264f.

146 Did the companies pay deputies?: Ibid., p. 265.

148 Hoped to impress: Testimony of Charles E. Lively, *WVCF,* pp. 356ff.

149 "A delicate sense of right and wrong": *NYT,* July 21, 1921.

150 "And did you think that was right?": Testimony of Charles E. Lively, *WVCF,* p. 360.

Chapter Eight: "Even the Heavens Weep"

153 A phone message confirmed: Savage, p. 66.
154 Hatfield made no secret: *Wheeling Intelligencer,* July 30, 1921.
154 Hatfield's arrest: *Wheeling Intelligencer,* July 29, 1921.
155 "I am very anxious": *Wheeling Intelligencer,* July 30, 1921.
155 Sheriff Hatfield had already left: Lee, pp. 67–68; Huntington *Herald-Dispatch,* Aug. 10, 1921.
155 The journey to Welch: Testimony of Mrs. Sid Hatfield, *WVCF,* Vol. 2, pp. 733ff.
157 Another flight of steps: Savage, p. 66.
157 "Shoot 'em with one gun": Lee, pp. 69–70.
158 A victory that came too late: *Charleston Gazette,* Aug. 2, 1921.
158 Account of shooting: Testimony of Mrs. Sid Hatfield, pp. 731–36; Testimony of Mrs. Ed Chambers, pp. 737–40; *WVCF,* Vol. 2; *Charleston Gazette,* Aug. 2, 1921; *NYT,* Aug. 3, 1921.
159 "Well that is all right": Testimony of Mrs. Ed Chambers, p. 739.
159 Work to do: Lee, pp. 67–68.
159 Evidence is "absolute": *Charleston Gazette,* Aug. 2, 1921.
160 Matewan in mourning: *Charleston Gazette, Wheeling Intelligencer,* Aug. 4, 1920.
160 2,000 workers laid down their tools: Huntington *Herald-Dispatch,* Aug. 4, 1921.
160 The UMW placard: *Charleston Gazette,* Aug. 4, 1921.
160 The graveside service: Mooney, p. 88.
162 Editorial comment: *Wheeling Intelligencer,* Aug. 3, 1921; *UMW Journal,* Aug. 15, 1921.
162 Lively's press conference: *NYT,* Aug. 7, 1921.
162 Keeney's plans: *Charleston Gazette,* Aug. 2, 1921.
162 "About 40,000 idle miners": *Wheeling Intelligencer,* July 30, 1921.
162 "Not willing to have them killed": *Charleston Gazette,* Aug. 2, 1921.
163 The strictures of martial law: Mooney, p. 89.
163 They descended on Montgomery: Ibid.
163 "The boys are good to me": Gorn, pp. 267–70.

164 "They are spineless": Mooney, p. 89.

164 Morgan could hear them plainly: Ibid., p. 89; testimony of Ephraim Morgan, Walter Allen trial, Reel 2A, TTT.

164 "Fill the jails": Testimony of J. W. Meadows, ibid.

165 Morgan's limited background: www.wvculture.org/history/morgan .html.

165 Morgan turns down request: Lunt, p. 124, citing Morgan letter to C. O. Bruere, Sept. 13, 1921, Morgan papers.

165 A tragi-comedy of errors: Savage, p. 75; statement of William M. Wiley, *WVCF*, pp. 513ff.

166 Chased them home: *NYT*, Aug. 14, 1921.

166 Supreme Court ruling: *NYT*, Aug. 20, 1921.

166 A menacing assortment: Testimony of J. W. Meadows, Walter Allen trial, Reel 2A, TTT.

166 "Making a demonstration": *NYT*, Aug. 20, 1921.

167 "We were worn out": Mooney, p. 90.

167 Denied any connection: *NYT*, Aug. 25, 1921.

167 "Wash my hands": *NYT*, Aug. 20, 1921.

167 "No armed mob": *NYT*, Aug. 22, 1921.

167 "A mystery": *NYT*, Aug. 25, 1921.

168 "A helluva lot of telepathy": Spivak, pp. 69–70.

168 Savoy Holt's role: Testimony of Charles Tucker, Walter Allen Trial.

169 McKeaver saw the miners: Testimony of J. S. McKeaver, Walter Allen Trial.

169 Local 404 members raised $200: Testimony of Ed Reynolds, Walter Allen Trial.

169 Most showed up in blue bib overalls: Testimony of Arthur Burns, Walter Allen Trial.

169 "Redneck" not yet in wide currency: Though some dictionaries say the term was coined as early as 1830, it does not appear in H. L. Mencken's *The American Language* (New York: Knopf, 1963; originally published in 1919 and revised in 1936). And as late as 1950 in his magisterial *Southern Politics in State and Nation* (New York: Knopf, 1950, pp. 230–31), the justly revered V. O. Key uses the term briefly only in his chapter on Mississippi, along with "peckerhead" and "peckerwood," as a synonym for rural Southern whites.

169 A new problem: Mooney, p. 90.

170 Better reason than they knew: Gorn, p. 269.

170 Typical of her relationships: Ibid., pp. 272–75; Testimony of Ephraim Morgan, Walter Allen Trial, Reel 2A, TTT.

170 Reaction of Keeney and Mooney: Mooney, pp. 90–91.

170 "Sellout" and "traitor": Gorn, p. 272.

171 Chafin's background: Lee, pp. 88ff; Testimony of Don Chafin, *WVCF,* Vol. 3, pp. 1053–57.

171 Chafin's arrangement: Gleason; Testimony of William R. Thurmond, *WVCF,* Vol. 2, pp. 867 ff.

172 Net worth about $350,000: Testimony of Don Chafin, *WVCF,* Vol. 2, p. 1064.

172 Given a choice: Lee, p. 90.

172 Heiser's fate: Gleason; Lee, p. 91.

172 Brandishing a pistol: Lee, pp. 92–93; *NYT,* Sept. 25, 1919.

173 Do what you can: Testimony of Don Chafin, Walter Allen Trial, Real 2A, TTT.

173 Total strength to 3,000: Ibid.; Savage, p. 82, citing *On Dark and Bloody Ground,* Oral history project, Ann Lawrence, director.

174 The defense perimeter: *TBOBM,* pp. 12, 23; Savage, p. 82.

174 Morgan appeals to Weeks: Laurie and Cole, p. 316.

175 "Inflamed and irritated": *NYT,* Aug. 26, Aug. 27, 1921.

175 Weeks dispatched Bandholtz: Rich, p. 162; *NYT,* Aug. 27, 1921.

175 Bandholtz background: Fifty-ninth annual report of the Association of Graduates of the U.S. Military Academy, West Point, N.Y., Jan. 8, 1928; Major General Harry Hill Bandholtz, biography, Office of the Chief of Military History General Reference Branch; *Grand Rapids Press,* May 8, 1925.

175 Service in Hungary: "General Bandholtz and the Hungarians," www. geocities.com/ihunsor; www. usembassy.hu/bandh.htm.

176 Had Morgan done all he could?: Testimony of Col. Stanley Ford, *WVCF,* pp. 1032ff.

176 They did not dally: Mooney, p. 91; Rich, p. 161; Laurie and Cole, p. 316; Berman, p. 211; Testimony of Col. Stanley Ford, *WVCF,* pp. 1032ff.

177 Bandholtz was even blunter: Mooney, p. 92.

177 He wired Washington: Rich, p. 162, fn. 39, citing Cassius M. Dowell, *Military Aid to the Civil Power,* p. 198.

177 Hurried to the White House: *NYT,* Aug. 27, 1921.

178 Mother Jones's view: Ibid.

178 Get Morgan to redo the request: Laurie and Cole, p. 318; *NYT,* Aug. 30, 1921.

178 In the same mode: Ibid.

178 Mitchell's career: Grant; www.airpower.maxwell.af.mil/airchronicles/cc.mitch.html.

179 Mitchell at Kanawha Field: Maurer and Senning; Lunt, pp. 39–40.

180 Keeney and Mooney were struggling: Mooney, pp. 92ff.

181 Mooney once more read Bandholtz's message: *NYT,* Aug. 27, 1921.

182 Bandholtz sent the news back to Washington: Laurie and Cole, p. 319.

Chapter Nine: "I Come Creeping"

183 When trouble started: Testimony of Charles Medley, John Wilburn Trial, Reel 5, TTT.

184 He encountered Mooney and Keeney: Mooney, pp. 94–96.

184 "To hell with Keeney": Testimony of Jack Brinkman, John Wilburn Trial, Reel 4, TTT.

185 Chafin took the call: Testimony of Don Chafin, *WFCF,* p. 1059, and Walter Allen Trial, Reel 2A, TTT.

185 Back at the breastworks: Ibid.

185 He called the AP bureau: Mooney, p. 94.

186 Chafin dispatched him: Testimony of Don Chafin, Walter Allen Trial, Reel 2A, TTT.

186 Chafin sent 200 deputies: *TBOBM,* p. 28.

186 Brockus's mission: Testimony of Capt. J. R. Brockus, Walter Allen Trial, Reel 2B, TTT; Memorandum of J. R Brockus on Sharples Battle, Aug. 28, 1921, Mingo County File.

187 "We've come after you God damn miners": Testimony of Marion Williams, John Wilburn Trial, Reel 4, TTT.

187 Prudence demanded retreat: Testimony of Capt. J. R. Brockus, Reel 2B, TTT.

187 They found themselves prisoners: Testimony of Fulton Mitchell, Walter Allen Trial, Reel 2B, TTT.

187 "They were shooting women and children": Testimony of James Blount, ibid.

188   Charnock's failed mission: *NYT*, Aug. 30, 1921; Lunt, p. 130, citing John H. Charnock to Morgan, Aug. 30, 1921, Morgan papers.

188   "A monster powder keg": *Charleston Gazette*, Aug. 29, 1921; *NYT*, Aug. 30, 1921.

188   Signs of an imminent explosion: Mooney, pp. 95ff; *TBOBM*, p. 30; Testimony of William McKell, *WVCF*, p. 943; Testimony of Ed Reynolds, Walter Allen Trial, Reel 2A, TTT.

189   "Throw the harness on": Testimony of Burrell Miller, Walter Allen Trial, Reel 2B, TTT.

189   "Fight, guard or die": Testimony of John Brown, John Wilburn Trial, Reel 4, TTT.

189   Most came from the Kanawha Valley: *TBOBM*, p. 30.

189   Many arrived on flat cars: Testimony of Ira Wilson, Walter Allen Trial, Reel 2A, TTT.

189   Ed Reynolds's "outlaw train": Testimony of Ed Reynolds, ibid.

190   "Some would say": Testimony of Dr. W. F. Harliss, John Wilburn Trial, Reel 4, TTT.

190   A more poignant ballad: "Even the Heavens Weep."

190   Morgan again wired Weeks: *NYT*, Aug. 30, 1921.

190   A proposition Chafin scorned: Ibid.

191   "Danger of attack imminent": E. F. Morgan to John W. Weeks, Aug. 30, 1921, Mingo County File.

191   Harding still resisted: *NYT*, Aug. 31.

191   The president's proclamation: Ibid., Mingo County File.

191   He sent Bandholtz back: *NYT*, Sept. 1, 1921.

191   Weeks made clear: John W. Weeks to E. F. Morgan, Aug. 31, 1921. Mingo County File.

192   Wilburn's advance: Testimony of Jack Brinkman, John Wilburn Trial, Reel 4; Testimony of Ira Wilson, Walter Allen Trial, Reel 2A, TTT.

192   "To show those redneck SOBs": *TBOBM*, p. 36 citing Michael E. Workman interview of Cecil Hutchinson, Sept. 12, 1991.

192   "That's for Sid": Testimony of J. C. Hardesty, Trial of John Wilburn; Testimony of Jack Brinkman, Trial of John Wilburn, Reel 4, TTT.

193   Morgan appointed Eubanks: Testimony of Ephraim Morgan, Walter Allen Trial, Reel 2A, TTT.

193   Volunteers from all over: *Charleston Gazette*, Sept. 1, 1921; *Huntington Advertiser*, Aug. 31, 1921; *Bluefield Daily Telegraph*, Sept. 8, 1921.

194   The defenders' passwords: Joe Savage, "Stopping the Armed March."

194   Headquarters in the Aracoma Hotel: *TBOBM*, p. 34.

194   The union miners' passwords: Testimony of Charles Tucker, Walter Allen Trial.

195   "The best thing is clear out": Mooney, p. 99.

195   "All fire and dynamite": Ibid., p. 67.

195   The pincers strategy: Testimony of Ed Reynolds, Walter Allen Trial, Reel 2A, TTT.

197   Defense forces alignment: *TBOBM*, p. 39; Meador, "The Red Neck War"; R. B. Adams.

197   Hollingsworth staved off disaster; *NYT*, Sept. 2, 1921; *Charleston Gazette*, Sept. 2, 1921.

198   "Unless troops sent by midnight": Walter Thurmond to Rep. Goodykoontz, Sept. 1, 1921, Mingo County File.

198   "Contemptuously ignored": Huntington *Herald-Dispatch*, Sept. 2, 1921.

198   The planes dropped copies of Harding's proclamation: *NYT*, Sept. 1, 1921.

198   More menacing cargo: Testimony of E. W. Eubanks, Walter Allen Trial, Reel 2B, TTT; *TBOBM*, p. 42, citing interview of Henry White by Michael Workman and Lee Maddex.

198   Re-established National Guard: *NYT*, Sept. 1, 1921.

199   One final effort: *NYT*, Sept. 2, 1921.

199   Carried little weight: Encounter with Murray: Testimony of Col. Stanley Ford, *WVCF*, vol. 2, p. 1034.

199   "Like sweeping the ocean with a broom": Testimony of Col. Stanley Ford, ibid., p. 972.

200   "I have nothing to say": *NYT*, Sept. 2, 1921; Huntington *Herald-Dispatch*, Sept. 2, 1921.

200   Bandholtz wired Harbord: *NYT*, Sept. 2, 1921.

200   The orders went out: Laurie and Cole, p. 322.

200   "A large quantity of teargas": *NYT*, Sept. 2, 1921.

200   Mitchell was to stay home: Laurie and Cole, p. 322.

200   "Ill-advised and ill-timed": *NYT*, Sept. 3, 1921, citing Bandholtz to Adjutant General, U.S. Army, Sept. 1, 1921.

201   Saved the bridge: *Huntington Advertiser*, Sept. 2, 1921.

201   "No sense of fear": *Bluefield Daily Telegraph*, Sept. 3, 1921.

201 "We couldn't fire a shot": *Huntington Advertiser,* Sept. 4, 1921.

202 Bombers had landed: Lurie and Cole, p. 322.

202 Infantry arrives: Ibid.

202 Against declaring Federal martial law: Rich, pp. 165–66.

202 "A law for rulers and people": *ex parte Milligan,* 4 Wallace, 2 (1866).

203 Bandholtz's instructions: Rich, p. 167.

203 "The only way for a square deal": *Huntington Advertiser,* Sept. 1, 1921.

203 "Not a single shot will be fired": *NYT,* Sept. 3, 1921.

203 "Obey the direction": Ibid.

204 Harding's cruise: Ibid.

204 Labor Day parade called off: *NYT,* Sept. 5, 1921.

204 "A broad enveloping movement": *NYT,* Sept. 4, 1921.

204 Wilson encounters Blizzard: Article by Boyden Sparkes reprinted from *Leslie's Weekly,* n.d.; *WVCF,* Vol. II, pp. 876–79; *NYT,* Sept. 4, 1921.

205 Only 33 bullets left: *Charleston Daily Mail,* Sept. 4, 1921.

205 Boyden Sparkes's visit to the front: *Charleston Gazette,* Sept. 9, 1921.

206 "I was amazed": *Roanoke Times,* Sept. 9, 1921.

207 "Under the influence": Lont, p. 137, citing Report of Maj. Charles Thompson to commanding general, provisional brigade, Sept. 6, 1921, Mingo County File.

208 Families strolled streets: Savage, pp. 160–61.

208 Only 400 guns turned in: *Charleston Gazette,* Sept. 5, 1921.

208 "It was Uncle Sam that did it": Savage, p. 164.

208 Miners carried their dead away: *NYT,* Sept. 3, 1921.

208 Between 10,000 to 20,000: Laurie and Cole, p. 321.

208 "You could hear it for miles": Testimony of Ira Wilson, Walter Allen Trial, Reel 2A, TTT.

Chapter Ten: Requiem for a Rebellion

211 "It was self evident": Testimony of Philip Murray, *WVCF,* Vol. 2, p. 670.

212 "The miners have yielded": Editorial paragraph, *The Nation,* Sept. 14, 1921.

212 "Nothing but trouble": "Personal Views of Sen. Kenyon," *WVCF,* Jan. 25, 1922.

212 Lewis seeks out Davis: *NYT,* Sept. 4, 1921.

213 His only obligation: *NYT,* Sept. 8, 1921.

213 Bandholtz refused: Lunt, p. 141, citing Bandholtz to Morgan, Sept. 6, 1921, Morgan papers.

213 Bethel's memorandum: Lunt, p. 141, citing W. A. Bethel memorandum, Nov. 16, 1921, records of the Department of Justice.

213 Daugherty let the matter drop: Corbin, p. 239, citing Harry M. Daugherty memorandum for Assistant Attorney General John Crum, March 3, 1922, Record Group 60, General Records of the Department of Justice.

213 "It may embarrass State officials": Corbin, p. 239, citing Crum memo to L. H. Kelly.

214 "Every effort will be made": *NYT,* Sept. 6, 1921.

214 Mingo County Defense League: Mooney, 99–100.

214 Lewis-Morgan exchange: Lunt, p. 143, citing Lewis telegram to Morgan, Sept. 19, 1921, and Morgan to Lewis, Sept. 22, 1921, Morgan papers.

215 Charged with treason: Lunt, p. 159; also see Jefferson County Circuit Court, orders and opinions, Kanawha County Circuit Court indictments and grand jury proceedings and Logan County Circuit Court indictments, Reel 1, TTT.

215 Treason provision in West Virginia Constitution: Lunt, p. 159.

215 "Larceny of a chicken": *NYT,* May 3, 1922.

216 Billed the state $125,000: Lunt, p. 159.

216 Woods's charge to the jury: Ibid., p. 161.

216 Blizzard acquitted: Ibid.

216 Carrying the alleged traitor on their shoulders: Mooney, p. 123.

217 Jury could not reach a verdict: Lee, p. 112.

217 Allen such a minor figure: Lunt, p. 162; Cain.

217 Judge Wood stymies the defense: Cain.

217 Wood rejected their motions: Defense contentions on jury instructions, Walter Allen Trial, Tape 1, TTT.

218 The state dropped charges: Ibid.

218 Billy Sunday's role: Jordan, citing *New York Journal,* April 15, 1922.

218 Coal supplies were abundant: Perlman and Taft, p. 482.
218 A steadfast ally of District 17: Corbin, pp. 237, 248.
219 "A landslide into the gutter": Mooney, p. 127.
219 One last stab: Corbin, "Frank Keeney Is Our Leader."
220 Fred Mooney's death: Mooney, p. x.
220 Police were driven back: Zieger, p. 91.
220 "Property-minded citizens scared": Leuchtenberg, p. 242.
220 "It ill behooves": Zieger, p. 106.
221 A facetious amendment: Leuchtenberg, p. 263.
221 "Help your struggling brothers": Testimony of W. R. Thurmond, *WVCF,* Vol. 2, pp. 938–39.
222 "We wouldn't revolt": *Charleston Gazette,* Aug. 28, 1921.
223 They turned up nothing: Lt. E. L. Brine to director of military intelligence, Sept. 4, 1921, Mingo County File.
223 "Two communists had ensconced their hides": Mooney, p. 122.
224 Native-born population: Jordan.
224 The union did what it could: Testimony of Frank Keeney, *WVCF,* pp. 196–97.
224 "There were no aliens": Spivak, p. 102.
224 "I could not absorb": Mooney, p. 48.
224 Unreliable allies: Corbin, p. 240.
224 That language did mean: Testimony of Frank Keeney, *WVCF,* p. 196.
224 "I hope I never will": Lane, pp. 86–88.
225 Their view of themselves as American citizens: Corbin, p. 243.
225 The bedrock of the miners' claim: Testimony of Fred Mooney, *WVCF,* p. 20.
226 Keeney moved swiftly: Testimony of Frank Keeney, *WVCF,* p. 190.

Bibliography

Archival Sources

Alderman Library, University of Virginia. Papers of William Jett Lauck (MSS#4742). These are papers and scrapbooks relating to West Virginia labor conflicts collected by a longtime United Mine Workers Union consultant.

Eastern Regional Coal Archives. Craft Memorial Library. Bluefield, West Virginia. H. C. Lewis Collection. Includes: Trial transcripts of the trial of Sid Hatfield et al. for the murder of Albert and Lee Felts (cited in notes as HTT); and Felts, Tom, "The Terror of the Tug," unpublished MS dealing with Sid Hatfield and Jessie Testerman Hatfield (cited in notes as Felts MS.).

Library of Congress. American Civil Liberties Union Archives. (Cited in notes as ACLU.)

National Archives. War Department. Adjutant General Files. RG407, AGO 370.7 Mingo County. (Cited in notes as Mingo County File.)

West Virginia and Regional History Collection, West Virginia University Library. Miners' Treason Trial Transcripts. Circuit Court of Jefferson County, West Virginia. Six Reels of microfilm, 1, 2, 2A, 3, 4 and 5. (Cited in notes as TTT.)

Books

Adams, Graham, Jr. *Age of Industrial Violence: 1910–1915.* New York: Columbia University Press, 1966.

Adams, R. B. "Blair Mountain from the Other Side." In Ken Sullivan, ed. *The Goldenseal Book of the West Virginia Mine Wars.* Charleston, W.Va.: Pictorial Histories Publishing Co., 1991.

Allen, Frederick Lewis. *Only Yesterday: An Informal History of the 1920s.* New York: Harper, 1964.

Berman, Edward. *Labor Disputes and the President of the United States.* New York: Columbia University Press, 1924.

Cohen, Stan. *King Coal: A Pictorial Heritage of West Virginia Coal Mining.* Charleston, W.Va.: Quarrier Press, 1984.

Cooper, John Milton. *Pivotal Decades: The United States 1900–1920.* New York: Norton, 1990.

Corbin, David Alan. "Frank Keeney Is Our Leader and We Shall Not Be Moved." In Gary M. Fink and Merl Reed, eds. *Essays in Southern Labor History.* Southern Labor History Conference, 1976. Westport, Conn.: Greenwood Press, 1977.

_____. *Life, Work, and Rebellion in the Coal Fields: The Southern West Virginia Miners, 1880–1922.* Urbana: University of Illinois Press, 1981. Cited in notes as Corbin.

Daniels, Josephus. *The Wilson Era: Years of War and After 1917–1923.* Chapel Hill: University of North Carolina Press, 1946.

Dictionary of American Biography, Vol. IV. New York: Scribner, 1932.

Dix, Keith. "Mechanization, Workplace Control and the End of the Hand-Loading Era." In *The United Mine Workers of America: A Model of Industrial Solidarity?* University Park, Pa.: Pennsylvania State University Press, 1996.

Dubofsky, Melvin. *The State and Labor in Modern America.* Chapel Hill: University of North Carolina Press, 1994. Cited in notes as Dubofsky.

_____, and Foster Rhea Dulles. *Labor in America: A History.* Wheeling, Ill.: Harlan Davidson, 1999.

_____, and Warren Van Tyne. *John. L. Lewis: A Biography.* Abridged edition. Chicago: University of Illinois Press, 1986.

Foner, Eric, and John A. Garraty, eds. *The Reader's Companion to American History.* Boston: Houghton Mifflin, 1991.

George, Alexander, and Juliette L. *Woodrow Wilson and Colonel House: A Personality Study.* New York: Dover, 1964.

Gorn, Elliott J. *Mother Jones: The Most Dangerous Woman in America.* New York: Hill and Wang, 2001.

Hunt, Edward R., ed. *What the Coal Commission Found: An Authoritative Summary by the Staff.* Baltimore: Williams and Wilkins, 1925.

Johnson, James P. *The Politics of Soft Coal: The Bituminous Industry from World War I Through the New Deal.* Urbana: University of Illinois Press, 1979.

Jones, Virgil Carrington. *The Hatfields and the McCoys: The Bloodiest Family Feud in American History.* Marietta, Ga.: Mocking Bird Books, 1994. (Originally published by the University of North Carolina Press, 1948.)

Jordan, Daniel P. "The Mingo War: Labor Violence in the Southern West Virginia Coal Fields, 1919–1922." In Fink and Reed, eds. *Essays in Southern Labor History.* Southern Labor History Conference, 1976. Westport, Conn.: Greenwood Press, 1977.

Lambie, Joseph T. *From Mine to Market: The History of Coal Transportation on the Norfolk and Western Railway.* New York: New York University Press, 1954.

Lane, Withrop. *Civil War in West Virginia.* New York: Oriole Chapbooks, nd. Originally published in 1921.

Laurie, Clayton D. and Ronald H. Cole. *The Role of Federal Military Forces in Domestic Disorders: 1877–1945.* Army Historical Series, Vol. II. Washington, D.C.: Center of Military History, United States Army, 1997.

Lee, Howard B. *Bloodletting in Appalachia.* Morgantown: West Virginia University Press, 1969.

Leuchtenberg, William. *Franklin D. Roosevelt and the New Deal.* New York: Harper, 1963.

Lunt, Richard D. *Law and Order vs the Miners: WV 1906–1933.* Charleston, W.Va.: Appalachian Editions, 1992. (Originally published in 1979 as an Archon Book.)

McCartin, Joseph A. *Labor's Great War: The Struggle for Industrial Democracy and the Origins of Modern American Labor Relations, 1912–1921.* Chapel Hill: University of North Carolina Press, 1997.

Meador, Michael. "The Red Neck War of 1921: The Miners March and the Battle of Blair Mountain." In Ken Sullivan, ed. *The Goldenseal Book of the West Virginia Mine Wars.* Charleston, W.Va.: Pictorial Histories Publishing Co., 1991.

———. "The Siege of Crooked Creek Gap." In Ken Sullivan, ed. *The Goldenseal Book of the West Virginia Mine Wars.* Charleston, W.Va.: Pictorial Histories Publishing Co., 1991.

Mooney, Fred. *Struggle in the Coal Fields: The Autobiography of Fred Mooney*, J. W. Hess, ed. Morgantown, W.Va.: West Virginia University Library, 1967.

Murray, Robert K. *Red Scare: A Study in National Hysteria, 1919–1920*. New York: McGraw Hill, 1964.

Perlman, Selig, and Philip Taft. *History of Labor in the United States, 1896–1932, Vol. IV, Labor Movements*. New York: Macmillan, 1935.

Rich, Bennett Milton. *The Presidents and Civil Disorder*. Washington, D.C.: The Brookings Institution, 1941.

Russell, Francis. *The Shadow of Blooming Grove*. New York: McGraw-Hill, 1968.

Savage, Joe. "Stopping the Armed March: The Nonunion Resistance." In Ken Sullivan, ed. *The Goldenseal Book of the West Virginia Mine Wars*. Charleston, W.Va.: Pictorial Histories Publishing Co., 1991.

Savage, Lon. *Thunder in the Mountains: The West Virginia Mine War 1920–21*. Pittsburgh: University of Pittsburgh Press, 1990. Originally published by Jalamap.

Smith, Gene. *When the Cheering Stopped: The Last Years of Woodrow Wilson*. New York: Time Reading Program, 1966.

Spivak, John L. *A Man in His Time*. New York: Horizon Press, 1967.

Sullivan, Ken, ed. *The Goldenseal Book of the West Virginia Mine Wars*. Charleston, W.Va.: *Goldenseal Magazine*, 1991.

Sullivan, Mark. *Our Times: America, the Birth of the 20th Century*. Abridged edition, Dan Rather, ed. New York: Scribner, 1996.

Taft, Philip. *Organized Labor in American History*. New York: Harper & Row, 1964.

Topper, Sherwood. "The Dust Settles: Felts Papers Offer More on Matewan." In Ken Sullivan.

Wilson, Edmund. *The American Earthquake*. Garden City, N.Y.: Doubleday, 1958.

Zieger, Robert H. *John L. Lewis: Labor Leader*. Boston: Twayne, 1988.

Periodicals and Web Sites

Blankenhorn, Heber. "The Miners at Cleveland." *The Nation*, September 27, 1919.

Burkinshaw, Neil. "Labor's Valley Forge." *The Nation*, December 8, 1920.

Cain, James M. "Treason to the Coal Operators." *The Nation*, October 4, 1922.

Capozzola, Christopher. "Mother Jones: The Most Dangerous Woman in America." *The Progressive*, September 2001.

Cole, Merle T. "Birth of the West Virginia State Police, 1919–1921." *West Virginia History*, Vol. XLIII, No. 1, Fall 1981.

_____. "Martial Law in West Virginia and Major Davis as Emperor of the Tug River." *West Virginia History*, Vol. XLIII, No. 2, Winter 1982.

Fisher, Lucy Lee. "John J. Cornwell, Governor of West Virginia, 1917–1921, Part II." *West Virginia History*. Vol XXIV, No. 4, July 1963.

Geiger, Joe and Greg Carroll. "West Virginia's Mine Wars." Compiled by the West Virginia State Archives at wvculture.org/history.

Gleason, Arthur. "Private Ownership of Public Officials." *The Nation*, May 5, 1920.

Grant, Rebecca. "The Real Billy Mitchell." *The Journal of the Air Force Association*. nd. www.worldwar1.com/dbc/ mitchell.htm

Hadsell, Richard M. and William E. Coffey. "From Law and Order to Class Warfare: Baldwin-Felts Detectives in the Southern West Virginia Coal Fields." *West Virginia History*, Vol. XL, No. 3, Spring 1979.

Laurie, Clayton D. "The United States Army and the Return to Normalcy in Labor Interventions: The Case of the West Virginia Coal Mine Wars." @ www.wvculture.org./history/journal.

Maurer, Maurer and Calvin F. Senning. "Billy Mitchell, the Air Service and the Mingo War." *West Virginia History*, October 1968, No. 1. Reprinted from *The Airpower Historian*. Maxwell Air Force Base. Montgomery, Ala., April 1965.

Phillips, Cabell. "The West Virginia Mine War." *American Heritage*, August 1974.

Scholten, Pat Creech. "The Old Mother and Her Army: The Agitative Strategies of Mary Harris Jones." *West Virginia History*, Vol. XL, No. 4.

Wolfe, Alan. "Strangled by the Roots." *New Republic*, May 28, 2001.

Public Documents

The Institute for the History of Technology and Industrial Archeology, West Virginia University. *The Battle of Blair Mountain (West Virginia):*

Cultural Resource Survey and Recording Project, Morgantown, W.Va., 1991. The report is based on a research effort conducted in response to controversy over the issuance of mining permits in Logan County. Its objective was to identify and possibly preserve key historic sites relevant to events of the summer of 1921. Cited in notes as *TBOBM*.

U.S. Senate, Committee on Education and Labor. *West Virginia Coal Fields, Hearings Pursuant to S. 80, to Investigate Recent Acts of Violence in the Coal Fields of West Virginia and Adjacent Territory and the Causes which Led to the Conditions which now exist in Said Territory.* 67th Congress, 1st Session, 1921. 3 Vols. Washington: Government Printing Office, 1921. Cited in notes as *WVCF*. Unless otherwise noted all references are to Vol. 1.

Doctoral Dissertation

Bailey, Rebecca J. "Matewan Before the Massacre: Politics, Coal and the Roots of Conflict in Mingo County, 1793–1920." Department of History, West Virginia University, 2001.

Television Documentary

Even the Heavens Weep. Produced by WPBY in Huntington, W.Va., 1985. Humanities Council of West Virginia Funding.

Index